Growing Beyond Prejudices

foreword by
ROBERT McAFEE BROWN

Growing Beyond Prejudices

OVERCOMING HIERARCHICAL DUALISM

DAVID L. SHIELDS

TWENTY-THIRD PUBLICATIONS
Mystic, Connecticut

Twenty-Third Publications
P.O. Box 180
Mystic CT 06355
(203) 536-2611

Library of Congress Catalog Card Number 85-52141
ISBN 0-89622-283-7

Cover design by George Herrick
Edited and designed by Helen Coleman

FOREWORD

In an era when prejudice is on the rise and is being used as a manipulative tool by those in power, whether residing in Washington or Moscow, we need all the help we can get, not only in understanding and exposing them, but even more in learning how to combat them. David Shields's book provides a wide variety of tools for achieving both of those ends. Although written particularly with educators in mind, his pages also speak to theology students and, indeed, to all who are involved in the educational process in whatever location and at whatever level.

This widespread appeal is grounded not only in the universal extent of the problem being studied, but in the diverse nature of the resources employed to cope with it. At first glance, the subjects of the first four chapters—Rosemary Ruether, John Dewey, Norma Haan, and Juan Luis Segundo—would seem a most unlikely combination of ideological companions, and yet each makes an indispensible contribution. Ruether provides the key to the subsequent discussion by her analysis of "hierarchical dualism" as a root cause of prejudice, and each of the succeeding thinkers offers a dimension of response—experience and the "quest for certainty," moral psychology and the search for "moral balance," compassion and the commitment to justice—out of which the author then weaves a skillful synthesis of his own.

If the first four chapters seem theoretical, which they are, the reader need only be assured that an important base is being constructed on which, in Chapters Five and Six, intensely practical and immediate suggestions are offered for dealing with, and seeking to reduce, prejudice in the classroom, and therefore in the lives of those who carry attitudes far beyond the classroom.

v

Clearly, no single discipline can resolve the deep-rooted prejudices endemic to our society, and it is cause for rejoicing in the present instance that a religious educator seeks the help of educational philosophers, moral psychologists, and even liberation theologians. It is out of these rich resources that Dr. Shields distills twelve summary statements on the nature of prejudice (in the Introduction to Chapter Five) and devotes a final chapter to translating the material gathered and analyzed into specific proposals for moving from "prejudice to pluralism."

I write these lines at the completion of a teaching career in theological education, much of which has been devoted, even when the terms were not used, to the attempt to challenge prejudice. I only wish the material in these pages had been available to me at the beginning, rather than at the end, of my years in the classroom.

ROBERT MCAFEE BROWN
EMERITUS PROFESSOR OF THEOLOGY AND ETHICS
PACIFIC SCHOOL OF RELIGION

PREFACE

Prejudice is a problem with many faces: sexism, racism, and classism are just a few of the masks it wears. A profound problem facing contemporary Americans, prejudice lurks within families, communities, schools, parishes, businesses, wherever we find people at odds with one another. Women seek equality with men, people of color struggle to break the monopoly of the white majority, labor strikes out at management, gays march to gain recognition of their basic rights. These liberation movements face a common challenge, prejudice. Prejudice is at the root of our broken human relationships.

Few would argue that prejudice is a serious social problem, but what can be done about it? If you were to ask people on the street, you would probably hear education mentioned most frequently as the solution. There is wisdom in this response. Education, as it seeks to broaden knowledge and shape attitudes and values, is often our best hope for building on the strengths of existing society and purifying it of ignorance, undesirable responses. When educators seek to promote understanding, responsible citizenship, and sensitivity to the physical and social environment, prejudice is reduced.

It is one thing to say that prejudice reduction is vital, but quite another to accomplish it. While prejudice reduction may be near the top of the agenda for educators, few have been equipped to undertake the task. Teacher training institutions rarely offer courses on prejudice and there is a paucity of good works on the topic. Having been given no better alternative, many teachers resort to ineffective admonitions and lectures. But good intentions are not enough to combat prejudice. Hopefully this book can help to fill the void.

In the following pages, I seek to lay the foundation for an educational model designed to challenge and overcome prejudices. While the book has been written primarily with the religious educator in mind, this is not intended as a limitation. As the great philosopher Alfred North Whitehead wisely said, all education is religious. While the intended readership includes all educators, I have drawn specifically from the Christian tradition for a good share of the insights contained in this book. It is my tradition and, consequently, it is the one I know best. Nonetheless, most if not all of the ideas are adaptable to other contexts and traditions.

The task of prejudice reduction has particular urgency for those within the church. Prejudice reduction is at the very core of what it means to be involved in authentic Christian education. It is not an optional goal appended to the primary goals of learning about the Bible, church history, and theology. Prejudice reduction is a necessary prerequisite to understanding the relationship between God and humanity. For how can one communicate meaningfully about a loving Creator when the children of God are holding each other hostage, threatening to destroy the whole human family? How can one teach effectively about Christ our Redeemer while most of humanity lives in the squalid unredeemed conditions of devastating poverty? And how can one speak convincingly of a community gathered by the Spirit when our churches are divided by sex, race, and class? Only as students become aware of the challenge of prejudice and begin to take steps to meet the challenge are they in a good position to grasp the gospel in its depth and breadth.

To journey from prejudice to a genuine embrace of human pluralism requires a good supply of compassion, courage, and humility. As difficult as the journey may be, however, an even greater task awaits those educators who would invite others to walk the road with them. We in the educational field, not having arrived at some comfortable destination, can only confront the prejudicial attitudes and values of others while continuing to name these same destructive forces within ourselves. This is the challenge the reader is invited to embrace while travelling through the pages of this book.

The book develops through a five-step process. The opening chapter probes the work of historian-sociologist-theologian Rosemary Ruether. Ruether's work takes us on a journey into early human civilization where we find that the male-female relationship was the likely locus for the entry of prejudice into human history. Ruether also supplies valuable clues to the nature of prejudicial thinking. She notes that the "ingroup/outgroup" thinking of the culturally dominant group reflects stereotypes that are rooted in dualisms. Thus, for example, the early exploitation of women by ruling males was justified by stereotypes based on mind/body and spirit/nature dualisms. Men were valued as "mind" and "spirit" people; women were debased as "body" and "nature" people. In the course of history, this same pattern of "hierarchical dualism" was directed toward a variety of victims. Thus, sexism spilled into racism, classism, and various forms of ethnocentrism. Chapter One defines the problem of prejudice as one of hierarchical dualism and illustrates its breadth.

If dualisms are central to prejudicial thinking, as Ruether maintains, then a challenge to dualism is pivotal to any educational effort designed to undermine prejudice. During the past century, the educator-philosopher John Dewey spent a lifetime designing an approach to education that is explicitly anti-dualistic. In Chapter Two, Dewey's philosophy of experience informs a response to the problems of prejudice. Dewey's analysis of dualism compliments that of Ruether. While Ruether focuses on intergroup relations, Dewey spotlights the relationship between humanity and nature. He responds to the problem by detailing an organic philosophy of experience, a democratic social theory, and an educational program focused on a non-dualistic approach to inquiry.

Both Ruether and Dewey indicate that prejudice is rooted in the irrational and constitutes moral failure. In the third chapter, we turn to the psychologist Norma Haan for assistance in understanding the irrational and moral dimensions of prejudice. Haan's model of coping and defending ego processes will enable us to elaborate on the irrational dimension of prejudice. In addition, her model of moral development will reveal that immaturity — as well as irrationality — may be a wellspring of prejudice. Prejudices may not always be based on psychological distortion; they also may reflect normal, but underdeveloped, ways of understanding the nature of moral relationships.

The fourth chapter returns to Dewey's insight that undermining prejudices requires a method of thinking that does not itself reflect dualisms. For Dewey's educational approach to become operational, educators must pay attention to the process by which theologies are constructed. Also in the fourth chapter, we travel to Latin America to investigate the religious awakening known as liberation theology. As one liberation theologian notes, "the clue to this theology is the elimination of all and every dualism." In particular, we will examine Juan Luis Segundo's work on theological method. Segundo points to the necessity of beginning religious reflection within a faith community that lives in solidarity with the victims of injustice. From this vantage point, one employs "ideological suspicion" to challenge the cultural myths that perpetuate the unjust situation. When Segundo's method is used educationally, it can become a means for enacting a Deweyian response to problems of prejudice as they are manifested both within and outside the religious community.

Chapters One through Four offer an interdisciplinary analysis of prejudice and its potential resolution. Each chapter centers on an exposition of the work of a key theorist. In the fifth chapter, the insights from Ruether, Dewey, Haan, and Segundo are consolidated into the following twelve summary statements about the nature of prejudice:

1. Prejudices are based on a pattern of experience that is hierarchical and dualistic.
2. Prejudices reflect a desire to control the uncertainties of life.
3. Prejudices buttress the self-esteem of the prejudiced person.
4. Prejudices reflect and reinforce current distributions of social power.

5. Sexism is foundational for other forms of prejudice.
6. Different forms of prejudice are connected.
7. Prejudices are buttressed by adaptable steretypes.
8. Prejudices may reflect immature forms of moral reasoning.
9. Prejudices achieve stability through irrational psychodynamics.
10. Prejudices are justified through appeal to ultimate criteria.
11. Prejudices have negative psychological consequences for both "oppressor" and "oppressed."
12. Prejudices have physical consequences.

These statements are elaborated and illustrated in the fifth chapter and the reader is invited to use them to reflect on personal attitudes and beliefs. The chapter concludes with a return to the themes of experience, democracy, and inquiry.

The final chapter offers a range of practical suggestions for reducing and preventing prejudice. Included is a description of a teaching model that coordinates cognitive, attitudinal, and behavioral approaches to prejudice reduction. Based on the work of the key theorists explored in Chapters One through Four, the model offers a practical guide for dealing with problems of prejudice in a variety of educational situations and contexts.

Many of the ideas contained within these pages were first elaborated while working on my doctoral dissertation at the Graduate Theological Union, Berkeley. I am profoundly indebted to the fine scholars and friends who served on my committee: David S. Steward, chair, Robert McAfee Brown, Karen Lebacqz, and Norma Haan. Their intellectual and emotional support was invaluable. Many other people also contributed to the development of this book, some of them unknowingly, and it is my pleasure to acknowledge a few of them. Rosemary Ruether generously responded to correspondence at a key stage of writing and I am grateful to her for lending me an unpublished section of manuscript. Vicky Johnson has been a steadfast source of encouragement, help, and advice, and I am deeply thankful.

I would also like to thank Brenda Bredemeier, who read the book in its entirety not once but several times. Her suggestions significantly enhanced the final product. Rachel Dupuich graciously read an early version of the manuscript and her questions, comments, and clarifying remarks aided my own thinking and writing about a difficult topic. Finally, the people of Twenty-Third Publications were immensely helpful in assisting me in the art of crafting a book, particularly Helen Coleman, John van Bemmel, Richard Haffey, and Neil Kluepfel.

There are several other people whose indirect contributions to this book were so valuable that they deserve special mention. Jean Blomquist, Mary Hunt, and Gay Chessell were particularly important influences on my reluctant beginnings in feminist thinking. Reg and Peg Schultz-Akerson, Cindy Hinkle, Terri Fisher, Frank and Charaline Yu Maxim, Barb Bornemann, Brian and Mary Stein-Webber, and other members of the Covenant Community Group, have been a constant support and inspiration; all have been models of living in contradiction to prejudice. To these individuals and to the many others who have hugged me along the way, I am deeply grateful.

CONTENTS

Foreword   v

Preface   vii

CHAPTER ONE   Sexism and Dualism:
Ruether Presents a Challenge   1

Hierarchical Dualism   3

Dualism and the Church   12

The Perpetuation of Hierarchical
Dualism   22

Combatting Hierarchical Dualism   28

The Next Steps   34

CHAPTER TWO   Restructuring Experience:
Dewey's Response to Dualism   39

Sources of Dualism   40

Experience   45

Responding to Dualism Through
Education   57

CHAPTER THREE   Morality in the Balance:
Dialogues and Distortions   67

Structural-Developmental Theory   69

Coping and Defending Ego Functions   74

Table 1—Coping and Defending Ego
    Process Model   76

    Interactional Morality   81

    The Development of Morality   95

    Table 2—Levels of Interactional
        Morality   96

CHAPTER FOUR   Compassion and Justice:
                Theological Method in Liberation
                Theology   107

                    What Is Liberation Theology?   110

                    Method and Content: A Look at
                        Christology   125

                    Theological Method   129

                    Dewey Revisited   142

                    Avoiding Theological Distortion   145

CHAPTER FIVE   The Nature of Prejudice
                and The Structure of Change   149

                    Through the Looking Glass   150

                    Toward a Common Language   167

CHAPTER SIX   Reducing and Preventing Prejudice:
                A Model for Teaching   177

                    Action, Attitudes and Beliefs   193

                    Preventing Prejudice   201

                Notes   209

                Bibliography   237

                Index   243

Growing Beyond Prejudices

CHAPTER ONE

SEXISM AND DUALISM: RUETHER PRESENTS A CHALLENGE

On May 4, 1983, Thong Hy Huynh, a shy seventeen-year-old Vietnamese refugee, was stabbed to death by a fellow high school student in the quiet university town of Davis, California. One student explained to a reporter why the Vietnamese students were frequently attacked: "The only people who get bothered are the people who make themselves outcasts. ... They have to make themselves more acceptable."[1]

At about the same time, Eileen Gardner, writing for the prestigious Heritage Foundation stated, "There is no injustice in the universe. As unfair as it seems, a person's external circumstances fits his level of inner spiritual development."[2] Her statement was designed as an explanation for physical handicaps and was contained in a position paper advocating the reduction of funding for programs to assist the physically challenged! She was later hired as a consultant by the United States Department of Education.

1

Also in 1983, Patrick Buchanan, then a columnist for the *New York Post* and later the White House Communications director, inferred that the dreaded disease AIDS was a deserved retribution to the gay community.[3]

These news reports are instances of prejudice. Unfortunately, they are by no means unique or even unusual. Hardly a day goes by without similar stories arriving on our doorsteps or flooding our living rooms via papers or television. Has something happened? Not long ago it seemed that prejudice was on the wane. The Civil Rights movement of the fifties sounded the trumpets against racism and ushered in progressive Civil Rights legislation; students of the sixties protested against the war and helped us gain an awareness of ethnocentric tendencies latent within us; in the seventies women challenged perhaps the most deeply rooted prejudice of all—that lodged within the intimacies of male-female relations. The spirit of hope hovered above the chaos of the times and many of us looked for the creation of a new world of justice and harmony.

Then, in the 1980s, the tide turned. Our dreams were washed away like so many sandcastles beneath growing waves of intolerance and bigotry. A decade of Civil Rights legislation, once a focus of national pride, is now being challenged and dismantled. The KKK is again on the rise, as is the activity of neo-Nazi groups. Resentment is mounting against feminists, gays, racial minorities, and others whose images do not reflect the face of middle America.

Prejudice is alive and well. But what precisely is it? If we look to its Latin roots, we find the term *praejudicium,* which simply means a judgment based on earlier decisions or experience, a judgment based on precedent. In English, prejudice (from pre-judge) acquired the meaning of a judgment made without sufficient warrant. Prejudice involves a predisposition toward a group of people that is not derived from adequate information. As one popular aphorism holds, prejudice is a vagrant opinion without visible means of support.

Technically, prejudices may be positive or negative. A positive prejudice would involve a favorable disposition toward a group for no adequate reason. More frequently, however, prejudice is used in the negative sense; it is an unfounded antipathy toward a group or a particular person because of his or her group membership. It is in this sense that the term prejudice is used in this book.

Prejudice is a serious problem. But what motivates it? How is it learned? Most importantly, how can we reduce or eliminate its influence in our homes, schools, churches, and jobs? These are difficult questions, and we need to use a range of resources in our efforts to provide answers. One problem that immediately confronts us is the bewildering array of prejudices. There is racial prejudice, gender prejudice, religious prejudice, class prejudice, national prejudice, age prejudice—to name only a few of the more obvious. If we are to begin our journey toward understanding and controlling prejudices, we need a way to make sense out of all this diversity.

I have found the concept of "hierarchical dualism" to be remarkably useful in understanding the commonality beneath the varied forms of prejudice. It is not a concept I invented. It comes from my study of feminism and, particularly, feminist theologians. In this first chapter we shall explore prejudice through lenses provided by these scholars. Rather than try to survey the whole field, I have chosen to concentrate on the work of one influential member of the feminist theological community, Rosemary Radford Ruether. Ruether was selected for special attention because of her probing analyses of the historical issues surrounding the development of hierarchical dualism and because of her careful attention to the connections among different forms of prejudice and discrimination.

Hierarchical Dualism

It has been commonly observed that the Western way of thinking is highly dualistic. Dualistic thinking is basically "either-or" thinking. Either something is light or it is dark; it is either hot or it is cold. The world is divided into opposite categories and opposing principles. Reality is divided into subject-object, natural-supernatural, body-soul. People are polarized into insiders and outsiders, haves and have nots, the strong and the weak. Dualistic thinking emphasizes what is dissimilar about two related concepts, ideas, or groups of people. What they may share in common is minimized.

Among the most influential dualisms that have prevailed over the centuries in Western philosophy and religion are dualisms between mind and body, spirit and matter, culture and nature. Dualisms such as these can also be called "hierarchical" because they are thought to reflect another fundamental dualism: good and bad. According to this dualistic mentality, mind, spirit and culture are viewed as opposite to and superior over body, matter and nature. While numerous philosophers and social commentators have objected to this pattern of dualistic thinking, the present generation of feminist theologians have added an important and often overlooked dimension. They have chronicled in some detail the manifold ways in which these dualisms have been connected with the categories of male and female.[4] In the pages ahead, we shall look at the early evolution of sexism and how it paved the way for other forms of group oppression.

THE ORIGINS OF HIERARCHICAL DUALISM

To understand the origin of hierarchical dualism, one must look back to the dawn of human history. Ruether believes that sometime prior to the classical urban civilizations, all of which can be characterized as dualistic and sexist, there was a period of integration, "we might say primitive innocence, before the rise of the dualism of dominance and subjection."[5] At this time, males and females had different social functions based on their biological suitability for various tasks, but the distribution of and rewards from work were equal. Basically, men were the protectors and hunters while the lives of women were centered in gathering food and child-rearing. Neither set of tasks was considered more important or worthy than the other. The essential equality of the period was reflected in ancient religious myths, populated by equally powerful and attractive male and female deities.

The integration of primitive life did not survive, however. Eventually the integrated view of humanity dissolved into a dualistic "self-other" view that divided people into more and less valued groups. Ruether suggested in early work that the rise of prejudice and discrimination did not occur until the advent of the classical civilization somewhere around the second millennium before Christ.[6] Prior to this period, people did not have a significant sense of their own individuality; the "I" was merged with the "we." Without a stable sense of individuality, Ruether reasoned, there was no basis for distinguishing others who might then become the target of prejudice.

In Ruether's more recent works, however, she has proposed "a different model of the original dualistic thinking and hierarchy that emphasizes the role of group ego."[7] Ruether now maintains that "the self-other dichotomy in its earliest forms was understood collectively rather than individualistically."[8] Thus, even though people did not experience themselves individualistically during the early tribal period of human history, they still had a collective sense of "our tribe" over against other tribes. Ruether elaborates:

> The tribal group, as the collective self, was a primary basis for human boundary-drawing, over against the "other," as non-human nature and as other human groups with whom one recognized no common humanity. The confusion of the self-other with the good-evil duality seems to have occurred very early in the history of human consciousness.[9]

Ruether's tracing of hierarchical dualism back to tribal cultures seems to be adequate anthropologically.[10] And her more recent work clarifies her thesis in relation to the underlying motivation for hierarchical dualism. Interpreters of Ruether have sometimes concluded, not without reason, that she views socio-economic motives as paramount in the formation of hierarchical dualisms.[11] Although this motive is frequently present, Ruether notes that between groups of equal power there is still a tendency to think of the other group as inferior.[12] This tendency cannot always be interpreted as a desire to gain or maintain economic or political power. Rather, it is motivated by a desire to feel high self-esteem; positive self-assertion (of oneself or of one's group) is gained by attributing negative qualities to an "other." Thus, the motive for prejudice may not always include a desire to exploit the other for political or economic gain; it may be to exploit the other for psychological gain, to enhance one's own sense of self-worth.

As tribal groups began to develop some sense of "otherness," the concept appears to have further been applied to the females within one's own group. There is nothing particularly surprising about this. Sexual identity is certainly among the most obvious and pervasive of all human differences, and the natural divisions of labor that accompanied human development provided a means for highlighting this difference. While there was no intrinsic need to turn this difference into a hierarchical dualism, it occurred quite early as Ruether notes:

> The males of tribal groups particularly became the centers of their own definition of the collective self over against the "other" as female, as other tribes and as non-human nature. We know that many tribes do not even have an inclusive word for "human." Their word for their own tribe functions as equivalent to the word human reducing outsiders to non-humans. Similarly, the word for human in many languages is identical with the word for "male," reducing women to a subsidiary status.[13]

THREE ALTERNATIVE FORMS OF HIERARCHICAL DUALISM

Sometime during the late tribal period, women came to be seen no longer as equals, but as possessions of males. In *New Woman/New Earth: Sexist Ideology and Human Liberation,* Ruether discusses three different but connected forms of hierarchical dualism and outlines the historical development of each. According to Ruether's chronology, the cultural history of women can be divided into three phases: (1) The Conquest of the Mother (i.e. women are subordinated to men), (2) the Negation of the Mother (i.e. women are evil), and (3) The Sublimation of the Mother (i.e. women are viewed idealistically, but considered irrelevant to real life). While the historical introduction of each form occurred in the order listed, one phase does not replace the previous one so much as add a new alternative conceptualization of women.

The image of woman as subordinate to man, the phase Ruether calls the "Conquest of the Mother," occurred primarily as urban cultures began to emerge out of the earlier tribal and village cultures. Urbanization brought with it the need for greater planning and organization. From their position as hunters, warriors, and tribal leaders, men generally took control of the political and military arena. In contrast women, whose lives had been centered in production and reproduction, generally entered the economic domain of the classical civilizations.[14]

With the movement toward urbanization also came a greater tendency toward exploitation. The discovery of farming and the organization of political and economic systems made it possible for divisions of labor to favor one segment of humanity over another. Who was to enjoy the new privileges afforded by the development of civilization? Since men generally occupied those cultural roles in which time was, perhaps for the first time in history, freed from the compulsion of necessary tasks, they were in an advantageous position to develop a cultural ideology. To justify their inherited monopoly of political and social power, "the cultural spokesmen for ruling-class males began to develop ideologies of both class and female inferiority to justify their position."[15]

The ruling males did not have to search far to find raw material for developing an ideology of superiority. The dualisms of mind and body, spirit and matter were ready at hand. These dualisms had also emerged with the development of urban civilization, a form of life that was less integrated with nature than the earlier tribal cultures. The person was viewed as a mind ruling over a body, as a hump of material clay infused with life by a governing spirit. Since child-bearing was imagined as intimately tied to the cycles of nature, women were thought to be more bodily and material than men who, by comparison, were more mind and spirit governed.

Ruether asserts that the first stage of women's cultural history, characterized by males' subordination of females, was followed by a second phase in which there was an outright negation of women. This second phase in the cultural history of women, the "Negation of the Mother," is well reflected, for example, in Greek philosophy. Plato believed that the soul is a spiritual being that resides in the body as an alien in a lower world. What is interesting for our purposes is to note how Plato connected this body-soul dualism with male-female dualism. In his creation myth, *Timaeus,* Plato relates how the soul is put into a male body as a testing place. If it lives virtuously, it is allowed to return to the spiritual world. If it fails and succumbs to the body, it will pass into the form of a woman at its second birth. Women were basically viewed as evil, as temptations to drift from the good life of contemplation.

Aristotle, no less than Plato, articulates hierarchical dualisms and develops a comprehensive view of society that relegates women to a servile position vis-à-vis free Greek males. For him, free Greek males represent the ruling "reason" that must subjugate the "body people," represented by women, slaves, and barbarians.

Ruether has labeled the final phase of the cultural history of women the "Sublimation of the Mother." An apparent reversal of images occurs during this phase. Rather than being debased, women are romanticized. These new idealistic images of women are shallow, however, for they mask an old reality—women are still denied equal participation in the centers of power. The most profound example of this phase occurred during the romantic reaction following the French Revolution. During this period of history, women—who had not long before been cast in the role of the devil's cohort— came to be seen as both more moral and more spiritual than men, though still less rational! This transformation in the stereotypic image of women would appear to run counter to the interest of dominant males, but in reality it was a change dictated by changes in culture.

The advent of industrialization profoundly altered the

structure of society. And with industrialization came secularization, the orientation of life around the things of this world rather than God. Religion, which had been at the center of cultural life, began to move to the periphery. Old values gave way to new values.[16] Secularization readjusted the focus of value away from an otherworldly spiritual realm toward a material reality. The "real world" became synonymous with the world of material existence, of products and work. During earlier periods when the material world was less valued or viewed as the seat of evil, women were imaged as closely tied to nature and the material world. Now, however, women came to be seen as naturally spiritual and moral, traits which became the basis for excluding them from positions of socio-economic power!

The change in values, however, left men with a feeling of shallowness. There was still a longing for the old values that had become antiquated. Men sought a compensatory sphere of morality and sublimated sexuality that could be maintained at the fringe of "real life," and chose the home as a nostalgic realm where out-dated values and suppressed desires could be given expression. Ruether writes:

> The Home and Womanhood were to be everything which this modern industrial world was not. . . . Here in the Home, patriarchy and the rights of birth still held sway as the natural aristocracy, even though this concept was everywhere else overthrown in democratic politics. . . . Here emotionality and intimacy held sway in a world dominated outside by unfeeling technological rationality. Here sublimated spirituality combatted the crude materialism of industrial competition. . . . Above all, the Home was the realm of piety and nostalgic religiosity, cultivated by women, to which men repaired to comfort their spirits against the insecurity of a new world governed by scientific rationality that left little place for the old faith.[17]

The home-work dualism so prevalent today is rooted in this romanticization of women. While many people would have us believe that men have always been associated with the sphere of production—that is, the world of work—and women with the consumer support system—that is, the home—this is actually a fairly recent invention. Before industrialization, the home had been an economic center of production, the source of businesses. But the industrial revolution progressively removed all self-supporting functions from the home, refashioning the family as a unit completely dependent on an economic system outside of itself. Although men had already enjoyed a virtual monopoly on political power, industrialization provided the opportunity to extend that monopoly to the economic realm as well. To this end, the image of the female had to change. Dualisms of fact and value, public and private, objectivity and subjectivity—all of which became popular in the modern world—became the touchstones for the new stereotypes. Women, who had been too corrupt and earthy to participate in the lofty worlds of politics and religion, now became too moral and spiritual to participate in the dirty world of economics. The female role was refashioned from that of an active laborer to that of a dependent manager of a consumption-oriented home and an "ornament to her husband's economic prowess."[18] An ideology of "true womanhood" which promoted the idea that women were somehow "naturally" suited for dependent domestic life arose to justify this marginalization of women.

These three phases in the cultural history of women illustrate variations within the general structure of hierarchical dualism. What is common to each phase is a dualism in which "the other" (i.e. the woman) is reduced to a stereotype. The stereotype serves a particular function, namely, to enable a social comparison process by which females can be seen as less deserving of social power and privilege than males. The stereotype, however, can reflect variously an image of a simple subordinate, an evil antagonist, or a childlike image of a lost good. In all cases, the projected image of "the other" serves to maintain the power of the dominant male.

SEXUAL SYMBOLISM AS MODEL

Ruether maintains that sexual prejudice and discrimination were the first of all forms to arise and that they have provided a highly adaptable model for the exploitation of one human group by another throughout history. Once dualisms arose and their positive and negative poles identified with male and female respectively, it was but a small step for the cultural elite to extend the negative descriptions to other groups. As Ruether notes:

> A similar view of the subjugated people as both objects of exploitation, and as irrational, passive and yet dangerously sensual, has marked the traditional view of white males toward all "inferiors": workers, peasants, and colonized, especially non-white, colonized peoples.[19]

Two advantages accrued to the male population by using the mind-body dualism to understand male-female relations. First, the alienated male, fearful of his own sensuality, was able to locate the source of trouble outside of himself; it is women who are sexual body-objects. Secondly, by imaging women in terms of bodiliness, men were given justification for subjecting them to the rule of "mind" people, namely elite males. The utility of this pattern of thinking led to its being reapplied numerous times throughout history to various other peoples. That the psychic model of sexual prejudice provided the model for other forms of prejudice is evident in the way exaggerated sexuality has entered the stereotypes for many other oppressed groups. The irrationality of the projection is made transparent by noting how frequently it clearly contradicts reality:

> It matters very little that the Jew was hardly orgiastic in the Middle Ages, that the heretics persecuted by the Church were themselves practitioners of rigid asceticism, or that official communism is highly puritanical. Invariably these agents of the powers of evil are seen by dominant society both as blasphemers of the received faith and order of society, and also as people who indulge in lascivious sexual practices and infect the rest of society with spreading debauchery.[20]

The way sexism is interconnected with other forms of group prejudice will attract our attention again as we continue to explore the nature of hierarchical dualism. We turn now, however, to the influence of the church on the development of dualistic ways of thinking. We shall see that the consequences of dualisms fostered within the church have contributed not only to the development of specific group prejudices but also to an imperialistic orientation toward nature that has led to the current ecological crisis.

Dualism and the Church

The three forms of hierarchical dualism discussed earlier have all been characteristic of the Judeo-Christian tradition. The subordination of women can clearly be seen in numerous legal codes and ritual practices of the ancient Israelites. The social structure of the Hebrew nation was definitely patriarchal and the biblical writers reflected the cultural assumptions of their time. In the Ten Commandments, for example, wives are listed together with houses, slaves, oxen and asses as property of men which the neighbor is not to covet (Ex. 20:17). Occasionally the biblical texts go beyond a simple subordination of women and we find images of women as basically more corrupt than men. Ruether believes the story of Genesis 3 is illustrative. It provides a reversal myth designed to legitimate patriarchy, and reflects a growing misogynism throughout the Western world:

> In the story of Adam's rib the male is the original human prototype. Reversing natural experience, he is described as giving birth to the woman with the help of a father God. . . . A misogynism developed, both in Greek literature and in the later strata of Old Testament and talmudic Judaism. These texts expound the evilness of women and trace the origins of evil in the world to female figures, such as Eve and Pandora.[21]

The identification of evil with "the first woman" has had a particularly devastating effect on real historical women. Regardless of the intent of the original author, the continual repetition of the story throughout the centuries has molded the cultural imagination to such a degree that periodic outbreaks of misogynist paranoia could be expected. It would not be too strong to state that the brutal murder of hundreds of thousands of so-called witches throughout history has had a direct root in this imagery. The incrimination of Eve is typical of the "victim-blaming" pattern of thinking characteristic of prejudice. Formed in the cultural context of patriarchy, the victims of patriarchy are blamed for its evils.[22]

Although the third form of hierarchical dualism where "the other" is romanticized seldom finds its source in biblical texts, it developed within the Christian church. Ruether notes, "Christianity typically produces a schizophrenic view of women. Women are split into sublimated spiritual feminity (the Virgin Mary) and actual fleshly women (fallen Eve)."[23] The church offers the world two basic images of femininity. Women can be "virgin mothers" and thereby achieve their intended spirituality, or they can be evil "Eves." Real women of flesh and blood, of course, always failed to live up to the ideal of both virgin and mother, and consequently the evil temptress continued to be the dominant image of femininity provided by Christianity, at least until the modern period.

To gain a better understanding of the role that Christian theology has played in the development and perpetuation of prejudices, it will be helpful to contrast two ancient patterns of dealing with the polarities of existence: the prophetic dialetic and apocalyptic dualism. We will show how the dualistic model was appropriated and used by the early Church, particularly in its polemics against Judaism, and how it developed its own set of dualistic categories. We will then turn to look at the interrelation of Christian dualisms with Western imperialism, American racism, and the current crisis in ecology.

DIALECTIC OR DUALISM?

Although Ruether criticizes dualistic modes of understanding reality, she does not deny that human experience contains many polarities. We experience life as both good and bad, as graceful and as sin-ful. We experience both hope and despair. Ruether, however, returns to the prophetic tradition for a non-dualistic way to understand these polarities.

The prophets employed a *dialectic* of judgment and hope. In this context, the difference between a dialectic and a dualism is that in the latter the poles (e.g. judgment and hope) are split apart and applied to two different groups; in a dialectic both poles are viewed as characterizing oneself or one's own people. For the prophetic community, the concepts of divine judgment and promise served as principles of discernment by which the faith and failings of their own community were judged. When the people acted with disregard to the foreigner or the widow, they were told that they were under God's judgment; yet, at the same time, the same people were heirs to God's promise of redemption. In the prophetic dialectic, the judgmental word is valid only when spoken from within the community addressed.

During the time between the Old and New Testaments the Jewish people were subjected to one of the worst periods of persecution they had known. Partially in response to the great suffering of the people, a new religious perspective developed called apocalypticism. The apocalyptic writers borrowed the polarities of the prophets but turned them into dualisms. God's judgment was on the enemies of the Jews, while the Jews were the proper inheritors of God's promise. The world was divided into children of light and children of darkness, as one book of the time was titled. It was during this period that Satan was first introduced into the Judeo-Christian tradition as a force inspiring evil in the world. The apocalyptic view was still very much in evidence during the first century and it was highly influential in the early development of Christian thought.

CHRISTIAN ANTI-SEMITISM

The early Christian church faced a severe problem. It claimed that a certain Nazarene named Jesus was the Christ expected by the Jewish people, and yet the majority of the Jews rejected him as their Messiah. The Christians had to argue that their interpretation of the Jewish scriptures was more accurate than the Jew's own interpretations. To understand how the church resolved the problem it is important to see the convergence of three influences. First, the patriarchal traditions of the Hebrews had provided a model for ordering people in terms of value. Second, the advent of apocalypticism provided a precedent for viewing some human groups as bearers of evil and other groups as the gate for salvation. Finally, there was the influence of gnosticism, an eclectic and popular group of teachings which held that salvation was gained through secret knowledge that transported one out of the evil world of nature and into a purely spiritual existence.

Under the combined weight of these influences, Christianity began to adopt a series of dualisms. The doctrine of redemption was severed from that of creation and thereby a dualism between "nature and grace" emerged. The old prophetic dialetics between inward and outward obedience to God's word led to dualisms between letter and spirit, law and gospel. Usually in the New Testament writings we find these polarities discussed as dialetics, but the need to proclaim Christ as the fulfillment of the Jewish scriptures led to occasional slips into dualism. The New Testament itself contains a schism between "the Christian 'good guys' and the Jewish 'bad guys.' " The Jews were imaged after the negative side of the dualisms mentioned. They were people of the law, tied to the outer letter, bound by unredeemed nature. In contrast, Christians viewed themselves as people of the gospel, guided by the spirit, open to God's grace.[24] Thus, the Jews failed to recognize their own redeemer because they were legalistic hair-splitters concerned only with outward obedience. Christians, on the other hand, as people of love, recognized the true import of the inspired texts because they were "enlightened" by inward grace.

By pronouncing God's judgment on "the Jews" and claiming the messianic hope for "the church," early Christianity adopted the dualistic-apocalyptic mode rather than the prophetic mode. In so doing, Ruether asserts that the church lost "the greatest moral achievement of prophetic Judaism, namely, the breakthrough from ideological religion centered in self-justification to a self-critical faith."[25]

CHRISTIAN DUALISMS

Ruether posits that the church inherited, both from Jewish apocalypticism and from Greek philosophy, a set of dualisms that fundamentally limited its capacity to create a liberating theology.[26] We have seen how some of these dualisms were manifested in Christian anti-semitism. We will now briefly examine some of the other influential dualisms that crept into early Christianity.

Classical Christian spirituality appropriated the Greek body-soul dualism. Accordingly, salvation is thought to come through repression of and escape from the body. This dualistic view of reality alienates persons from their own bodily existence. By extension, all perceptible reality is reduced to secondary status in relation to the otherworldly spiritual realm. Not surprisingly, the sexes came to be associated with this dualism. Classical Christian spirituality viewed man as "rational spirit"; woman was viewed as "sexual object."

The church, in contrast to the predominant biblical view, also developed an individual-community dualism. In old Israel, God was viewed as the redeemer of the nation: the Hebrew people understood as a collective unity. Similarly, in the New Testament Christ is often imaged as the savior of the world. But early in the Church's history, the individual was removed from the communal context and viewed as the recipient of God's saving activity. The individual concept of salvation also implied an individualistic approach to sin, resulting in a petty and private concept of evil. Rather than focusing on such communal manifestations of evil as injustice and violence, sin was individualized as sexual deviation and negative emotion. In contrast to this individual/communal dualism, Ruether notes that even in St. Paul the individual's movement toward conversion cannot be separated from his or her membership in the community of reconciliation.

Ruether maintains that Christianity has also employed a number of dualisms in its images of God.[27] In these images of God, we also find again the fundamental male-female dualism. The patriarchal culture out of which Christianity arose led to God being imaged as the Great Patriarch who stands above and outside nature and the world. God is seen as a transcendent "Subject" that reduces creation to the status of inferior "object." God is the "sky-Husband-Father" over the earth as "wife." In the Old Testament, this analogy is transferred to the relation of Yahweh-husband and Israel-wife, while in the New Testament it becomes the relation of Christ the bridegroom to the church, his bride.

IMPERIALISM AND CHRISTIAN DUALISM

As noted earlier, the same psychic pattern of hierarchical dualism that underlies sexism can readily be expanded to include whatever "other" a ruling power finds it advantageous to oppress. When self-identity is built on identifying oneself with positive qualities alone—repressing and projecting the negative side of dualistic pairs—then there is a strong motive for imperialism. By subjugating other people, conquerors can remake them in accordance with their own stereotypic images while reaping political, economic, and psychological advantages at their expense. Thus, native Americans, robbed of their homelands and herded onto reservations, suffer from high rates of alcoholism and depression while the white settlers praise themselves for their civilizing (i.e. "Christianizing") influence. In the "Christian" West, where technological development created the potential for massive economic and political exploitation, imperialism took a firm hold.[28]

Western imperialism is largely a result of a deeply rooted Christian hierarchical dualism, the dualism of saved and damned. As Ruether notes, "White imperialism springs from the Christocentric view of history."[29] Christians view themselves as "the saved," God's elect people, commissioned to conquer all other nations in the name of Christ. The great commission to preach and baptize is given a secular translation, justifying the seizing of foreign lands and the annihilation of independent cultural identities. In more recent and secularized times, the Christian West simply becomes the Democratic West, the "Free World," and the imperialistic mentality continues unaltered.

The view of the church that fosters imperialistic tendencies is called "Constantinianism" by Ruether. In this model of the church there is a "suppression of the messianic dialectic of the Gospel and an ideological use of the messianic symbols of the Gospel to baptize the empire."[30] This is the predominant social use of Christianity in the advanced industrialized nations of the world.

RACISM AND CHRISTIAN IMAGES OF WOMEN

Racism takes many different forms and certainly predates the rise of Christianity. In this section I will limit the discussion to the interaction of sex and race in the American South. Within this limited scope, the images provided by the Christian tradition have played a key role in the development of the cultural life of the people. Ruether notes that American slavery depended not only on a rigidly racist anthropology that defined blacks as inferior "by nature," but also on a destruction of the black family and the structuring of black women into a system of white male sexual dominance. To understand this complex of connected prejudices and discriminatory practices, it is helpful to remember the legacy of Christian female symbolism that was mentioned earlier.

There are two primary women at the core of the Christian tradition and these two women provide opposite models of the feminine potential. There is Eve the sinful temptress, and there is the holy, but non-imitable, Virgin-Mother Mary. Throughout most of Christian history, real women were painted with the template of Eve. But with the coming of industrialization and late Romanticism, women began to be idealized and the Mary image became, in secularized form, predominant. This fantasy, however, was actually only possible for the privileged classes since the real condition of most women required dehumanizing labor.

In the South, Ruether asserts, the Eve-Mary dualism took racist form. The elite white patriarch ruled over a society divided by sex, race, and class. Within these categories, white and black females were made opposites. The white woman was imaged after the Virgin Mary. She was the delicate ornament of the parlor, representing the class and racial ideal of pure virginal feminity, excused from difficult labor and dressed to reflect the cultural ideal of chastity and simple beauty. The black woman, on the other hand, was the polar opposite— imaged as a secular Eve and exploited for sex and labor. The abuse of the black woman, in turn, required the suppression of the rights of the black male as husband, father, and householder. The black man was relegated to the bottom of the hierarchy, reduced to an asexual beast of burden.

The period following the Civil War did not see any significant improvement in the disrupted condition of the Southern black family. Having eliminated official slavery, white society remained unwilling to replace it with socio-economic integration. Black women were still made available to white patriarchs on demand. The inevitable sexual guilt that accompanied this exploitation was often repressed and projected onto the black male. Thus, black men became scapegoats for white guilt:

> Repressing its sexual guilt, white male society projected its pathology upon the black male. He became the walking symbol of white fears of retribution. He was fantasized into a dark sexual "beast," with outsized penis, ever about to assault the barricades that protected the white man's "virginal" females. Hundreds of black men, their genitals ripped from their bodies, were left to twist on trees as sacrificial victims of this obsession.[31]

Ruether suggests that the frequent failure of black liberation groups and women's liberation groups to cooperate is partially an outgrowth of this history.[32] According to Ruether, white terrorism against black males remains the ultimate existential reference point for most black liberation movements. Perceiving themselves as powerless, black males in such groups compensate by exaggerating their own black masculinity. The powerful black male, machine gun in hand, functions as an appealing image to black men who feel castrated by white society.

When white feminists dialogue with members of the black movement, Ruether concludes, they are usually ignorant of the history of racism and its effects. When these feminists offer their critiques of the "feminine mystique," a problem that is derived from the image of the ornamental white lady, they are too often unaware of the racist underpinnings of this image. Most black women have been subjected to a different form of oppression than most white women, and the two forms of exploitation cannot simply be collapsed into a single analysis of patriarchal oppression. Cooperative efforts among liberation movements, which fortunately are becoming more frequent, require sensitivity to the unique historical circumstances that have given rise to each form of oppression.

CHRISTIAN DUALISM AND THE ECOLOGICAL CRISIS

Up to this point we have concentrated our attention on the way in which dualisms have influenced prejudice. We should not overlook the fact that dualism has also facilitated another major social problem: the ecological crisis. Though we hear about it less frequently than we did a decade ago, the ecological crisis still presents one of the most serious threats to human survival. Toxic dumps, acid rain, nuclear waste, pollution of rivers and lakes all present a monumental challenge to our continuing existence. Ruether maintains that the mindset behind imperialism is closely linked to that which justifies a domination of nature. She notes:

> The ethic of technological mastery and political domination is culminating in a world divided by a forest of penis-missiles and counter-missiles that could destroy mankind many times over. The ethic of mastery, also, by ignoring the organic harmonies that link man [sic] with animals and plants, sky and earth, pollutes the environment and turns the city into a technological wasteland, undermining the social and ecological fabric of all existence.[33]

Since Lynn White's essay on the "Religious Roots of Our Ecological Crisis,"[34] it has been common to trace the domination of nature back to the Old Testament mandate to subdue the earth. Ruether takes exception to this position, pointing out that Hebrew religion in the pre-exilic period had not developed a negative view of nature.[35] Ruether argues that two important elements that define nature as a sphere for human domination are absent from pre-exilic Hebrew religion. One element is a view of consciousness as somehow apart from or transcendent to visible nature. The second element is the integration of the spirit/nature split into class and race relations.

These two elements, however, were typical of classical Greek philosophy as Ruether notes:

> Here the authentic self is regarded as the soul or transcendent rationality, over against bodily existence. The relation of spirit to body is one of repression, subjugation and mastery. Material existence is ontologically inferior to mind and the root of moral evil. Moreover, the language of hierarchical dualism is identified with social hierarchy. The hierarchy of spirit over body is expressed in the domination of males over females, freed men over slaves.[36]

Apocalyptic Judaism also developed an alienated view of nature. The "world," according to the apocalyptic vision, has fallen from the sovereignty of God and is under the domain of diabolical powers. Salvation, according to the apocalypticists, comes either through spiritual escape from this world or through God's destruction of this world to be followed by the creation of a new heaven and earth.

Early Christian theology created a fusion of Platonic dualism and apocalyptic Judaism. Generally, nature was tied to evil, but not entirely. The Christian view of nature took on much the same character as its view of women. There was a split between two opposing possibilities for nature — sacramentality or demonicality.[37] Nature, restored to the sovereignty of God through Christ, was exemplified in the sacraments. Here, in the sacral sphere of the church, nature was restored as the image and incarnate presence of God. But outside of this redeemed sphere, nature was considered demonic.

The image of nature as the seat of principalities and powers of evil eventually came into conflict with the needs of the budding sciences. In order to render nature safe and available for human use, it had to be liberated from its image as the playground of the devil. Francis Bacon sought to bring the scientific project within the blessing of the Christian community by arguing that the domination of nature through science was actually the fulfillment of the Christian hope for the redemption of nature.

By the nineteenth century the Judeo-Christian God concept was largely secularized. The former idea of the Christian redemption of nature evolved into the notion of "human progress." The idea of progress, though, still reflected the same underlying spirit-nature dualism that had informed the Christian mission of redemptive science. Males, identifying themselves with transcendence, made technology the vehicle of a progressive incarnation of "spirit" into nature. Progress was to be achieved by molding nature to conform to the desires of the technocrats. But nature was not respected of itself and consequently its harmonies and balances were ignored. It was simply there to be used. The human-nature relationship reflected the model of male-female relations. Thus we often speak of the rape of nature. The end result, as Ruether notes, is that "within two centuries this pattern of thought and activity has brought humanity close to the brink of the destruction of the earth."[38]

The Perpetuation of Hierarchical Dualism

We have explored the historical roots of hierarchical dualism and have noted the role played by the Church in its development. We turn now to the contemporary world in an effort to understand the powers that sustain prejudice. Why does hierarchical dualism persist? For purposes of discussion, the mechanisms that Ruether identifies for the perpetuation of hierarchical dualism can be divided into two major categories. First there are *psychological processes* that result in distortions of our perceptions of the world around us. Borrowing from the psychoanalytic tradition, the key psychological processes that Ruether isolates are repression and projection. The second category is *socialization processes*. Because our language, customs, manners, habits, and lifestyles reflect hierarchical dualism, children learn it from their experience in our homes, schools, churches, and businesses.

THE PSYCHOLOGICAL PROCESSES

According to Ruether, the psychoanalytic revolution is one of the most important changes in consciousness that divides us from our ancestors of even a century ago. Prior to Freud it was common to regard consciousness as a direct reflection of "reality." Because of the psychoanalytic revolution, however, there has come to be a broad recognition that our perceptions of reality are frequently distorted by irrational motives buried deep within our psyche. The way we choose our friends and lovers, for example, may reflect submerged desires related to our relationships with parents and siblings. The recognition that our beliefs, attitudes, values and perceptions may reflect unconscious motives is of central importance to women. While other analytic tools can be used to criticize the injustices of oppressive social structures, the psychoanalytic revolution is helpful in understanding the irrational dimensions of sexism. In spite of this liberating potential, however, Ruether believes that Freud's psychoanalytic theories have been "the enemy, not the friend of women."[39]

Because of Ruether's negative evaluation of the way in which psychoanalysis has been developed in relation to women, it is not surprising that she spends little time discussing in detail the psychological mechanisms that underlie and perpetuate hierarchical dualism. She does, however, make use of Freud's concept of defense mechanism. According to Freud, when individuals feel under psychological attack (either from external sources or from their own inner impulses or conscience), they may alleviate the pain and maintain their sense of self-identity by unconsciously falsifying or distorting their perceptions. For example, if my conscience "tells me" that I'm basically evil, I may unconsciously redirect the condemnation to others, thereby labeling others as evil.

Freud discussed several defense mechanisms, but the two most frequently mentioned are repression and projection. Ruether also highlights these two processes or mechanisms.

To extend the quote mentioned above, Ruether writes:

> Freud's psychoanalytic revolution has been the
> enemy, not the friend, of women. Yet the psycho-
> analytical discovery of repression and projection is
> too important a tool for revealing the processes of
> male sexism itself to be simply rejected by women
> because it was originally shaped within a male
> ideological description of experience.[40]

Repression operates by forcing a threatening memory,
idea, or perception out of consciousness. For example, repression may prevent a person from seeing something in easy view,
or it may distort what is seen in order to protect the ego from
a perceived threat.

Ruether, unfortunately, offers little elaboration on how
repression operates to maintain hierarchical dualism other than
to suggest that the mind-body dualism is maintained through
a repressed sexuality.[41] By repressing one's sexuality, an image
of the self as "transcendent ego," only incidentally clothed in
a body, can be maintained. Bodiliness becomes a threat to the
independent ego. Ruether suggests that until recent times males
in particular have experienced their own bodiliness as
threatening.

Ruether has not taken advantage of another aspect of
Freudian thought that is related to his concept of repression.
Repression, according to Freud, operates not only on the immediate anxiety-creating object, but on any object that becomes
in some way closely associated with the original anxiety-producing object. Thus, if one's body is experienced as threat,
it is not only one's sense of bodiliness or sexuality that must
be repressed but related ideas as well. Repression may come
to operate on a host of similar phenomena, including all sensual, material reality generally. This necessity to repress
associated ideas, memories, or perceptions may lie beneath the
tendency for one dualism (e.g. mind-body), once established,
to spawn further dualisms (e.g. spirit-matter, other world-this
world, eternity-history).

The second Freudian defense mechanism highlighted by
Ruether is projection.[42] When a person feels anxious about

something, another way to handle the anxiety is to attribute its cause to the external world. Instead of saying, "I have sexual desires for her," for example, one might say, "She's tempting me." Through the use of projection, the ego transforms what is actually neurotic or moral anxiety, which arises from within the self, into an objective threat coming from the environment.

As was the case with repression, Ruether elaborates little on the role of projection in the maintenance of hierarchical dualism. However, her analysis points to projection and repression operating together to create various forms of hierarchical dualism. In the prototypic case of sexism, Ruether suggests that many males cope with their fear of intimacy by repressing their own sexuality while, at the same time, projecting a heightened sexuality onto women. Consequently, a partial aspect of female existence—their bodiliness—becomes for these males the total definition of femininity. The result, of course, is a stereotype. A stereotype takes a limited aspect of a person or group and exaggerates it as if it were an adequate image for the whole. The stereotype is maintained by repressing— or otherwise defensively processing—any data contrary to the projection.

The reader may experience difficulty with this brief description of the psychological processes underlying hierarchical dualism. Indeed, Ruether may be guilty herself of creating a stereotype of the prejudiced person. What Ruether is attempting to do, however, is make explicit psychological dynamics which are often only implicit in our everyday interactions. By exaggerating the subtle she helps us see what we might not otherwise see. In the third chapter we will return again to the psychological processes underlying hierarchical dualism and expand upon the hints that Ruether has dropped.

THE SOCIOLOGICAL PROCESSES

Prejudice and oppression are not the same thing. While prejudice is often a form of justification for inequitable power distributions, it need not be. Prejudice can exist in situations in which there is no discrimination. Ruether makes note of this:

The perception of the other as inferior. . . rationalizes
exploitative relationships with them. But the two need
to be distinguished. The perception of the other as
evil is not just the ideological superstructure of exploitative relations, as Marxists would have it. It
already is found in situations where groups coexist,
each thinking of the other as inferior. But when one
conquers the other, then the ideology of superiority
of the dominant group stifles and suppresses the corresponding sense of self of the other.[43]

Sexism is not really equivalent to sexual prejudice nor
is racism equivalent to racial prejudice. Sexism is sexual prejudice combined with enough coercive power to dominate the
other sex. Racism is racial prejudice joined to a power structure that allows whites to exploit nonwhites. While anyone can
be prejudiced, sexism is uniquely a male problem and racism
is uniquely a white problem. Ruether does not make this point
explicitly, but it is implicit within passages such as the above
and it has been made by several social scientists.[44] The distinction between prejudice and oppression (sexism, racism,
heterosexism, etc.) becomes important when we turn to the
sociological mechanisms that support hierarchical dualism.

We might also note that the term hierarchical dualism
itself has a deliberate ambiguity. Most often we have used it
to describe a way of organizing perceptions of value. Thus,
it has a psychological meaning. Hierarchical dualism also has
been used to designate that philosophical outlook wherein reality
is divided into opposing forces (e.g. mind and body or spirit
and matter). Thus it has been used to designate a philosophical
perspective. We now turn to a third meaning. Hierarchical
dualism can be used to describe a pattern of social relationships
or institutional structures. It can have a sociological meaning.
In this third sense, hierarchical dualism can be used to describe
a situation of oppression. The three forms of hierarchical
dualism, of course, are mutually reinforcing.

Socialization—the process of informally and formally
training the young to assume their adult roles—brings all three
meanings of hierarchical dualism together and provides a mechanism through which the prejudices of an elite are combined

into power arrangements that lead to oppression. Young children learn to organize their experience in dichotomous value-laden categories (hierarchical dualism in the psychological sense) by repetitive contact with cultural ideologies (hierarchical dualism in the philosophical sense) through their participation in social relationships and institutions that reflect differential power among various social groups (hierarchical dualism in the sociological sense).

The importance of the socialization process becomes evident when it is realized that oppression almost always requires at least the partial cooperation of those who are oppressed. It may seem odd that some people would willingly submit to subordinate status, but this is frequently the case. The cooperation of the oppressed is gained through persuading them that things are as they should be. "Women belong in the home." "Blacks are great athletes, but they're lousy executives."

Ruether contends that when one group has power over another, an "ideology of inferiority" becomes embedded in the subordinated groups' socialization processes. Not only does the dominant group see the oppressed group through stereotypic lenses colored by projection, but the subjugated people themselves internalize the stereotype as part of their own self-image. Ruether writes:

> In order to understand the sociological workings of psychic projection, we must see the way the projection tends to be internalized by the subjugated group. The projected images dictate the social role they are allowed to play. This in turn molds their own self-image so that they largely take on the appearance, not only in the presence of the oppressors, but even in their own eyes, of the character vested in them. This is reinforced by exclusion from educational and vocational opportunities for correcting and enlarging experience.[45]

Subjugated people are taught to see themselves as inferior to the dominant group and to restrict their aspirations to the limited range of poorly rewarded vocational and social options generally open to them in society. The lower class native American child, for instance, may easily embrace a self-image that incorporates a sense of shame and inferiority due to the way Indian people and cultures have been stereotyped in the language, media, and folklore of dominant culture. Full of self-doubt, the child is likely to exaggerate the significance of any failure experiences in school or work places and, consequently, aspire to only the most menial of job opportunities. Socialization processes, while powerful and pervasive, frequently go unrecognized. The mechanisms of socialization into sexist stereotypes may be particularly difficult to bring to consciousness, as Ruether notes:

> Oppression in society is never a matter of open force only. It always seeks to become socially incorporated and to operate through modes of cultural conditioning which make the subjects internalize the image projected upon them. Since, of all power relations, that between men and women is the most intimate, carefully hidden forms of persuasion are necessarily demanded in order to shape women to be what, according to male ideology, they are, and to lead them to internalize a self-image appropriate to this status. From their earliest years women are culturally conditioned to be willing cooperators in their enslavement and unconscious of their objective situation.[46]

Much work has been done by feminist sociologists to expose these socialization processes.[47] Perhaps language is the most important of these, for "language is the prime reflection of the power of the ruling group to define reality in its own terms and demote oppressed groups into invisibility."[48] Language is so taken for granted that its powerful role in shaping our perceptions of reality and value are usually completely unconscious. When, for example, a religious tradition continually visualizes the divine in exclusively masculine terms (Father, King, Lord), the worshippers' perception of ultimate value cannot help but slant toward the male even though God may still be affirmed as beyond sexuality.

Combatting Hierarchical Dualism

Ruether's responses to the problems of hierarchical dualism focus on the communities she knows best: women and the church. She makes no claim to speak for all oppressed people, not even for all white, Christian women. She believes it is important for all those interested in promoting equality to be open to a variety of expressions of liberation and to seek points of commonality while recognizing differences. In this spirit, the following discussions of the church and women's consciousness-raising are offered not only for their potential contributions to Christians and women, but for what they might suggest for other institutions and oppressed groups.

THE CHURCH AS A LIBERATING COMMUNITY

There can be no doubt that the church often has acted like a powerful engine pulling the train of human liberation down the wrong track. Earlier in this chapter, we explored some of the ways the church has fostered patterns of hierarchical dualism. But the church, Ruether argues, need not be nor has it always been associated with suppression of the human spirit. For many, it has been the inspiration for struggle against injustice and the source of hope for a better world.

The potential of the church to serve as an institutional base for liberation struggles has been hotly debated in feminist circles. Some have argued that patriarchy is so central to the church, there is no hope for its redemption. The classical statement about "no salvation outside the church" is reversed to read, "no hope for liberation to be found within the church." In her powerful and penetrating book *Beyond God the Father,* the feminist philosopher and theologian Mary Daly takes this position.[49] Daly's critique has focused on how religious symbols function in culture to legitimize the oppression of women. For her, the Father God of the church is a male idol. In a similar manner, she declares the core religious symbols of the church—Father, Son, Lord, Kingdom—to be unredeemably patriarchal; they buttress and justify male supremacy. For Daly, as Carol Christ observes, "the Father, Son and Spirit legitimate an 'Unholy Trinity' of Rape, Genocide, and War in which unrestrained power forces the submission of 'the other.' "[50]

If the church is to recover its potential to be a salvific

presence in the world, it cannot simply dismiss these critiques as feminist hyperbole. Too often, people who first encounter feminist theology dismiss it as an overreaction. Until one expends the effort to carefully study the patriarchal deformation of Christianity and explores the connections between images of women in the church and the littering of history with brutalized feminine bodies, it is easy to claim exaggeration.

Even a cursury study of church history will reveal how deeply ingrained misogynism has been. Only a century after the Apostle Paul set out to preach the good news of Christ, Tertullian, perhaps the most influential of the early Church "fathers," blamed women for Christ's death and declared, "The judgment of God upon your sex endures even today; and with it inevitably endures your position of criminal at the bar of justice. You are the gateway of the Devil."[51] The great theologian of the fourth century, Augustine of Hippo, denied that women had souls.[52] Thomas Aquinas said of women that they are "defective and misbegotten."[53] Martin Luther failed at humor when he quipped, "God created Adam master and lord of living creatures, but Eve spoiled all."[54] Nor was it funny when thousands of statements like these built to a climax in the witch hunts carried out in the name of the Catholic and Protestant faiths; conservative estimates indicate that a million people were murdered.[55]

It would be easy to dismiss the realities of our patriarchal past by simply declaring that the church no longer teaches that women are inferior and certainly we ourselves do not hold such a view. But as surely as our lungs breathe the air around us, our minds absorb the subtle yet pervasive subordination of women in our church life. It is present in the language that we use about God and ourselves, in our patterns of worship and leadership, and in the myriad of informal practices and norms that assign church tasks according to sexual identity rather than interest or capability. Women in the church are often softly exploited, gently abused.

Ruether shares many of the same concerns that motivate Daly's rejection of the church, but she finds hope where Daly only sees despair. In particular, Ruether and Daly diverge over their evaluations of the Christian scriptures. In elaborating her own position, Ruether writes:

> I regard patriarchy as a strong social additive, but not the norm or essential nature of the Judeo-Christian tradition. Else I would not be a Christian. I regard the authentic nature of the Judeo-Christian tradition as the prophetic-iconoclastic-messianic tradition; the tradition of critique of idolatry and ideology and the hope for the transformation of human reality in the direction of proximate and ultimate salvation and reconciliation with each other, with the world, with God. This norm is also the norm for the denunciation and purging of patriarchy from biblical faith.[56]

According to Ruether, then, the critique of patriarchal symbols and practices within Christianity need not come from a position outside the church nor need it destroy the essential Judeo-Christian tradition. Rather, the critique is essentially prophetic self-criticism. It is rooted in the biblical faith.[57]

But it is not just the glimpses of liberation that Ruether finds sprinkled through the Scriptures that give her hope. There is a spirit in the contemporary church that yearns to be freed from its patriarchal cage. Ruether finds hope, for example, in the increase of women entering the ordained ministry in the Protestant churches. If women enter the ministry in large numbers, she suggests, then the whole range of dualisms—God-human, soul-body, clergy-laity, sacred-secular—will have to be rethought because the sexist pattern that underlies them will be open to critical re-evaluation. As women's gifts are harnessed by the Spirit, Ruether suggests, church leadership will change from a paternalistic, hierarchical style to a dialogical form of leadership where all the people are the agents of the ministry and mission of the church.

Ruether believes women and clergy are natural allies even though the clergy have inherited misogynist tendencies from earlier generations. Both groups have experienced marginalization from "real life" in the modern world. Women have been confined to the home and the church has been removed from its central position in society and pushed to the sidelines. This common experience may be the basis for cooperation and a transformation both of church and society:

> If both the clergy and women have suffered from encapsulation in the domestic sphere, then they must see each other as allies in a common struggle to overthrow the false schism between "private morality" and the "real world." In order to pray Jesus' prayer that "God's will be done on earth," we must break apart the false schizophrenia between private "feminine" morality and the public world of technological rationality which renders the message of the Church "effete," while the Masters of War go about their "manly" activities. The message of the Church must be seen as the social mandate of human history, rather than private individual "salvation."[58]

To regain its liberating potential, Ruether recommends that the church engage in a reinterpretation of its key theological tenents:

> The destruction of the traditional dualisms of classical Christian theology demands a transformation of the semantic content of the religious symbols. . . . The key Christian symbols of Incarnation, Revelation and Resurrection cease to point backward to some once and for all event in the past, which has been reified as a mysterious salvific power in the institutional Church, and becomes instead paradigms of the liberation which takes place in people here and now.[59]

For Ruether, the incarnation does not refer simply to God becoming human in the person of Jesus; rather "to be incarnate" means to make God humanly present in today's world by being fully and bodily committed to the liberation of the oppressed. Revelation is not limited to a past communication of supernatural truths, but involves that redeeming and liberating insight that makes people aware of the need to live and act for justice and peace. The resurrection is not confined to an ancient miracle that happened to Jesus alone, or will happen to all after death. Resurrection is the present hope of the "new person" who is being born in the commitment and struggle of making a new world. By giving its religious symbols contemporary meaning, the Body of Christ may again feel the lifeblood of messianic hope rushing through its veins.

CONSCIOUSNESS RAISING AND SOCIAL ACTION

While Ruether has pointed to the church as a vital institutional source for God's work of emancipation, she is less clear about how to enlist the support of grassroots women and men. She does, however, provide a brief sketch of a process that women might experience in coming to terms with their situation and the need to transform it. It is a process that holds together the need to change both one's own awareness and the social institutions that reinforce patriarchy.[60] One without the other is insufficient.

Ruether speaks of four interpenetrating stages to the liberation of women. The first stage is generally subjective and psychological. It involves raising consciousness and exorcising debasing self-images. Ruether speaks of anger and pride as theological virtues in this context.[61] Anger gives women the power to break free from their dependent attachments to males and overcome the debased images of women prevalent in our culture. Pride gives women the power to re-establish an authentic sense of personhood as the ground of their being. Anger and pride give back to women the power of self-definition.

The second stage is one of social action. The focus of attention must move beyond the individual to the corporate situation of women. One's own new awareness must lead beyond thought to action. One must work to overcome the way women as a group are entrapped by the systematic structuring of male-female roles.

Third, women must move beyond self-affirmation to self-criticism, particularly of their own class and racial contexts. Left by themselves, the first two steps tend toward the development of an apocalyptic consciousness that divides the world into good and evil. In this vision, women become the exclusive bearers of salvation, while men are denigrated as "male chauvinist pigs" with no possibility of redemption. However necessary and useful this apocalyptic division of humanity is in clarifying an oppressive situation, it is ultimately inadequate. Our common humanity must become the ultimate basis of denouncing exploitation and oppression.

Fourth, the projected vision of a new society of social justice must accommodate the ecological crisis. While nineteenth-century progressivism imagined that disadvantaged peoples could gradually be included in the privileges previously reserved for an elite, today it is essential to recognize that "infinite material demand inflicted on a finite earth is rapidly destroying the ground under our feet."[62] Ruether recommends that we move in the direction of social, political and economic equality that balances human need with the necessity to remain in harmony with nature.[63]

The Next Steps

Ruether argues that the roots of oppression in Western culture can be traced to an alienated dualistic world view inherited from the ancient world. A fundamental alienation was experienced throughout the ancient world which resulted in the projection of a series of hierarchically related dualisms: sacred and secular, spirit and nature, mind and body. The biological differences of male and female became oppressive when the despised bodily, natural, this-worldly reality was associated with women while men imaged themselves as inherently more sacred, spiritual, and rational. These projected identities justified male suppression of female. Furthermore, the projection of the negative side of dualisms onto women became the psychic model for the culture-creating males' view of other groups and set the stage for the exploitation of nature as well.

Ruether's line of argument to establish the foundational character of sexism for other forms of exploitation is suggestive. She has provided intriguing historical analogies between sexism on the one hand, and racism, anti-semitism, and imperialism on the other. It is unfortunate that Ruether has not yet carefully thought about the psychological development of the child in relationship to her historical work. There are interesting parallels between the development of the child and the historical development of hierarchical dualism. Just as gender was probably the first pervasive human difference to be recognized historically,[64] so too the maturing child learns his or her sexual identity prior to learning his or her racial, ethnic, class, or religious identity.[65] And just as gender differences became the first axis on which hierarchical relationships were established, so young children learn value-laden stereotypes for males and females before they learn stereotypes for other groups. Finally, just as sexism provided the historical model for other forms of human oppression, so the child—after once having learned to relate to an "other" hierarchically—is predisposed to relate hierarchically to other groups when they become clear in the child's mind.

Sexual oppression may be not only the oldest form of human domination, it is likely also the most pervasive.[66] Patriarchy is all but a universal phenomenon. This has particular significance when it is recognized that the relation between the sexes is generally closer, more intimate, and more sustained than that across other forms of human difference, thus providing an optimum setting for deep paradigmatic learnings. Given these observations—that sexual differences are the earliest developing, both historically and psychologically, that sexism is the most pervasive oppression, and that the relations across sexual differences are the most sustained and intimate— it is reasonable to conclude, with Ruether, that "the domination of women is the most fundamental form of domination in society, and all other forms of domination, whether of race, class, or ethnic group draw upon the fantasies of sexual domination."[67] As Ruether is quick to note, "This also suggests that the liberation of women is the most profound of all liberation movements."[68]

The point is clearly not that women are materially or even psychologically more oppressed than other groups. In fact it is difficult for many women even to see themselves as oppressed. Prejudice may exist in cruder and more obvious forms of exploitation in relation to racial or class differences. But

women, by virtue of the pervasiveness, antiquity, and paradigmatic character of their oppression, provide an important
reference point for understanding the meaning of the subjuga-
tion of one person to another.

Although Ruether has illuminated many aspects of hierarchical dualism and has painted with broad strokes her vision of what can be done to oppose it, she readily admits that
"we do not yet know how to begin to overcome" this way of
thinking. Nonetheless, she has given us many clues. She has
identified dualism as a central problem behind prejudice. In
the next chapter, we will pick up on the theme of dualism by
examining John Dewey's explicitly anti-dualistic educational
philosophy. Ruether also has pointed to the way psychological
defense mechanisms distort our perceptions of moral relationship. In the third chapter, we will look at the work of psychologist Norma Haan to further explore the moral psychology
behind prejudice. Finally, Ruether has suggested that we need
to rethink the way we do theology. In the fourth chapter,
Segundo's reflections of theological method will help us think
through the connection between liberation and how we think
and act in relation to divine reality.

For Discussion

1. Do you think prejudice and discrimination are serious problems today? Explain your response.

2. Explain "hierarchical dualism" in your own words and give
   an example from your life.

3. Do you think Ruether is correct in identifying sexism as
   the oldest and most pervasive form of prejudice? Why or
   why not?

4. From your experience, how has the church challenged prejudices and how has it supported them?

5. Explain your understanding of the difference between a dialetic and a dualism.

6. Some people have defined racism as "white prejudice plus power." Do you think it is possible for a native American to be a racist?

For Further Reading

Christ, Carol. "The New Feminist Theology: A Review of the Literature." *Religious Studies Review* 3:4 (October 1977), 203-212.

Daly, Mary. *Beyond God the Father: Toward a Philosophy of Women's Liberation.* Boston: Beacon Press, 1973.

Freeman, Jo. *Women: A Feminist Perspective.* Palo Alto, California: Mayfield Publishing Co., 2nd ed., 1979.

Ruether, Rosemary R. *Sexism and God-Talk: Toward a Feminist Theology.* Boston: Beacon Press, 1983.

Ruether, Rosemary R. *Faith and Fratricide: The Theological Roots of Anti-Semitism.* New York: The Seabury Press, 1979.

Ruether, Rosemary R. *New Woman/New Earth: Sexist Ideologies and Human Liberation.* New York: The Seabury Press, 1975.

CHAPTER TWO

RESTRUCTURING EXPERIENCE: DEWEY'S RESPONSE TO DUALISM

In this chapter we will be concerned with John Dewey's philosophy of experience and his program of education. It may seem odd that Dewey, whose career preceded Ruether's by half a century, follows Rosemary Ruether in our scheme. While Ruether is comfortable with a blend of contemporary critical theories, Dewey was the major force within the philosophical school of American pragmatism, an approach that many had pronounced dead. While Ruether calls for a major transformation of our social structures, Dewey worked for a program of gradual reform. And yet Dewey's work complements Ruether's in striking ways. His emphasis on a philosophy that is realized and tested in constructive action is certainly congruent with Ruether's philosophical and theological commitments. Most importantly, both Dewey and Ruether believe that hierarchical dualism is central to the problems plaguing society. Unlike Ruether, however, Dewey devoted a lifetime to building an educational approach to addressing the problems associated with dualisms. As we shall see, Dewey's extensive and insightful writings on the educational process provide a rich resource for those concerned with reducing prejudice.

This chapter is divided into three major sections. In the first, we will analyze the sources of dualism as described by Dewey, recognizing that he attributed the emergence of dualism to a "quest for certainty" motivated by the hazards of living in an insecure world. Although this quest can lead to false solutions that reflect dualistic thinking, it can also provide a motive for constructive action. Next, we will turn to Dewey's philosophy of experience and see how it seeks to undermine dualistic ways of viewing reality, in particular exploring the constructive role that human intelligence can play in creating a world in which humane values are realized. In the final section of this chapter, we will highlight the concepts of experience, democracy, and inquiry as developed in Dewey's educational writings. It is worth noting in advance that for Dewey education does not consist of a technological application of ready-made philosophies or theories of learning. Education is philosophy, and educational action is the source and test of philosophical reflection. Thus, the place to reduce dualisms is in education.

Sources of Dualism

Dewey offers a number of reflections on the sources of philosophical and cultural dualisms, focusing particularly on the difficulties inherent in living within the world. We will refer to these as the contextual sources of dualism since they come from the context in which we live. Dewey also frequently discusses a second source of dualisms, namely, the faulty use of our minds. We shall refer to this as the methodological source of dualism.

THE CONTEXTUAL SOURCE OF DUALISM

Dewey opens his book *The Quest for Certainty* with the line: "Man who lives in a world of hazards is compelled to seek for security."[1] In this one sentence Dewey summarizes his view of the existential context that has repeatedly given rise to dualistic thought throughout history. The world we live in is both precarious and predictable; it is permeated by surprise and yet it is mundane. This joining of the uncertain with the certain is the source of life's joy and mystery. Surprise breaks monotony and makes happiness possible. But surprise can also bring tragedy. When we open the box of the future it can be a present that delights us or a bomb that destroys us. These fluctuations of fortune create within us a fear of the uncertain. Wouldn't it be great if somehow we could live in a world that wouldn't make such a mockery of our plans, goals, values, and ideals? Wouldn't it be great if somehow we could control the uncertain?

Since it is impossible to eliminate the uncertainties of reality, Dewey suggests that our desire to do so often leads us to believe in a pretend world. The precariousness of life leads to a "quest for certainty" that frequently eventuates in elaborate false solutions to the problems of existence.

Dewey often focuses on Greek culture to illustrate how the quest for certainty can lead to dualisms. According to Dewey, the Greeks tried to equate ultimate reality with pure idea. The "real" world became the world beyond the world of our senses. By establishing a world of idea transcendent to the natural world of experience, "true" reality was freed from those fluctuations of fortune inherent in everyday life. Ideas are not subject to the forces of nature; they are not emaciated by droughts or chastised by storms. Thus, a dualism arose between the real world of idea and the illusory world of nature.

When the Greeks postulated a realm of idea beyond the experienced world, they not only created a dualism, they also created a problem for themselves. If the ultimately real lies outside the natural order, how does one relate to it? How does one get a foot in the door of the secure world of idea? For the Greeks, knowledge — gained through contemplation — was thought to provide access to the unchanging realm of idea. But even the Greek's conception of knowledge reflected their idea-nature dualism. Knowledge was divided into "true" or "high" knowledge, and knowledge of the matter of fact. The mind at work in those arts that deal directly with nature was less valued than the contemplative mind that connected one with the "ultimately real."[2]

Dewey points out that this depiction of reality was not without its ideological importance. The division of knowledge into nobler and baser forms suited the needs of a socially divided culture. Religious and philosophical "knowledge" was in the possession of an upper class who engaged in the leisure of reflection and who came to disdain the "matter-of-fact" knowledge of the lower classes.[3] Because the upper classes believed that they were the sole possessors of "true" knowledge, they viewed their domination of lower classes as only appropriate.

Dewey's analysis would be a historical curiosity were it not for his insistence that the quest for certainty is as relevant to contemporary thought as it is for analyzing historical developments. Many contemporary dualisms are still rooted in the desire to baptize the secure or the certain as the ultimately real:

> We have substituted sophistication for superstition, at least measurably so. But the sophistication is often as irrational and as much at the mercy of words as the superstition it replaces. Our magical safeguard against the uncertain character of the world is to deny the existence of chance, to mumble universal and necessary law, the ubiquity of cause and effect, the uniformity of nature, universal progress, and the inherent rationality of the universe.[4]

Dewey is suggesting that something akin to the secularization process has occurred in our quest for certainty. We no longer resolve the quest by appeal to some "other world" more real that the world of nature. Rather, we try to anchor certainty in science or natural law. But as the proverb goes, "the more things change, the more they stay the same." We are still motivated by a desire to gain control over the uncertainties of life, and our quest still leads us to construct an imaginary world in contrast to the world of everyday experience. We believe that there is a world of scientific explanation; if only we could gain access to it, all mysteries would dissolve.

Science becomes the new contemplation. The end result is again dualism; for example, a dualism between science (the realm of certainty) and religion (the realm of illusion).

THE METHODOLOGICAL SOURCE OF DUALISM

The uncertainties of the world foster within us a felt need for security. In itself, however, precariousness does not lead to dualism. Dewey elaborates his description of how dualisms arise by connecting dualism to a faulty method of understanding experience.[5] In particular, Dewey focuses on the process of abstraction that we use when we think about the world around us.

All thinking involves abstraction. When we look at a plate of carrots, onions, and squash, we abstract the category "vegetable." When we abstract, we engage in a process of mental selection. We notice certain things and overlook others. When we abstract the category carrot from a particular configuration of colors, textures, shapes, smells, and tastes, we have selected from the multitude of sense impressions those qualities that are relevant to the goal we have in mind, namely, identifying the vegetable. It is important to notice, however, that abstraction not only focuses our attention *on certain qualities,* it also takes our attention *away from other qualities.*

For Dewey, abstraction is a highly valued mental capability. However, attendant with the process of abstraction is the possibility of mistaking the abstracted object for the full experience. In other words, thinking can go awry if it mistakes its own products with reality. It would be like a potter molding a lump of clay into a beautiful bowl and then forgetting that the bowl is the product of human activity. Dewey writes, "Selective emphasis, choice, is inevitable whenever reflection occurs. This is not an evil. Deception comes only when the presence and operation of choice is concealed, disguised, denied."[6]

Dewey calls the products of our thinking, "eventual functions." In contrast, the "lump of clay" that comes to our experience is designated "antecedent existences." It is the confusing of eventual functions with antecedent existences that is the heart of what Dewey calls "vicious abstractionism."[7] Vicious abstractionism takes a mental construct and treats it as if it really is a part of objective reality.[8] To avoid vicious abstractionism, it is important to remember that mental constructs exist in the mind for purposes of conducting logical investigations. When they are separated from their function within logical inquiry and said to have independent existence, then trouble sets in. This is how we arrive at dualisms. For example, a distinction can be drawn between mind and body, which is useful for thinking logically about certain relations. But it is a mistake to project this reflective distinction back into pre-reflective reality. Mind and body, as experienced prior to the selections and abstractions of intellect, are organically connected.

Motivated by the quest for certainty, vicious abstractionism inevitably involves a disguised value choice.[9] We mentioned earlier that abstraction requires selective awareness. But on what basis is the selection made? According to Dewey, we generally pay attention to those aspects of experience that are somehow relevant to our needs or interests. We abstract from our experience enough information to label something a carrot, because food is of value to us. In vicious abstractionism, what is of value to the thinker is selected as the focus of attention, but then the choice is denied by assuming that it is reality rather than our interests that creates our preferred categories or concepts.[10] For example, valuing culture over nature may lead a person to isolate these categories for special attention. As yet there is no problem. But then the person may forget that culture and nature are abstractions and not reality itself. When this happens, reality is portrayed as fundamentally divided into culture and nature.

To further clarify the process of vicious abstractionism, let us look at how it might work in the case of racial prejudice. Let us say an individual watching the evening news witnesses a story about a murder suspect who has been apprehended. The accused murderer is black and above average in height, weight, and musculature. On the same program, our viewer sees another story about a swimming accident in which a young boy is saved by a passer-by, a thin, short, black man. After watching the news, our viewer remembers that the person in the first story was black and threatening in appearance; she didn't notice many of his other characteristics. In addition, she didn't remember the race of the second person. For her, in crime stories it is particularly relevant to notice and remember if the person involved is black. This confirms previous value assumptions and makes the world more stable and predictable because people fall into appropriate categories. She doesn't realize that her memory reflects a hidden value choice. She believes she is simply looking objectively at the world.

Let us summarize the points that have been made. All thought, according to Dewey, relies on the potential of the mind to make discriminations within experience. Thinking proceeds, for example, by making a distinction between subject and object, or between human culture and natural phenomena. Sometimes, however, the products of our thought are mistaken for reality itself. When this occurs, reality comes to be understood as constituted by hard and fast dualisms, such as subject and object, or humanity and nature.[11] Because we like to believe that what is of greater value to us is somehow more deeply rooted in the very nature of reality, we often forget that a value choice was involved in isolating mind from body or the human from the natural.

DEWEY'S RESPONSE TO DUALISM

Vicious abstractionism thrives when reflection becomes disconnected from ordinary experience. For Dewey, ordinary experience and its attendant problems and ambiguities must envelop the processes of inquiry if vicious abstractionism is to be avoided. Perhaps paradoxically the term "ordinary experience" in Dewey's vocabulary is itself not what we might ordinarily mean by the word experience. In the next sections we will attempt to clarify the complex relationships between experience, thought, and value.

Experience

To understand Dewey, it is important to distinguish two meanings for the word "experience." Most often, Dewey means by experience an unanalyzed event, a happening. Experience, as it first occurs, is not divided into the categories of our logic. This is what Dewey means by "primary" experience. It is to be distinguished from "secondary" or "reflective" experience, which is experience as it has been molded by the operations of human intellect. For Dewey, such terms as organism and environment, or subject and object, already move us a step beyond primary experience; they reflect discriminations made by the thinking person about experience. Experience exists, or better happens, prior to and during these reflective discriminations. it is from the unanalyzed totality—primary experience—that all philosophy and thinking must begin if it is not to fall into dualistic error.[12]

While, on the one hand, Dewey affirms that primary experience has not yet been transformed by the logical processes of thinking, he is equally adamant that primary experience is still not free from the influence of the experiencer. The individual does not passively receive experience. Even at the level of primary experience, the experiencer selects and organizes impressions from the environment, largely on an unconscious level. This is because the person is never simply a neutral observer. The person interacts with the environment out of some need or motivation. As Dewey states, "Every experience, of slight or tremendous import, begins with an impulsion."[13] As the outward movement of the person, impulsion proceeds from some form of need and terminates in a changed environment. Consequently, the environment itself is as much a product of the action of the person as it is a product of existences external to the person.

Because both the person and the environment are active in the process of experience, Dewey can refer to experience as a relational process between what the person does and what the person undergoes. The person shapes the environment and, in turn, is shaped by it. The relationship between the doing and undergoing gives experience its pattern and structure. It is vital to emphasize that, for Dewey, experience is far from uniform. Every experience possesses a fundamental uniqueness that is incomparable. In addition experience, to Dewey, involves a plurality of overlapping experiences, each having internal complexity and integrity. An experience can last for the smallest moment or develop and flow over a period of time. An experience is a blend of beginnings and ends, transitions and transformations, interruptions and continuations.

EXPERIENCE IS PART OF NATURE

It has been common in Western philosophy to create a dualism between experience and nature. One can experience such things as beauty and value, but these are said to be outside the natural world. Sometimes these qualities of human experience are dismissed as illusions; at other times they are held to be real, but owe their source to some supernatural agency. The separation of human experience from nature has often resulted in a view of nature as "dead matter." As we saw in the previous chapter, when we removed value from the natural order, we have travelled the first mile down the road toward ecological destruction.

Dewey is careful to avoid such dualisms by articulating a philosophy that places experience within the natural process. Experience is simply one kind of event within nature. Just as a chemical reaction occurs when certain chemicals are brought together, so experience occurs when two types of natural phenomena are brought together. Experience is the result of the interaction between an experiencing subject and an experienced environment. The interaction of these elements, distinguishable only in reflective experience, is the ultimate source of all experience.[14]

Nature, according to Dewey, consists of a variety of transactions that can be grouped into three evolutionary plateaus: the chemical-physical, the psycho-physical, and the human.[15] Each of these plateaus has unique qualities not present at lower plateaus, but there are no sharp breaks between them. At the chemical-physical level, matter interacts in very primitive and predictable ways. When hydrogen and oxygen are brought together under the right conditions, water is produced. The interactions that occur at the psycho-physical level are somewhat more complex. This is largely the level of animal

life where drives and instincts reflect the primitive organization of mental processes. Finally, at the human level, experience
is possible. The differences between the plateaus reflect the
varying degrees of organized complexity. But each plateau is
a form of natural transaction; each is an occurrence of nature.
While value, beauty, and similar phenomena are appropriate
categories for speaking of natural transactions at the human
level, there is no need to see such abstractions in dualistic
discontinuity with physical or chemical interactions.

Dewey's way of responding to the experience-nature
dualism is typical of his philosophy. Where disjunction is
believed to exist, Dewey explores how the disjoined elements
reflect an underlying continuity. Every dualism, Dewey believes,
is premised on disjunction, an imagined break in experience
or nature. The break comes because the products of reflection
are thought to be more real than the continuity of primary
experience.

EXPERIENCE IS MORE THAN A SOURCE OF KNOWLEDGE

A second common dualism in Western thought is that between
the knower and the known, or subject and object. Dewey suggests that these dualisms reflect the exclusive interest in
epistemology characteristic of many philosophical discussions
of experience.[16] For many philosophers, experience is reduced
to a source of knowledge. In Dewey's view, this is much too
narrow an emphasis. For Dewey, "knowing" is only one way
to relate to or experience reality. And knowing itself can be
understood properly only when it is placed within a much
broader context of non-cognitive dimensions of experience.
When experience is equated with knowledge seeking, then the
experiencer is reduced to a knower and the environment is
reduced to objects to be known. This double reduction creates
an unbridgeable gulf between subject and object, which are
taken as the fundamental dimensions of reality. The path out
of the dilemma is to recognize that the subject-object distinction arises from one way of viewing the organism-environment
interaction, but it is not the only way. As Dewey explains:

If the one who knows things also stands in other connections with them, then it is possible to make an intelligible contrast between things as known and things as loved or hated or appreciated, or seen or heard or whatever. . . . If the one who is knower is something else and more than the knower of objects, and if objects are, *in relation to the one who knows them,* something else and other than things in a knowledge relation, there is something to define and discuss. . . . Knowing is a connection of things which depends upon other and more primary connections between a self and things.[17]

The relationship between subject and object is a little like the relationship between two lovers. Imagine the lovers in a fight. If each of the persons relates to the other only as an antagonist, then there is no way out of the dilemma, no way to overcome the separation. But if the lovers view the argument within a broader context that also accepts the other as friend, companion, helper, storyteller, confidant, etc., then the role of the other as antagonist is not exaggerated into the whole definition of the other. So it is with the knowledge relation. The knower-known dualism results when the knower and the known are viewed exclusively in terms of the knowledge relation. To keep the functional nature of knowing evident, a third perspective is required. If the knower and the known are to be distinguished for functional reasons, it must also be remembered that objects are appreciated, valued, feared, etc. as well as known.

The overcoming of subject-object dualism is central to challenging prejudice. Prejudice reduces members of outgroups to the status of objects. The prejudiced person does not experience outgroup members in their full human wholeness; rather, members of outgroups are reduced to objects knowable by their group-identifying characteristics and stereotypic traits. Black people are known as *black* people, not as sad, joyful, sentimental, anxious people who are also black. For prejudice to be overcome, the victims of prejudice must be experienced in their concrete individuality.

EXPERIENCE IS MORE THAN THE IMMEDIATE PRESENT

A third dualism that Dewey challenges with his philosophy of experience is that between experience and thought. In this dualism, the world of the senses and the world of meaning are severed. As was noted in connection with Greek culture, such dualisms often have ideological significance. When experience and thought are separated, the dualism can provide the basis for stereotyping groups as primarily mental or primarily sensual. Dewey, in contrast, is critical of any view that reduces experience to what is immediately present to the senses. In this connection, he disputes both empiricist and rationalist notions of experience. Empiricists are those who hold that knowledge must be derived directly from experience; rationalists, on the other hand, generally hold that the human mind can grasp truth apart from specific experiences.[18] However, empiricists and rationalists frequently share the view that experience in itself is limited to what is sense. Thus, in their view, experience is devoid of meaning until interpreted.

For Dewey, experience can be devoid of meaning, but it need not be. Sense data cannot be isolated in a way that would make it an independent, original datum for cognition. For Dewey, the very perception of a sense quality involves integration with existing meaning structures: "Any sensuous quality tends, because of its organic connections, to spread and fuse."[19] The view of experience that equates it with sense data overlooks the active, selective role of the mind in the very perception of data. The proper contrast, according to Dewey, is not between experience and thought, but between experience that is funded with meaning derived from intelligent activity, and experience that is not.

The dualistic approach to experience and thought provides one base for similar dualisms, such as that between means and ends, the real and ideal, the practical and the moral, the material and the spiritual.[20] When these distinctions are perceived dualistically, the first in each pair is seen as more directly related to experience, the second to thought.

INTELLIGENCE IN EXPERIENCE

In response to the precarious nature of existence, humans engage in a quest for certainty, seeking to diminish the anxieties of living in an uncertain world. While the quest for certainty can lead to dualisms, it need not. It can spur people to use their intelligence to formulate a plan of action. In response to a flood, one can assert an otherworldly existence untouched by suffering, or one can build a dam. In the latter instance, the quest for certainty becomes a powerful, positive motive for the reconstruction of the environment, making it more conducive to human life and growth.

To better understand the role of intelligence in Dewey's philosophy of experience, it will be helpful to point out the future-oriented nature of his pragmatic philosophy.[21] According to Dewey, experience is expanded and deepened when it is pregnant with meaning. And the way experience becomes meaning-full is by the perception of connection between what is now and what will be. Experience is meaningful when it reflects our anticipations, our expectations of the conclusions toward which the present is moving. We experience a log on the beach as a chair because we can anticipate sitting upon it.

In maintaining that experience is meaningful to the extent that it is anticipatory, Dewey also sought to indicate the vital role that activity plays in human experience. A person is an agent who actively transforms the environment in anticipation of consequences. Experience is meaningful when it suggests action that can be performed to bring about desired results.

It would be easy to misunderstand Dewey at this point. Experience that is rich with cognitive significance is not necessarily better than less cognitively potent experience. Experiences can be enjoyable, for example, without being intellectual. To say that an experience is laden with cognitive meaning, however, is to say that it is useful for purposes of knowledge or intelligence; it is useful for reflective experience. But reflective experience is only one dimension of life. In fact, it is in primary experience where the qualities of objects are had, enjoyed, and suffered, that human life is primarily lived. We spend more of our time simply experiencing our world than we do cognitively reflecting on it. But reflective experience can enrich primary experience. Knowledge can increase our joy. Let me offer a brief illustration. I enjoy chocolate chip cookies. When I am eating one, I don't analyze my experience or try to break the experience down into constituent parts. I simply revel in the taste. But knowledge is not irrelevant to that experience. If I know the recipe, I can more likely reproduce similar experiences. Knowledge is important to primary experience because it perceives connections within experience; by carefully analyzing how our actions can effect desired environmental changes, we can transform the quality of our primary experience. Thus, reflective experience makes possible the greater actualization of values in primary experience.[22]

Intelligence is able to perform this function in part by discriminating between what Dewey calls the consummatory and instrumental aspects of experience. A helpful way to understand what Dewey means by the consummatory aspect of experience is to keep in mind two related meanings. First, the consummatory aspect of experience refers to that which gives the experience its unique quality or flavor. The particular taste sensation of this cookie at this point in time is part of the consummatory dimension of my experience. A second way to view the consummatory dimension of experience is to think of it as the outcome of a series of temporal events that have flowed to a climax. Orgasm in love-making is probably a good illustration of this aspect of the consummatory dimension of experience. Of course, the consummatory dimensions of experience can be negative as well as positive.

The instrumental aspect of experience allows one to logically systematize experience. While I cannot reproduce in logical analysis all of the features of eating a particularly enjoyable cookie, I can systematize some of the experience in terms of the interaction of flour, sugar, butter, spices, chocolate, salt, heat, etc. By analyzing the instrumental aspects of experience, I can gain some control over the nature of the consummations to be achieved. Since every experience has an irreducible dimension of uniqueness, the control will never be complete, but even partial control can greatly improve the likelihood that I will enjoy my experiences.

I have used the trivial example of cookies to illustrate the use of intelligence. But Dewey applied the same idea to massive social problems as well. Whenever there is a problem that needs resolution, the goal of intelligence is to find a means by which the environment can be reconstructed so that our experience of the world will be enhanced.

The appropriate application of logic is the key to the constructive use of intelligence, according to Dewey. For intelligence to perform fruitfully, it must make use of the generalized properties of experience. While primary experience is permeated with qualities that are not finally comparable, thought (or reflective experience) deals with what can be generalized. "For practical purposes we think in terms of classes, as we concretely experience in terms of individuals."[23] The role of philosophy and logic is to guide thinking in its attempt to resolve particular issues by providing appropriate methods of dealing with generalized concepts. Logic is an aid to inquiry.[24] In summary, the role of philosophy and logic is to provide means to guide the use of intelligence; the role of intelligence is to grasp the relationships of nature so that objects can be regulated in such a fashion that valued consummations can be realized.

HABIT AND INTELLIGENCE

It was noted earlier that all experience begins with an impulse derived from some form of felt need. This is as true of animal life as human experience. But in highly developed forms of life, impulses do not necessarily lead directly to action.[25] With the first urge to eat, we do not necessarily gobble the first thing in sight. Under the influence of the environment, primarily the social environment, impulses are shaped and organized into specialized functions that Dewey refers to as habits. For Dewey, action is governed by habit in situations where the exchange between the person and the environment is unproblematic. For example, we habitually dress in a certain way, eat at designated times, greet people with conventional lines. Habits are ways of acting that involve minimal thought because the patterns of action have been made routine.

But what about those situations in which a problem interrupts the usual operation of a habitual pattern of behavior? For example, what happens when the habit of reaching into the refrigerator for a snack no longer produces food? According to Dewey, human intelligence is a specialized form of habit that comes into play in problematic situations.

The proper function of intelligence is to respond to uncertainty by restructuring problematic situations so that they are no longer problematic. Intelligence, however, may be used incorrectly. Under the influence of the quest for certainty, people may respond to a problem by spinning a web of ideas rather than by planning a constructive action. Rather than confronting famine with the development of new farming techniques, the thinker might declare the "soul" to be what is ultimately real, thereby supposedly dissolving the problem. In contrast, Dewey sees intelligence as a highly specialized and flexible habit that can be used to transform nature, including human culture. In relation to culture, the role of intelligence is often to reorganize our habits so that outmoded patterns of behavior can be made more responsive to present demand. If current habitual patterns of male-female behavior are revealed to reinforce the subordination of women, for example, the role of intelligence is to construct new habits. This conceptualization of the relationship between intelligence and habit, it should be noticed, negates the dualism of thought and action, a dualism in which thought flies off into irrelevancy, and action deteriorates into theory-less activism.

THOUGHT AND VALUE

Dewey's view of the relationship between intelligence and experience helped him avoid such common dualisms as that between thinking and feeling, science and art, and fact and value. All of these dualisms represent a disjunction between the instrumental and consummatory dimensions of experience. To help us understand how he responded to these dualisms, it will be useful to outline his view of esthetic experience.

In Dewey's view of experience, immediacy plays a prominent role. Immediacy refers to the pervasive unique qualities of primary experience. The qualities of an experience that are perceived in their immediacy are those that lead up to and participate in the consummatory dimension of experience. These immediate qualities are subordinated in much of experience by the abstraction process of thought, but at other times they dominate and the experience has a flow that characterizes it as *an experience*.[26]

Esthetic quality is to some degree present in all experience. Correspondingly, "esthetic experience is always more than esthetic."[27] Experience is always a blend of the instrumental and consummatory, the cognitive and non-cognitive. The experience that later reflection would call particularly esthetic is one in which various elements, not in themselves esthetic, "become esthetic as they enter into an ordered rhythmic movement toward consummation."[28] A sunset, for example, may be observed as an instance of light refraction under a particular set of environmental conditions. In such a case, the experience is primarily instrumental and cognitive. But the same event can be esthetically experienced as a unique, unrepeatable instance of harmony between a configured environment and an appreciative observer. In the latter instance, the dimensions of the experience create an esthetic quality enabling one to designate the temporal flow as *an experience*. The experience has an unfolding, rhythmic quality that leads toward a felt consummation.

The instrumental and consummatory dimensions are united in primary experience. They can be distinguished for purposes of analysis as light can be refracted through a prism into different colors. But they are originally united. Similarly, the esthetic qualities of an experience are not distinct from its cognitive qualities. The recognition of this fact is the key to overcoming dualisms. Thinking and feeling emphasize different dimensions of experience, but they are not separable. Although we think more in relation to the instrumental dimensions of experience, thinking is rooted in experience as immediately felt and has itself esthetic qualities; feeling, in turn, is not devoid of meaning but requires the infusion of meaningfulness for its fullness.

Dewey responds to the dualism of science and art in a similar way. In his view, science and art again emphasize different dimensions of experience. Each discipline works from the same range of experiences, but emphasizes different aspects. Art works toward the development of experiences that are worth having in themselves; science seeks to understand the means through which consummations can be realized, problematic situations resolved.

Dewey also opposes any ultimate separation between fact and value. When experience is primarily had and enjoyed, it is funded with value. This in no way separates it from nature, or makes it any less objective. When experience is primarily analyzed, it is tested for fact. But this does not remove it from value. Thus, when experience is viewed instrumentally, it is constituted by facts, but when it is viewed in its consummatory dimensions, it is permeated by values.

Facts and values, like means and ends, are not independent, separable phenomena; the terms are relational. A value judgment is predictive: it is a claim that a particular experience is worth having. Thus, facts and values share a predictive, probabilistic character. Facts relate primarily to the means by which ends can be reached, and values relate primarily to what ends are worth pursuing. But ends are never fully just ends; they are also means to further ends. Consummations are not only worth having in and of themselves, but also in terms of further experiences to which they lead.

For Dewey, the ultimate value is growth. What has value is an experience that opens the person to broader, more meaningful, more esthetic experiences. Thus, a value judgment consists of a judgment about what constitutes a growth experience. For Dewey, this is not a purely subjective evaluation. Value judgments involve propositions that can be empirically evaluated just as factual propositions do.[29]

Having arrived at the theme of growth, we are ready to turn to Dewey's educational philosophy. It would be easy to think of education as a field of application for philosophy. But this was not Dewey's view. His approach to education is not separable from his philosophy of experience. Dewey developed, tested, and refined his ideas about experience from his practice of education. The problems of education were the source for a great deal of his philosophizing. As the reader may anticipate, a key problem that Dewey faced in his educational work was that of dualism.

Responding to Dualism Through Education

For Dewey, education is the process of expanding and reorganizing experience so that it becomes richer in its esthetic qualities and broader in its cognitive meaning. Education is a, or better, *the* moral imperative.[30] But education itself has been plagued by the same dualisms prevalent elsewhere. It is not surprising that Dewey's attack on dualism took the form of a lifelong crusade to restructure education. In the following sections, we will look at the educational implications of three major themes that run throughout Dewey's diverse educational writings: experience, democracy, and inquiry.

EXPERIENCE

Experience emerges from the interaction between a person and an environment. It is the result of a doing and an undergoing; the person acts and, in turn, is acted upon. If either the person or the environment is viewed dualistically, educational problems emerge. Let us look at a few of these dualisms and their effect on education.

One of the most prevalent dualisms is that between mind and body. Not surprisingly, this dualism frequently finds educational expression. It often happens in the classroom that the continuity between mind and body is cut, and mind comes to be equated with the passive side of experience and body with the active side. Bodily activity becomes disjoined from mental "receptivity." When a teacher expects students to sit quietly and still in their chairs and absorb information into their minds, this dualism is evident. The body is imaged as the enemy of mental development. In Dewey's words, "bodily activity becomes an intruder."[31] Dewey suggests that many of the discipline problems experienced in education may have their source in this mind-body dualism. Disruptive behavior may represent the child's inarticulate protest against the severing of the body from its organic connection to meaningful activity. Similar to the mind-body dualism is that between subject and object. This dualism can be expressed educationally as a split between the person, viewed as a receptacle and holder of knowledge, and subject matter, seen as a body of external material to be learned. When subject matter is equated with an independent body of knowledge that is only externally related to the ongoing pursuits of the individual, then rote learning easily takes the place of true education. Subject matter simply becomes foreign matter injected into more or less disinterested individuals.

The supposed split between nature and humanity has also been influential in the development of educational practice. The separation between "natural" sciences and the "humanities" is one example of this disjunction. In contrast, for Dewey the natural sciences are organically related to the humanities. It is the humanities that give science a depth of meaning:

> Perception of meanings depends upon perception of connections, of context. To see a scientific fact or law in its human as well as in its physical and technical context is to enlarge its significance and give it increased cultural value.[32]

Science is thus not opposed to the humanities. In Dewey's view, science is the study of means through which values can be enhanced, lives can be made more meaningful, and society more equitably structured.

The reader is reminded that these dualisms — mind-body, subject-object, nature-humanity — not only create rifts within educational practice, they also foster an environment that is likely to cultivate prejudices. It is not that the separation between the sciences and the humanities, for instance, directly teaches prejudices. But when science is severed from the cultural arts, the learner is encouraged to think dualistically and may easily use such a dualism to designate some people as realistic and rational while dismissing others as superstitious and emotional.

Dewey's prescription for avoiding these and other dualisms is to hold the doing and undergoing phases of experience together. Experience becomes educative to the degree that connections are perceived between what a person does and what consequences result.[33] Education must be an active process of reorganizing experience through transforming the environment and broadening the connections that one brings to experience. When learning is tethered to meaningful action, the mind is engaged with what the body is doing, the subject matter of the school expands the meaning of the life experience of the person, and scientific information is placed at the service of social values.

Education, for Dewey, is centered in activity. It involves coming to know how to direct activity intelligently to achieve anticipated ends. Dewey can thus define education as "that reconstruction or reorganization of experience which adds to the meaning of experience, and which increases ability to direct the course of subsequent experience."[34]

Dewey's emphasis on activity can be misleading, however. Activity does not always involve body movements. Participation in communication is one form of highly significant activity. In fact, communication lies at the heart of social activity. For Dewey, participation with others in activities where meanings are shared is the primary structure of the educational process. Dewey's view of education as a social process in which meanings are broadened and communicated through joint endeavor highlights the element of social organization. For Dewey, the optimal social organization for both the school and society is democracy.

DEMOCRACY

Dewey felt that only in democratic societies does education become one with the moral process. To understand this statement, it is helpful to examine Dewey's description of the three functions of education.[35] First, education must provide an organized and gradated means for the learner to acquire the accumulated knowledge and wisdom of a complex culture. However, the society should not be simply presented as it is. The second function of the school environment is to eliminate, so far as possible, the undesirable elements of existing society. Because the school environment is smaller and more manageable than society as a whole, it can be organized to reflect the best traditions of the broader society. The final educational task is closely related: The school's role is to see that students receive the opportunity to escape from the limitations of the social group in which they were born.

In Dewey's view, democratic societies provide the best possibility for these three functions to come together in a unified whole. What Dewey means by a "democratic society," however, is a combination of description and prescription. Although he based his thought on the "democracies" he knew, primarily the United States, he consistently and at times vehemently attacked the lack of democracy in these same societies. In Dewey's reformist view, the educator's task is to extract the desirable traits from the community life as it is and employ them to criticize the undesirable features.

Dewey identifies two basic criteria that can help determine the extent of democracy within any given society or community. According to Dewey, a democracy is a means of social organization in which participants share common interests and values and, secondly, where there are no artificial restrictions on the free and equal exchange among members of the society. In Dewey's words:

> Now in any social group whatever we find some interest held in common, and we find a certain amount of interaction and cooperative intercourse with other groups. From these two traits we derive our standard. How numerous and varied are the interests which are consciously shared? How full and free is the interplay with other forms of association?[36]

Dewey's endorsement of democracy reflects his view of experience. Experience becomes rich with connection and meaning as it is shared. If something infringes on the free sharing of experience, then experience is crippled. Similarly, society benefits when there is free sharing of experience among all its members. When boundaries exist that prevent free social exchange—such as prejudice and discrimination—then democracy is undermined. Unfortunately, modern society is characterized by many social divisions. Dewey, like Ruether, suggests that dualisms may reflect the underlying divisions within society. In Dewey's words:

> The origin of these [dualisms] we have found in the hard and fast walls which mark off social groups and classes within a group: like those between rich and poor, men and women, noble and baseborn, ruler and ruled. These barriers mean absence of fluent and free intercourse. This absence is equivalent to the setting up of different types of life-experience, each with isolated subject matter, aim, and standard of values. Every such social condition must be formulated in a dualistic philosophy.[37]

The division of society into more and less privileged groups is often reflected educationally by a separation between "technical" education in preparation for an occupation and a "liberal arts" education oriented toward appreciation of culture. Such a division serves the interests of a society divided into a labor and leisure class, but is counterproductive to democracy.[38] The class divisions of modern society also perpetuate the old dualisms of theory and practice, knowledge and action. Socially privileged people value theory above practice and knowledge above action. For Dewey, educators must be involved in social reorganization if such fundamental dualisms are to be overcome and if society is to become more democratic.

INQUIRY

In education there is often a separation between thinking and doing. Thinking is treated as if it were an entirely internal process going on within the mind of the individual student. Doing, in contrast, is treated as a matter of skill, habit, or trial and error. For Dewey, however, thinking is one form of experience, enveloped on all sides by another form of experience. Thinking, or reflective experience, begins and terminates in non-reflective or primary experience. The artificial severing of thought from primary experience results in what would otherwise be a puzzling phenomenon: "No one has ever explained why children are so full of questions outside of the school...[yet there is a] conspicuous absence of display of curiosity about the subject matter of school lessons."[39] One reason for the disinterest of many students is the gulf between the kind of thinking that goes on in the classroom, on the one hand, and the life activity of the students, on the other.

One reason why thinking has become dissociated from action is the need to acquaint students with a large body of accumulated information that society has acquired over generations. This cannot be done solely through direct experience. Much of our valuable experience is indirect. Children are able in a few years to journey the full path of human history because language can impart to the child the vast store of information gained through centuries of experience. Language allows students to learn not only from their own experience but also indirectly from the experiences of others, both those immediately present and those far removed in space and time. While the use of indirect experience is vital, it has its attendant difficulties:

> There is always the danger that symbols will not be truly representative; danger that instead of really calling up the absent and remote in a way to make it enter a present experience, the linguistic media of representation will become an end in themselves. Formal education is peculiarly exposed to this danger.[40]

If the vast meaning available through indirect experience is to be made accessible to the child in usable form, it must be joined with ongoing direct experience. When learning through language becomes dissociated from activity that directly affects the environment, then the child may learn to verbalize far more information than the child knows how to meaningfully employ. Thought becomes dissociated from experience and easily becomes absorbed in the products of its own reflection. As noted before, this can become a source of vicious abstractionism.

To avoid these difficulties, Dewey offers a view of inquiry that can guide educational practice. He abstracts from the procedures of science five generic features of reflective experience.[41] In short, these are: (1) a felt interruption, (2) formulation of a problem, (3) suggestions and hypotheses, (4) abstract reasoning and inference making, and (5) testing by action.

All reflective thinking, for Dewey, begins when the equilibrium of habitual action is disturbed in some way. The disruption is *felt* before it is cognitively formulated. At this point, past habits may prevail, in which case no problem will be intellectually formulated and the restructuring of experience will not occur. However, if the situation is sufficiently indeterminate or the individual sufficiently sensitive to the possibilities for growth, inquiry will move to the second stage: formulation of a problem.

When a problem has been tentatively formulated, the mind spontaneously produces guesses, wishes, hunches. These reflect common-sense wisdom and may be adequate to meet the needs of a particular situation. However, the heart of the third phase is the refinement of these spontaneous thoughts into clearly formulated ideas and hypotheses. The next phase, that of reasoning, is for Dewey the key in the process of reconstructing experience. It is at this phase that ideas are related directly to one another and are not dependent directly upon sense experience. Ideas and hypotheses are put within an abstract framework of already logically connected ideas and tested for consistency and potency. The final phase is that of returning from the abstract back to the specific context and testing consequences.

Dewey's assertion about the process of inquiry is firm: it begins in a non-cognitive experience, moves through a cognitive formulation that eventually is transformed to a more abstract and symbolic level, and terminates with a return to the practical, particular, and experiential. Dewey's process of inquiry represents an integration of the theoretical and the practical.

Dewey also integrates two levels of cognition. The first is common sense. Common sense corresponds primarily to the third phase of inquiry. Practical problems give rise to suggestions and guesses that come "popping into the head." It is an unsystematized process but may serve to meet many of the everyday needs of life. But common sense also provides the substance that is reworked in more formal inquiry. The second level of cognition is that of the more formal procedures characteristic of the fourth phase of inquiry. The procedures of scientific investigation are reflected in this level of cognition.

In his theory of inquiry, Dewey has avoided dualisms between ends and means, thought and action, theory and practice, common sense and science. These dualisms, however, plague education where externally imposed artificial problems sever ends from means, theory from practice, formal disciplines from common-sense cognition. Such dualistic education, while it does not teach prejudice directly, nevertheless encourages a right-wrong, up-down, inside-outside style of thinking that seeks to divide nature and people into opposing forces. It is a style of thinking that readily accommodates prejudice.

Dewey's model of inquiry is one of his most important contributions to education. It is an admirable effort to systematize a procedure for keeping thought integrated with action, intelligence tethered to primary experience. We shall reflect further on Dewey's model of inquiry in the final chapter.

For Discussion

1. How has the "quest for certainty" influenced your ideas?
2. Explain "vicious abstractionism" in your own words and give an example from your life.
3. Describe how you see the following dualisms operative in today's world: mind-body, subject-object, humanity-nature, thinking-feeling.

4. How has your educational experience reflected dualisms?

5. How might Dewey's approach to inquiry be used to challenge prejudice?

6. With what aspects of Dewey's philosophy do you disagree?

For Further Reading

Dewey, John. *Democracy and Education.* New York: Macmillan, 1916.

Dewey, John. *Experience and Education.* New York: Collier Books, 1938.

Dewey, John. *How We Think.* Boston: D.C. Heath and Company, 1933.

Dewey, John. *The Quest for Certainty: A Study of the Relation of Knowledge and Action.* New York: G. P. Putnam's Sons, 1929.

CHAPTER THREE

MORALITY IN THE BALANCE: DIALOGUES AND DISTORTIONS

There is a considerable difference between characterizing a person as tall, outgoing, and musical, on the one hand, and designating the person as prejudiced on the other. The term *prejudice* connotes a moral evaluation. It is not good for a person to be prejudiced. The moral dimension of prejudice was implied in the last two chapters, but was not directly discussed. In this chapter we will turn to the social sciences to help us understand the moral psychology of prejudice.

Moral issues have been notoriously difficult for scientists to investigate. In recent years, however, psychologists have made great strides toward understanding the dynamics of moral relationships. In this chapter we will focus on Norma Haan's theory of morality and moral development. Her work is particularly enlightening for our purposes because it brings together two important dimensions. First, Haan expands and clarifies the psychoanalytic notion of ego processes. The reader

67

may recall that Ruether appealed to the ego processes of repression and projection to help her understand sexism. In Haan's work, these defense mechanisms are organized into a larger model of both coping and defending ego processes that clarifies the relationship between appropriate and inappropriate ego functioning. Haan's central thesis is that when people use "coping ego processes" they act in rational and accurate ways, but when people use defensive processes they sacrifice accuracy for the sake of maintaining a coherent sense of self.

The second relevant aspect of Haan's work is her model of moral reasoning and moral development. For Haan, morality is a form of interpersonal knowledge and skill that develops through a five level sequence. (See Table 2, p. 96.) The person's level of development puts a ceiling on the person's ability to think and act in a morally mature manner. A person who is able to reason only at Level Two, for example, would not be able to act in a very mature manner. However, even people who have developed to the highest moral level may still not act in a mature manner; how people actually behave will reflect both their level of moral development and the specific ego processes that they use. When people are defending—using ego defense mechanisms—they will not be living up to their full potential. We shall see that prejudicial thinking and behavior may reflect immature reasoning, defensive ego functions, or a combination of the two.

In advance of the more detailed discussion, let me offer the reader a synopsis of the chapter's logic. It is suggested that a self-identity formed under the influence of hierarchical dualism cannot be maintained without the use of defensive psychological maneuvers. As a consequence, prejudiced people inevitably resort to defensive processes when they relate to those people who are the objects of their prejudice. This defensiveness is reflected in defective communication and results in dominated and distorted moral exchange.

This chapter is organized into four sections. The first section introduces structural developmental theory, the basis of Haan's formulations. The second section presents Haan's ego processing model. The third section presents Haan's model of interactional morality, reserving for the final section a specific analysis of moral development and moral education.

Structural-Developmental Theory

Haan is an eclectic thinker who has synthesized elements from both the psychoanalytic and structural developmental traditions. Further, she has avoided the frequent pitfall of the eclectic—that of weighing all contributions equally. Haan has employed structural developmental theory as her basic paradigm. By incorporating psychoanalytic insights into her work, however, Haan has succeeded in developing a more flexible and open view of structural developmental theory than most other advocates.

In this section the basic tenets of structural developmentalism will be outlined. While this approach has been used to investigate numerous problems within psychology, we will focus on moral development; examples from other areas will be used only when they add clarity. To make the distinctive features of the structural development approach evident, it will be contrasted with a competing approach to moral development, social learning theory. While the structural developmentalist focuses on the meaning-construction processes of the developing individual, social learning theorists concentrate on how the growing child internalizes the norms of adult culture. In addition to contrasting these two approaches, Haan's unique contributions to structural development theory will be contrasted with the more strict approach of other advocates, such as Piaget and Kohlberg.

STRUCTURE AND CONTENT

People do not think and behave in totally random ways. There is a logic underlying most of our thoughts and a pattern to our actions. Often we are not even aware of the rules or principles that underlie our thinking and behavior. When we speak, for example, we follow a very complex set of linguistic rules even though we are not conscious of them. The underlying rules are called a linguistic structure. Similar structures underlie our cognitive reasoning, our social judgments, and our moral reasoning and behavior.

Social learning theorists believe that the organization of an individual's thought and action is learned directly from watching others and being rewarded for correct behavior.[1] Particular patterns of thought and action are shaped through modeling and reinforcement. In contrast, structural development theorists believe that the organization of thought and action does not come solely from outside the individual. All people are born with a tendency to give coherence and order to their perceptions, to structure information. Rather that merely witnessing events in the environment and passively internalizing them, people witness events, perform actions, and integrate new information into existing structures of thought. The environment presents an individual with a wide variety of experiences, and the individual "makes meaning" out of these experiences. By assimilating experience into already existing structures of thought and by elaborating those structures to accommodate new information, the person develops increasingly sophisticated patterns of thought and behavior. According to structural development theorists, there are only a few basic structures. Cognitive structures, which pattern one's interpretations of the physical world, and linguistic structures are the most studied, but moral structures have also been given considerable attention.

To better understand the concept of structure, it will be helpful to highlight the distinction between the *content* of thought and its underlying *structure*. Specific information, beliefs, and values represent the content of thought. Thus, for example, a person's belief that "honesty is the best policy" is an element of content. A researcher can tap into the contents of a person's thought rather easily. In contrast, psychological structures cannot be demonstrated directly; they must be inferred from a collection of observations. For example, let us say we are interviewing a child and the following dialogue occurs:

Q: How do you decide when it would be OK to break a promise?

A: Generally, I think it is important to keep promises, but sometimes you have to break them, like if your best friend might be hurt if you keep it.

Q: Do you think it is always wrong to lie?

A: Most of the time. People won't trust you unless you tell the truth. But sometimes you have to lie a little to protect your friends.

The child's specific beliefs about promises and truth-telling are aspects of moral content. Beneath the specific responses, however, a pattern begins to emerge. In response to both questions, the child appealed to friendship as the determining factor. If further questioning resulted in the same pattern, then the interviewer would conclude that this person's moral structure defined loyalty to peers as a key value for determining what is right. It is not that the child is specifically aware that this principle is at work. Structures lie beneath the surface of thought, providing thought with organization and coherence. A structure is an organized pattern of mental operations that can be applied to a wide range of subjects.

Closely related to the distinction between structure and content is the distinction between competence and performance. Not all structures are equally adequate. The linguistic structure underlying the speech of a three year old is likely to be less flexible and differentiated than the linguistic structure of an adult. The capacities inherent in a person's structures define their range of competence. For example, a child who does not have a stable understanding of numbers (a structural competence) will not be able to solve problems of mathematics (a performance). Of more interest, however, is the fact that even if a person does possess the requisite structural capacities to resolve a problem, that does not mean the person's performance will demonstrate it. As we shall see, Haan suggests that ego processes regulate the way psychological structures operate.

Quantitative vs. Qualitative Growth

Social learning theorists view development as a relatively continuous and homogeneous process of learning new bits of information. Complex behavior is learned later than simple behavior only because the requisite skills and information repertoires need to be developed through modeling and reinforcement. The learning model is predominantly a quantitative one: development involves the continuous addition of new skills and pieces of information.

Structural developmentalists believe that growth consists of two types of change. Quantitative change occurs as the developing individual acquires more information. But growth involves qualitative transformations as well, in the way in which individuals understand and organize information. The individual is not a passive receiver of data; rather, the individual actively seeks new information and organizes it into patterns of meaning. In the process of development, these structures undergo qualitative transformations that can be charted through a regular sequence.

Most work done from within the structural development perspective has used a cognitive developmental framework. This closely related set of theories defines human growth in terms of the sequential development of logical structures of thought. Jean Piaget, the pioneer of cognitive developmentalism, suggests that the child passes through several stages of cognitive functioning.[2] Each stage represents a coherent set of interrelated mental processes or operations.

Hypotheses about stages of development are the cornerstone of cognitive developmental theories. These theorists hold in common the view that human growth can be characterized as development through an orderly, invariant, culturally universal sequence of stages, with each succeeding stage more adequate than the preceding. Each stage reflects a closed system of definable mental operations. Both Piaget[3] and Kohlberg[4] have provided detailed models of moral development stages.

While Piaget and Kohlberg employ a "stringent" structuralist perspective, Haan advocates a more flexible interpretation. Theories postulating invariant, logic-based stages may be appropriate, Haan maintains, for characterizing the development of children's understanding of the relatively stable physical world. But moral behavior is not so stable. A person who acts one way in one situation will not necessarily respond the same in other situations. Due to the fluctuations in moral behavior, the process of moral growth may not fit a neat system of tightly defined stages. Nonetheless, Haan still believes that morality does develop and the developmental process isn't haphazard. To distinguish her view from that of the strict structuralists, Haan prefers to use the term "level" rather than "stage" to describe the phases of growth. In contrast to stages, levels are not necessarily irreversible and invariant. We shall return to Haan's model of moral development in the final sections of this chapter.

THE UNIVERSALITY OF MORALITY

Society is the ultimate moral reference point for social learning theorists. What is right is equivalent to society's norms, and the task of moral growth is to learn those norms. Consequently, social learning theorists take a relativist stance toward morality. What is right is relative to the view of the culture. Moral behavior is typically classified as either "pro-social" or "anti-social" depending upon whether it conforms to accepted social values.

Cognitive developmentalists, like Kohlberg, take a strict universalist position. Kohlberg maintains that his six-stage model of moral development represents a culturally universal sequence. People at the highest level of moral reasoning, Kohlberg believes, will draw the same conclusions, given similar moral dilemmas, no matter what their culture or circumstance.

Haan seeks to navigate a course midway between cultural relativism on the one hand and cultural imperialism on the other. She concurs with Kohlberg's belief that society cannot serve as the ultimate point of reference for morality, but disagrees with his claim that mature individuals across all cultures will arrive at the same moral resolutions. Rather than arriving at the same conclusion, Haan believes mature people will use similar procedures in seeking resolution. The dimension of universality in Haan's model relates to the processes that people use to reach moral decisions. According to Haan, morally mature individuals may reach different conclusions in different cultures or situations, but they will use similar processes to reach their conclusions.

In summary, structural development theorists seek (a) to identify and describe psychological structures that underlie reasoning and behavior patterns, and (b) to chart the development of those structures through qualitatively distinct phases of growth. As a structural developmentalist, Haan has described the growth of moral structures. Before we turn to Haan's theory of moral development, however, it will be helpful to consider the personality theory in which it is embedded.

Coping and Defending Ego Functions

THE PSYCHOANALYTIC BACKGROUND

Haan worked as a child clinical psychologist before she entered the field of psychological research. As a clinician, she was trained in the post-Freudian psychoanalytic tradition. One of the lasting contributions of Freud and his followers, she believes, is the recognition of how frequently and easily our perceptions of reality can be denied, falsified, or distorted.[5] According to psychoanalytic theory, the most frequent cause of these distortions is the ego's desire to minimize anxiety. Psychoanalytic theorists have developed a taxonomy of ten commonly recognized defense mechanisms. These defense mechanisms are processes available for the ego to protect itself from id impulses, from the punitive actions of the superego, and from perceived environmental threats. It is not necessary, however, to adopt the psychoanalytic view of entities like the id or superego to appreciate the significance of the ego defense mechanisms.

THE PIAGETIAN BACKGROUND

Early in her career, Haan began to reach out beyond the confines of psychoanalytic theory. In particular, she took an interest in the cognitive-developmental work of Jean Piaget[6] and his colleagues. This large body of studies highlights the constructive, reality-oriented processes of the child and the development of cognitive structures. While the Freudian tradition primarily reflects a focus on psychopathology and the mechanisms by which self-deception can occur, the Piagetian tradition emphasizes normal and accurate mental functioning. Haan's coping and defending model is an attempt to combine insights from each of these traditions into a theory of personality focused on ego processes.

THE COPING-DEFENDING-FRAGMENTING MODEL

The beginning point for Haan's process model of the ego is the ten classical defense mechanisms. Haan believes, however, that the view of the functioning ego is deficient if only these processes are included: "The conceptualization of ego functioning requires, besides recognition of defense mechanisms, explicit and systematic consideration of the role of coping mechanisms."[7] The key hypothesis that Haan develops is that defense mechanisms are distorted ways of handling information that is normally handled in a coping, that is to say accurate, manner.

In the model first developed by Haan and Kroeber,[8] they list ten generic processes, each having two possible modes of expression — one coping, the other defending. For example, the generic process of *sensitivity* can be displayed as coping *empathy* or as defensive *projection*. Empathy and projection are closely related; they are both ways of handling the same problem, namely, the need to identify the inner state of another. Empathy does this without distorting the available information, while projection distorts. Table 1 illustrates the coping and defending ego process model by summarizing the coping and defending mechanisms associated with six of the more common generic processes.

In 1969 Haan expanded the model to include three modes of expressing each generic process.[9] To coping and defending was added fragmenting. Fragmenting processes might be conceptualized as extreme forms of the defense mechanisms. However, while the defense mechanisms still connect one to objective reality, even while distorting it, the fragmenting processes violate all sense of rationality.[10] Fragmenting processes are most clearly evident in psychotic patients, though healthy individuals may temporarily fragment under

TABLE 1

Coping and Defending Ego Process Model

Problem to Be Solved	Coping Solution	Defending Solution
1. MEANS-ENDS SYMBOLIZATION What is the relationship among events?	LOGICAL ANALYSIS – Step by step reasoning; conclusions based on evidence	RATIONALIZATION – Logic used to justify decision; conclusions based on desire
2. SENSITIVITY What is the other person feeling?	EMPATHY – Accurately perceives what other is feeling	PROJECTION – Objectionable feelings and attributes within oneself are attributed to others
3. SELECTIVE AWARENESS Where do I focus my attention?	CONCENTRATION – Attention focused on relevant items and issues	DENIAL – Attention limited to items and issues that do not conflict with self-interest
4. DIVERSION Where do I express my feelings?	SUBLIMATION – Feelings expressed toward appropriate people and objects	DISPLACEMENT – Feelings vented on people or objects not responsible for the feelings
5. TRANSFORMATION How do I handle primitive impulses?	SUBSTITUTION – Impulses comfortably transformed into socially approved effects	REACTION FORMATION – Impulses rigidly turned into their opposite (e.g. hostility becomes excessive altruism)
6. RESTRAINT How do I handle feelings that can't be expressed?	SUPRESSION – Feelings controlled until they can be appropriately expressed	REPRESSION – Feelings unconsciously and purposefully forgotten

76

extreme stress. While the addition of fragmenting processes is an important supplement to the model, fragmenting processes do not have special relevance for our purposes; only the coping and defending processes will be emphasized in this chapter.

In Haan's scheme the three modes of functioning are organized in a hierarchy of utility. In terms of the long-range resolution of problems, coping is best and fragmenting is worst. In everyday life, an individual will cope if possible, defend if necessary, and fragment only if all other options fail. Unfortunately, people cannot always cope. The primary determinant of which mode is employed in any given context is whether or not one can accurately assimilate information without threat to one's sense of self-coherence. If the new information is too dissonant or threatening, it will be distorted and made innocuous. Threatening or stressful situations may elicit defending and, if extreme, fragmenting processes. In addition, people have preferred hierarchies of coping and defending processes. While one person may tend to repress frequently, another may respond to stress with an abundance of denial. The coping and defending hierarchies of an individual comprise a significant dimension of a person's personality.

In any given act, various coordinations of internal structures and external factors need to be integrated. As a result, a person uses a variety of processes at once. On careful examination, it will usually be found that a person is neither entirely coping nor entirely defending, but is utilizing some combination of both.

PROCESSES AND STRUCTURES

Ego processes accomplish two primary tasks. First, they coordinate one's psychological structures. In any given action, information from various structures must be brought together and coordinated. For example, if I am going to type a sentence, I must coordinate information from my psychomotor structures about the mechanics of typing; information from my linguistic and cognitive structures about the meaning of words, sentence construction, and logical development; and information from my structures of social cognition that provide me with a picture of the interests and motives of my intended audience. To accomplish my tasks effectively, each of these structures must contribute and the contributions of each structure must be coordinated and integrated. That is the first task of the ego processes. The second task is similar, but instead of mediating internal structures, the coordination is between internal and external factors, that is, between one's psychological structures and the fluctuating circumstances of situations. In this case, information originating from the environment is transmitted to the internal structures and integrated with these psychological meaning systems. To catch a ball, for example, information received through my eyes must be coordinated with cognitive structures that interpret the ball's movement so that I can move my body accordingly.

A crude analogy would hold that the psychological structures are like the processing chips of a computer and the ego processes are like the circuitry that connects the internal components and coordinates them with input from the keyboard, modem, or other external devices. Coping processes are analogous to properly functioning circuitry, but defensive processes are like electrical short circuits that distort information.

The coping and defending processes can help to explain the often observed disparity between capacity and performance. We do not always live up to our potential. In Chapter Seven of her book *Coping and Defending,* Haan sets out in detail her view that a person's structural capacities work properly only when the person is coping and when the person's different structural formulations are compatible and can be merged to achieve a solution. On the other hand, Haan says, a person's structural capacities fail to work properly when the situation is stressful to the point of forcing defensive processing, or when various structural formulations are incompatible and lead to contradictory solutions.

The relationship between ego processes and structural capacities means that when a person fails to act in a fully mature manner, the failure may have either of two causes. It may be that the individual does not have the requisite structural capacities, and therefore cannot perform the task. Alternatively, it may be that the person has the capacity, but ego defense distorts the manifestation of structural competence.[11] This raises the question of whether prejudice is a structural problem or whether it is at root a problem of ego processing. This issue will be taken up next.

PREJUDICE: STRUCTURE OR PROCESS?

Human failings may have their source either in deficient structural capacities or in the use of psychological defense. We have identified prejudice as a moral problem. Is it due to an immaturity in the person's structure of moral reasoning or is prejudice a reflection of a person's use of defensive ego processes? The differences are important. If prejudice is defined as a structural problem, then the weight of the error rests outside the individual. This is because structures reflect accurate, though sometimes incomplete or selective, interpretations of reality. Thus, an explanation of prejudice that emphasizes psychological structures would discuss the impact of social practices and cultural ideologies on the individual. If one believes the locus of hierarchical dualism is in defense mechanisms, on the other hand, then the weight of the error rests within the individual. Explanations for prejudice would focus on the deviant psychological needs of the prejudiced person. A process interpretation of prejudice emphasizes the irrational.

Ruether and Dewey agree that hierarchical dualisms are irrational. Dewey, for example, points out that in every dualism there is an element of denial. It is Ruether, however, who has emphasized and tried to delineate the irrational dynamics. She suggests that male sexism has its genesis in repression and projection. According to Ruether, a fear of intimacy and sexuality underlies sexism. In addition to repressing feelings of their own sexuality, Ruether suggests, males project this feared dimension as a stereotype of females. Consequently, women, in the imaginations of men, become little more than sexual beings.

The thesis that prejudice is uniquely tied to the psychological processes of repression and projection is problematic, however, in light of data collected by Haan. She has not found these processes to be particularly salient or more characteristic of males than females. The lack of any particular pervasiveness of repression and projection may be interpreted in at least two ways. The first option is that prejudice is primarily structural and therefore does not rely extensively on psychological defense. Alternately, the repression-projection syndrome may be highly specific in content and only come into play when problems of relating across human differences are faced.

An adequate explanation of prejudice may require that both structure and process dimensions to the problem be identified. Ruether is probably accurate in suggesting that hierarchical dualisms originated historically through the operation of elite, male, ego defense mechanisms. At one time in human evolution, repression and projection probably played a particularly significant role in the development of cultural ideology. However, once a hierarchical dualism has become entrenched in culture, the psychological mechanisms necessary for its perpetuation change. Psychological defense no longer needs to play such a critical role. If everybody believes the earth is flat, that information will be integrated into the child's structural interpretations of the physical world. Similarly, an accurate, or coping, self-interpretation that is constructed within a culture where prejudicial images of people are common will undoubtably mirror those distorted images. In contemporary culture, and probably for the past many centuries, prejudices have simply been passed on to the young as part of cultural reality.

There are several reasons for suspecting that hierarchical dualism has a structural base. Structures tend to evolve very slowly while ego processes tend to be quite fluid and adaptable. The durability and cultural pervasiveness of hierarchical dualism is consistent with a structural interpretation. Further, a structural view is consistent with variations in the content of prejudice. While hierarchical dualism remains consistent, the specific content of a prejudice may change. We saw, for example, how the imagery of women radically shifted under the influence of romanticism. Finally, structures are indicated when there is a consistent pattern to a variety of specific contents within a person's thinking. We have seen how different prejudices—such as racism, sexism, and anti-semitism—all have the same basic structure, namely, hierarchical dualism.

To hypothesize that hierarchical dualism is a structural phenomenon, however, does not mean that ego defense is not operative in prejudices. While the specific processes of repression and projection may no longer play a particularly salient role, some form of defense is still required. Since victims do not conform to the rigid stereotypes of prejudicial thinking, dominators must shield themselves from conflicting information. The point is that no particular set of defenses, namely, repression and projection, is needed. Data contrary to current stereotypes can easily be fought against by use of whatever defense mechanisms an individual prefers. Similarly, fear of sexuality need not continue as the emotive force behind sexism once sexism has become a dominant cultural pattern. The emotive force may simply be a desire to maintain a coherent sense of self. Even the subordinate party often defends against a liberating new insight because her sense of self-identity is threatened.

We noted in the introduction to this chapter that prejudice is fundamentally a moral issue. If hierarchical dualism is a structure-like phenomenon, then we are likely to find it integrated with moral structures. To help us better understand this structural interpretation, we turn now to Haan's theory of morality and moral development.

Interactional Morality

BACKGROUND

Norma Haan's moral development theory is highly indebted to, though substantially different from, the seminal work of Lawrence Kohlberg.[12] According to Kohlberg's groundbreaking theory, the developing individual passes through a series of stages of moral growth on the road toward moral maturity.[13] Everyone passes through the stages in the same order, and once a new stage has been obtained, the person does not revert to earlier stages. Kohlberg postulates that each higher stage is "better" than lower stages in two senses.[14] First, at each higher stage a person recognizes a wider range of relevant moral considerations and is better able to prioritize them. Second, Kohlberg postulates that these psychological advances, formally referred to as differentiation and integration, correspond to philosophical criteria for moral adequacy, thus making each higher stage ethically superior to lower stages. For Kohlberg, each higher stage moves closer to development of the principle of justice, which is the defining characteristic of Stage 6, the highest stage.

Moral reasoning, from Kohlberg's viewpoint, is basically deductive. As children mature and develop in their logical functioning, they become better able to apply moral rules or principles to situations of moral conflict. For example, a person at Stage 4 may reason that a poor man should not steal an expensive drug to save his dying wife because society is based on everyone operating according to its rules and there is a law against stealing. In contrast, a person at Stage 5 might respond to the same dilemma by approving the theft since laws are designed to preserve and promote human life; thus, saving the wife's life takes logical precedence over maintaining a law which, if kept, would contradict its own purpose.

For Kohlberg, morality is relevant only to those situations where individuals have conflicting claims. The man who wants to steal the drug for his wife is in a moral situation because his right to preserve life conflicts with the druggist's right to his property. The types of rights or claims to which Kohlberg is referring are those which can be publicly stated. Furthermore, a moral situation is one where an abstract moral principle can be employed to decide between competing claims. A moral principle, in turn, is "a mode of choosing which is universalizable, a rule of choosing which we want all people to adopt always in all situations."[15] For Kohlberg, sound moral principles are devoid of all personalized reference so that they can be deductively and impartially applied to all situations of moral conflict. It is Kohlberg's central thesis that there is really only one principle, that of justice, which can be used to adequately decide among competing claims.

Kohlberg's work on moral development has been criticized on various grounds. Of particular interest here is the possibility that it is biased in favor of elites. A number of studies employing Kohlberg's techniques have concluded that males develop faster[16] or further[17] than females. Similarly, middle-class American males progressed faster and further than youths from Taiwan, Turkey, Mexico, or lower-class Americans.[18]

Carol Gilligan,[19] in a celebrated study of the moral reasoning of women deciding whether or not to have an abortion, concluded that Kohlberg's formal principle of justice does not adequately address the moral aspects of women's experience. Women construct social reality differently from men, Gilligan argues. Women's moral concerns, rather than focusing on justice, revolve around issues of responsibility and care. Thus, Gilligan contends, males' moral decisions may be more or less adequately guided by the principle of justice, but women's moral development may be best characterized as moving toward the principle of nonviolence.[20]

Haan's theory, like Kohlberg's, is based on the premise that all people develop through the same moral structures. At the same time, however, Haan concurs with Gilligan's critique of Kohlberg's model, contending that he has failed to capture all, or even the most salient, structures of morality that people actually use.[21]

INTERACTIONAL MORALITY: BASIC DEFINITIONS

Interactional morality finds its philosophical roots in such theorists as Dewey, Quine, and Habermas.[22] A common theme in these approaches is that what we call "reality" is something we construct. This does not imply, of course, that there is no reality apart from the operations of the mind. It does assert, however, that reality as we know it is created by the active operation of mental and social processes in interaction with an external world. Furthermore, the two poles of the interaction are not separable. It is impossible to distinguish reality "as it is in itself" from reality "as it is humanly perceived and constructed." Since we cannot get outside ourselves and look at "naked reality," truth is equivalent to that upon which we can agree. Any idea or principle is true to the extent that we are consensual about it and it is useful to us.

For Haan, morality is the product of social construction. It is oriented toward the regulation and enhancement of our lives. Kohlberg's deductive approach to morality, where correct moral action is deduced from a principle, is replaced in Haan's system by an inductive process whereby members of a social unit develop mutual understandings about behavior that are acceptable to all. Moral "truth" is defined as any consensual agreement about privileges, rights, and obligations that enhances the lives of those who are party to it. Since moral truth must be constructed, the central process of interactional morality is moral dialogue. Through moral dialogue we enter into mutual agreements with one another, called moral "balances," which are the basis for all moral duties.

THE MORAL DIALOGUE

In Kohlberg's system, abstract role taking is the central process of moral decision making. In the process of moral reasoning, the individual imaginatively places himself or herself in the role of each party in the moral dispute in order to isolate the specific claims that each person can make. These claims are then ranked according to the justice principle. This procedure fits Kohlberg's individualistic approach to morality.

For Haan, morality is not centered in individual reasoning about justice. The core of morality is an interpersonal process of negotiation about how we can best live together. Haan points out that nobody fully knows the needs, thoughts, and feelings of another human being. Consequently, an abstract role taking is not enough. We must enter into dialogue if we are to reach equitable agreement about our mutual responsibilities. Dialogue prevents us from assuming that our view of a situation is the only way the situation can be viewed. Dialogue allows for a mutual consideration of one another's hopes, desires, fears, and expectations, leading to constructive moral resolution:

> Dialogue is an exploration of mutual thought—a
> joint reflective inquiry into the facts and parameters
> of the moral issue at hand. Initially, parties make

fumbling, awkward attempts to defend their views; but faced with antithesis, they back off in order to clarify the problem. Thus, statements of antithetical positions serve to identify the parameters of the issue. As its features are identified, elaborated, and finally simplified, the parties can begin fully to comprehend each other's views. For one person to understand another, attitudes of passivity, receptivity, and amity are required, and people must cast off their self-preoccupation. That people do recognize each other's moral positions is evidence of how important are moral motivations and how comprehensive the social embeddedness of humans.[23]

Every day we enter into moral dialogues. Deciding who is going to wash clothes and who is going to do the dishes involves moral dialogue. Any time there is disagreement or potential disagreement over someone's rights or responsibilities, whether of major proportion such as a discussion of gay rights, or of relatively minor significance such as deciding which TV program to watch, moral dialogue occurs. Through moral dialogue people seek common agreement about interpersonal rights and responsibilities.

It is easiest to think of moral dialogue as a verbal exchange between persons in a moral dispute. Such an image is useful for gaining a preliminary grasp on the dynamics of moral construction, but one must guard against three possible misconceptions. First, dialogue is not limited to verbal communication. Moral actions, for example, participate in moral dialogue, as do other non-verbal forms of communication. Many people find it difficult to talk directly about moral issues, and various indirect ways of communicating substitute. A second misconception arises if moral dialogue is thought to occur only when a person consciously intends to negotiate a moral issue. In actuality, we are often unaware, or only partially aware, of our moral negotiations. I may snap at a colleague without even realizing my desire to communicate that I am upset that she was late for an appointment. Nonetheless, my action communicates displeasure and is an element of a moral negotiation about what we can expect from one another. Finally, the image is misleading if moral dialogue is thought to be limited to discussion among individuals. Moral dialogue also occurs between groups of people. Arms negotiation, for example, is an important instance of moral dialogue aimed at reaching a moral balance between nations. Similarly, dialogue occurs between races, sexes, classes, and cultures. In moral dialogue between groups, the communicative mechanisms often are not verbal. Demonstrations, political activism, voting choices, wall graffiti, self-defense training, and bra burning are examples of the many mechanisms that have been used to communicate moral perspective.

THE MORAL BALANCE

Moral dialogues are aimed at achieving, maintaining, or restoring moral balances. What Haan means by a moral balance, however, is difficult to define precisely. In part, moral balance refers to an agreement between people about what each person will do for the other. In part, it refers to a subjective sense that a relationship is equalized. The concept of an equalized relationship is substantially different from a just relationship. Justice is an abstract principle that can be universalized. In contrast, an equalized relationship is too particular and nuanced to be captured by such a principle. Haan notes that people in relationship develop informal expectations about what they require of each other and will do for one another, both psychologically and materially. These expectations take on the character of informal "obligations." When two or more people are in "moral balance" they agree that each party has done, is doing, or will do for the other what is desirable for all.

Several illustrations may help to clarify the concept of moral balance. If I am in a relationship with someone and I know that she needs outdoor activity and she knows that I need time alone, then we will likely negotiate our time so that both of our needs are met. Such an arrangement represents a moral balance. Even though the agreement may not be formally stated, still I will feel offended if my solitary time is infringed upon without further dialogue.

Let us say, as our second example, that I have recently

suffered the loss of a family member. Because of my situation, I may receive more psychological support from my friends than I am able to give. The relationship is temporarily unequal, but it may still be accepted as equal because my friends trust that in their time of need I will be there for them. We can see from this illustration that a moral balance is a dynamic equilibrium that takes into account not only present action but past patterns of behavior and expectations about future behavior as well.

As a third illustration, let us suppose that my car breaks down and I go to a neighbor and ask to borrow his. Even though he owes me no particular favors, he lends me his car. Later that week while trimming my own hedge, I also trim his. The moral balance was temporarily upset, but my action restored it. The alert reader may object that only a stingy neighbor would consider the moral balance to be upset just because I borrowed his car. It is true that such an event is hardly cause for a serious breech of moral relationship. However, what if I borrowed it the next day, and the day after? Pretty soon my neighbor would no longer answer his door should I knock! Moral balance rests on the good faith assumption that there will be a mutual giving to the relationship. When one person gives to another, it is with the implicit understanding that the other will at some appropriate time reciprocate. This is not a legalistic exchange, but an open sharing of communal existence. Good faith in a relationship is often maintained through a subtle give-and-take.

It is difficult to label the kind of exchange described above as "just" or "unjust" because justice involves either an exchange of similar, comparable items or setting a priority of one value over another based on some logical relationship. Thus, it is just to steal a drug for a dying wife because the value of life preempts that of property or law. But borrowing a car and clipping a hedge cannot be readily compared. Who got the better deal? The point is that such a question is irrelevant. A moral balance, in contrast to justice, is created or sustained when there is a subjective sense that all parties are equally satisfied with the situation. One need not be able to universalize a decision based on an effort to equalize; often this decision will be tied closely to the particularities of the context and the unique characteristics and desires of the individuals.

Suppose, as a final illustration, that a worker says to his hard-driving employer, "I feel cheated" and the employer replies, "What is it you want? You get a fair wage. I provide medical benefits. You have paid holidays." The worker finds himself in an awkward position. He feels that he is not valued or respected, but all external criteria indicate otherwise. There is a lack of moral balance in this situation, but there is no concrete injustice. In everyday life, it is often difficult to explain why we feel cheated, or neglected, or taken advantage of. Such feelings may be vague and no specific overt wrongs identifiable. Still, the worker knows something is wrong; things are simply "out of balance." The employer is just, but she doesn't treat the worker with due respect. Moral balances incorporate these more subtle dimensions of relationship that cannot be captured in a list of publicly stated rights and duties.[24]

Moral imbalance is how Haan labels that condition when moral balance has been disturbed. When wrongs have been committed or disagreements arise about individuals' rights or responsibilities, as happens frequently, then the moral balance is upset and needs to be regained. Moral dialogue must occur to restore the balance—to restore common understanding and agreement—so social exchange can continue and life go on. A moral balance is restored when all parties agree that the solution is the best that can be found, given the limitations of the situation and the current resources of the parties involved. Again, agreement need not be publically or verbally stated.

The restoration of moral balance can occur in quite subtle ways. I remember observing a videotape of a simulation game from one of Haan's studies. In this particular session, a teenage girl violated an unspoken but clear agreement about how to play the game and thereby took advantage of one of her friends. At this point, there was a moral imbalance between the two girls. Later in the session, the offender took out her comb and gently combed the hair of the girl she had cheated. That act was a nonverbal form of moral dialogue;

it was an implicit apology and was her way of restoring moral balance.

We have again been talking as though moral balances are only between individuals. Just as moral dialogue occurs between groups, so the concept of moral balance can refer to intergroup relations. Moral balances between groups can take the form of legislation, formal contractual agreements, or informal norms about appropriate ways to interact.

MORAL "TRUTH"

Defining moral truth is an inevitable part of any moral theory.[25] To ask the question of truth is to ask what one really *ought* to do. As might be anticipated, in Haan's view there is no moral truth outside human discourse. Moral truth for interactional morality can be defined as as pragmatic consensus; it is reached through discussion and is equivalent to an agreement that enables participants to live together and enhance each other's lives.

This may sound like pure relativism, but it is not. Haan has not discarded the need for moral norms, but she has changed their focus. Typically, moral theories offer norms by which resolutions to problems can be described as moral or not. Haan believes that the social scientist cannot base a theory of morality on such norms without violating the limits of social science. Although it is beyond the scope of social science to define what *should be done,* the social scientist is not left without alternatives. Haan offers a view of moral norms that focuses on the process of moral construction, rather than on the outcome of moral decisions. By focusing on process, Haan points to an arena in which the social scientist is competent. Social science can identify distorted and deceptive processes; criteria for the avoidance of these distortions can be a source for moral norms.

Valid moral dialogues are aimed at achieving moral balances. Inherent in the concept of moral balance is the idea of agreement based upon accurate information about the needs and interests of all concerned parties. Only when a dialogue avoids the sources of distortion and deception is it validly defining the moral truth for that situation. Thus, the moral dialogue must meet certain conditions before it can count as a "truth-identifying" dialogue. The nature of a truth-identifying moral dialogue can be stated in terms of four criteria.[26]

1. Interdependence of Participants

For moral truth to be identified, all members of the group must have a stake in finding a resolution. Hypothetical discussions, for example, are not suited for the identification of moral truth. When dialogue is not rooted in interdependence, it drifts easily into abstract formulations, and the particularities of the specific situation are often ignored or distorted.

2. Equality of Participation

A moral dialogue that identifies moral truth must be free and equal. All participants must have free access to information pertinent to the issues and be free to discuss and question. A truth-identifying dialogue requires that each participant have equal chance to influence the ultimate decision.

3. Consensus Among Relevant Parties

A truth-identifying dialogue must include as participants all who will be affected by the conclusions reached, and the conclusions must be reached unanimously. All parties must accept the solution as the best that can be achieved, given the limitations of the situation and the particularities of the discussants. Any use of physical or psychological coercion to gain a resolution automatically invalidates the conclusions.

4. Situationally-Specific Resolution

Conclusions that have a chance of being "truths" must be empirically drawn, use common-sense language, be specific to the individuals and the particular nature of their joint dilemma, take all parties' self-interest into account, and satisfy the individuals in their everyday life.

These four conditions, of course, are quite stringent and are rarely, if ever, realized in actual moral dialogue. In our everyday lives we must—and do—accept conclusions of moral dialogues that do not meet all of these conditions. It is vital, nevertheless, to specify as precisely as possible under what conditions conclusions may be taken as "true," so that less than perfect conclusions will be viewed as tentative and so that we can seek means to achieve better dialogues.

VARIATIONS ON THE THEME OF MORAL BALANCE

Up to this point we have been considering only the most frequent form of moral balance. There are, however, other forms of dialogue and balance and these are discussed below.

1. Legitimate and Illegitimate Imbalances

The relationship between persons of unequal power or resources (e.g. adult and child) may lead to an objective imbalance that is still accepted as balanced because it is socially and emotionally legitimated by all parties' expectations. In the parent-child relationship, the parent is expected to give in much greater proportion than the child. This is accepted as normal and appropriate, even though imbalanced. Similarly, in some situations, physically able persons are expected to give more to physically challenged persons. Taxes, for example, may be used to construct wheel chair ramps even though the expenditure of funds benefits a limited group disproportionately to their representation within the general tax-paying public. These instances are called *socially legitimated imbalances* and are characterized by the party with greater physical or psychological resources accepting a larger proportion of financial, social, or personal responsibility. Negotiation, however, must still take place. For the person of greater resources to give too much is as inappropriate as to not give enough, and what is "enough" must be determined by negotiation. Paternalism results when the party of greater resources gives, or appears to give, without the informed agreement of the less advantaged party.

Socially legitimated imbalances occur between people or groups who have unequal power and/or abilities. The unequal distribution of advantage reflects factors beyond the control of the parties involved and the imbalance is legitimated through mutual consent. But there also are illegitimate imbalances. In almost all societies inequalities exist due to the social, economic, and political structures. There is no legitimate basis within Haan's procedural theory of morality for the individuals of greater power to use that power to dominate the dialogue. To do so is an example of "bad faith" and results in the disruption of the dialogue or causes unsatisfactory conclusions. When domination does occur, various resistance or protest strategies may need to be used by the "oppressed."

A second source of illegitimate imbalance occurs when one party enters into moral exchange insincerely. The "free-loader"—the person who appears to negotiate in good faith but secretly pursues self-oriented ends—presents a serious threat to moral exchange. If a participant should prove to be insincere, dialogue becomes futile and all that a sincere participant can do is be self-protective and withdraw from further exchange.

2. Legitimate and Illegitimate Regressions

Another variation of moral balance has been identified by Brenda Bredemeier, a sport psychologist at the University of California, Berkeley, and the present author.[27] Our research on the moral reasoning that occurs in play, games, and sport indicates that, in these contexts, a temporary transformation occurs in the way people reason morally. In the "world-within-a-world" of sport, for example, people often exhibit a regressed-like pattern of moral reasoning that structurally resembles that of a young child. While the moral reasoning of most adults is oriented toward an equalized moral exchange, sport participants frequently become quite egocentric. Moral reasoning within these unique contexts might be labelled legitimate regressions. It violates the usual norm that all participants seek a mutually beneficial solution, but the violation itself is accepted by all. This regressed-like moral reasoning is accepted as legitimate because the play, game, or sport activity has no "real life" consequences, participants mutually anticipate it and freely accept it, and the pleasure of sport participation partially rests on the release that it provides from the usual demands of everyday life. Illegitimate regressions, on the other hand, occur when this same type of egocentric moral reasoning is used to gain advantage through means that have not been accepted by all parties or when implications of the behavior affect real life. If an athlete, for example, deliberately injures an opponent to gain advantage for her team, that is an instance of illegitimate regression.

PREJUDICE AND MORAL IMBALANCE

Prejudice involves interpreting information about human groups through the use of stereotypes. Particular characteristics of some members of a group are selected and become the image for the whole group. This stereotyping is accompanied by a double denial: denial that those same characteristics are also present in the group to which the person doing the stereotyping belongs, and denial of true individuality to persons stereotyped. This process has serious moral implications.

The psychic patterning of hierarchical dualism makes "truth-identifying" moral dialogues a problem. On the one hand, valid moral dialogues are premised on the key concepts of freedom and equality. Truth-identifying dialogues involve freedom to negotiate as peers and equal consideration is given to the interests and needs of all parties. In contrast, hierarchical dualism involves domination and is based on an interpretation of self and others as unequal.

Hierarchical dualism may be looked at as a form of *rigid moral imbalance*. It shares features of both illegitimate regressions and illegitimate imbalances. Like an illegitimate regression, hierarchical dualism is limited in scope and uses a moral pattern that is not fully mature. And like an illegitimate imbalance, hierarchical dualism reflects unequal power or resources.

The moral default inherent in hierarchical dualism is disguised, though, because the dualistic categories create the illusion that the moral imbalance is socially legitimated. Dualisms are used as a justification—or, rather, rationalization—for unequal distribution of social benefit. Take, for example, the dualism of "strong" and "weak" that has often been used to interpret male and female respectively. If the sexes really could be so categorized, there would indeed be a socially legitimate imbalance in the way tasks requiring physical labor were distributed. But many women are more physically powerful than many men. Thus, when the dualism of strong and weak is used to keep women out of certain professions, it is appropriate to refer to an illegitimate imbalance.

Hierarchical dualisms ensure communication will be distorted and that moral imbalances will be constructed and persist. Let us say, for example, a black caucus forms to pressure the management of a corporation to alter its investment policies in South Africa. The managers, however, hold to subtle images of black inferiority. Consequently, information that they obtain from other whites will be given greater credibility than the information from the caucus. Communication is systematically distorted since the contributions by black members are not considered equally. The result is that administrative decisions are likely to perpetuate the moral imbalance of apartheid, perhaps under the guise that the investments are helping the blacks.

It is also the case that rigid moral imbalances are often supported by the disadvantaged party. As Mary Daly writes with regard to sexism: "The exploitative social caste system could not be perpetuated without the consent of the victims as well as the dominant sex, and such consent is obtained through sex role socialization."[28] Women, and other subordinate groups, cooperate in maintaining rigid moral imbalances because their self-identity was formed under the weight of cultural images. They often believe the stereotypes and eventually embrace them as their own. On an unconscious level, the old adage holds — "if you can't beat them, join them." Having internalized the dominator's view, the subjugated party has a difficult time believing that they could or should enter moral negotiation as equals.

Rigid moral imbalances occur not only with regard to macro-moral issues such as job opportunities, legal rights, and vocational channeling, but also in everyday interactions. In fact, it has been a consistent and essential theme of many feminist thinkers that personal and societal levels of action cannot be separated. This notion has been popularized by Sheila Collin's phrase, "The personal is political."[29]

In a society characterized by sexual injustice we would anticipate that the interaction and moral negotiations of everyday life would also be characterized by male dominance. As an illustration of this, researchers have consistently found that the differential power and status of females and males is reflected in everyday speech patterns. Zimmerman and West,[30] for example, found that in conversations between members of the same sex, the average number of interruptions occurring was no different for males and for females. However, in mixed sex conversations males interrupted females far more frequently than vice versa. Men also talk longer during their speaking opportunities than do women[31] and, as listeners, men reinforce women speakers significantly less than women reinforce men.[32]

In these studies we again see communication systematically distorted. If males consistently dominate interpersonal exchange, then the conditions for truth-identifying dialogue are absent and the moral imbalances that result are likely to favor the males. It is interesting to note that this domination of communication is hidden behind the stereotype of women as talkative.

In summary, it appears that hierarchical dualism results in rigid moral imbalances. But to better understand how this is possible, we need to look at hierarchical dualism in light of the development of moral understanding. This will enable us to see how hierarchical dualism can be lodged within moral reasoning patterns.

The Development of Morality

Up to this point in our discussion of interactional morality, we have assumed our reference is a morally mature person. From Haan's viewpoint, even very young children are capable of acting in morally mature ways if the conditions are not stressful or cognitively taxing. Nonetheless, children do improve in their grasp of the subtle meanings of moral exchange and they increasingly develop their moral skill.

Haan's theory hypothesizes that there are five "levels" of interactional morality.[33] Each level represents a more adequate way to approach moral exchange. These levels are summarized in Table 2. The levels are characterized by interlocking "structures." The primary structure, already discussed,

TABLE 2
Levels of Interactional Morality

Assimilation Phase

Level One: Power Balancing. The person is unable to sustain a view of others' interest apart from self-interest, and vacillates between compliance with others when forced and thwarting others when able to do so. Balances reflect self-interest except for situations where the self is indifferent or forced to compromise.

Level Two: Egocentric Balancing. The person is able to differentiate others' interests from self-interest, but does not understand that both may coincide in a mutual interest. People are viewed as essentially self-interested and out for their own good. To get what the self wants, trade-offs or compromises are made.

Accommodation Phase

Level Three: Harmony Balancing. The person differentiates others' interest from self-interest, but assumes that a harmony of these interests can be found by giving to others since most people are believed to possess altruistic motives. Balances are sought which rest on the good faith of all. People of bad faith are considered odd and dismissed from moral consideration.

Level Four: Common Interest Balancing. The person differentiates all parties' self-interests from the common interest of the group. Balances of compromise are sought which conform to the system-maintenance requirements of the group. Because the moral culpability of all is recognized, externally regulated patterns of exchange are sought that benefit all while limiting personal vulnerability.

Equilibration Phase

Level Five: Mutual Interest Balancing. The person coordinates all parties' self-interests and the common interest of the group in a search for a situationally-specific moral balance which will optimize everyone's interest. In such a search, the person recognizes the need to consider the specific values and desires, strengths and vulnerabilities, of the parties involved. Solutions may achieve harmony of interests or may represent compromises of interest, whatever the particularities of the situation and participants allow.

is the particular form of "moral balance" that each level seeks to achieve.

At the first level, moral balances that favor the self are thought to be appropriate. The person at this level has difficulty understanding that others have different interests and needs. It is not that Level One children are selfish, though adults may commonly misinterpret their actions as such. It is rather that their level of development limits their ability to recognize that others may have conflicting needs. Moral dialogue at this level is largely limited to asserting one's own desires. Balances achieved at this level are largely based on power. Either the child creates a balance that molds the behavior of others to the child's interest or the child's assertions are thwarted by others.

At the second level, the person still attempts to create moral balances that are tilted in his or her favor. However, at this level an understanding of reciprocity moderates the egocentrism. The Level Two person recognizes that others have a perspective of their own and a legitimate right to seek their own gain. A view of moral exchange as "trade-offs" is common. Equal exchanges of good or bad take place in a kind of tit-for-tat morality.

Then, between Levels Two and Three, a dramatic shift occurs. At Level Three, the individual attempts to create moral balances by overly accommodating the interests of others. At this level the person assumes a fortunate harmony between the interests of self and others. All people, with the exception of a few "odd" people, are believed to be good and to maintain their goodness in all situations. In creating moral balances the Level Three person generally gives to the other with the assumption that the other has one's own interests at heart too.

By Level Four a more accurate understanding of the fallibility of humanness leads the person to transform his or her image of both self-interest and others' interests into the new idea of the common interest. At this stage, one accepts the need for impersonal outside regulation. The person at Level Four believes it is important for everyone to make sacrifices to "make the system work." The "system" can refer to a family, a school, society as a whole, or any other collective. In order for the common interest to be served, the Level Four person subscribes to moral balances that can be characterized as "systematized structured exchanges." A legal system is the clearest example of a systematized structured exchange. These codified moral balances both define one's obligation to others and set limits on one's accountability.

At Level Five, equilibrium is reached between the interests of all and a search is begun for a solution that maximizes mutual interest. Mutual interest is distinguished from the common interest by its particularity. While the search for a common interest is reflected in a desire to find a common practice that everyone can follow for the benefit and protection of the whole social group, mutual interest is a search for a solution that optimizes the needs and interests of the particular individuals involved, given their unique situation. At Level Five, any given solution may not reflect equality, but equalization is achieved over a period of time.

Haan not only discusses the type of moral balance that people at each level seek to achieve; she also discusses "substructures" involved in moral exchange.[34] Substructures are interactional capacities that influence the frame of reference with which a person approaches moral relationships. Substructures help a person organize and interpret information during moral dialogues. There are essentially three moral substructures in Haan's model. Though the details of how each substructure is manifested at each level of development are beyond the scope of this book, brief mention of the basic dynamics of the substructures will help to illustrate how prejudice enters into the moral exchange.

1. Self and Others as Moral Beings and Objects

Interactional morality is based on incessant, detailed, and intimate moral concern and attention to others and to the self. Giving to others is always a matter of moral balance and exchange. The problem of moral growth is not the relatively simple one of learning to give ("altruism"), but, more complexly, learning how to exchange.

If a person does not take adequate account of their own needs and interests, then the moral balance is likely to be upset by "overgiving." By giving too much, the person (often unintentionally) obligates the other, and when the other does not respond to this imposed obligation, the giver will eventually feel used. Altruism, as traditionally viewed, only takes into account the inclinations of one party to give while it ignores the pragmatic consequences of the way giving fits into an exchange pattern.

It is also possible, of course, to give too little. In this case, the other will feel used and will need to seek reparations or will abandon the relationship. In the rigid moral imbalances imposed by hierarchical dualism, the errors of giving too little and giving too much are systematically imposed: The dominant party maintains position by requiring overgiving on the part of others while undergiving themselves.

2. Taking Chances on Others' Good Faith

The complexity of moral situations means that defaults are often not obvious, the means of redress not always clear, and the person who is so inclined can interact secretly in bad faith (the freeloader). Taking chances on others' good faith reflects a recognition of the complexity of moral relationship. One must risk that others interact in good faith in order to keep dialogue and interchange open. One must expect good faith, but there is a difference between naive and mature anticipation of others' good faith. Blind trust is naive. The mature anticipation of others' good faith includes not only the complex decisions of when, why, whom, and how much to trust, but also includes recognition of oneself as a worthy object for one's own moral consideration.

Hierarchical dualism also influences how this substructure operates. The dominant party expects to be trusted, but views with suspicion the motives of those in the disadvantaged position.

3. Righting Wrongs

Moral balances are complex and often informal. It is inevitable that wrongs will be committed. The mature person is able to use a variety of means to re-establish moral balance following wrongs. Procedures for restoring balance include forgiving, restitution, and reparation. What is required in a particular situation will vary with the wrong committed, the particular circumstances, and the nature of the relationship. But attempts to re-establish the moral balance require that people recognize when a wrong has actually occurred that needs righting. If there is no admission of wrong, there is no felt need for restitution and the imbalance will persist. Many moral imbalances are due to the inability to integrate inevitable wrongdoing with the remaining possibilities of restoring a moral balance.

Again, hierarchical dualism has profound influence on this substructure. Stereotypes hide the wrongs committed by the offender and moral imbalance is not perceived. When the dominant group does admit to wrong, it is shrugged off as an accident or oversight and rectified by apology without reparation.

MORAL DEVELOPMENT AND PREJUDICE

For another view of the ready-made opportunities where hierarchical dualism lurks, even in the upper reaches of Haan's structures, let us look at Haan's levels of moral development in reverse order.

The hallmark of Level Five moral reasoning is sensitivity to people and contexts. The person who operates at Level Five is responsive to the particularities of situations and individuals. All parties' interests and needs are given equal consideration, and balances are sought that coordinate all viewpoints. Level Five thinking is inconsistent with the stereotyping and value polarizing of hierarchical dualism. However, lower levels of moral reasoning, as we have seen, do incorporate hierarchical dualism within their structure.

Certain characteristics of Level Four reasoning lend themselves to an interpretation of human groups that is both hierarchical and dualistic. There is a tendency to reduce people to "objects," devoid of their particularity. The "systematized structured exchanges" that characterize this level are limited in their flexibility and can adapt to only broad classifications of people. Thus in a culture where sexist and racist stereotypes are rampant, these broad categories may be used as the basis for assigning moral rights and duties and evaluating moral worth.

The "hidden value choice" Dewey spoke of can be understood as selectively noticing those instances when disadvantaged groups are conforming to negative stereotypes while choosing to concentrate on positively valued traits in the dominant party. This selective perception of predetermined and value-laden attributes can readily be assimilated into a level of reasoning that wants to treat individuals in broad categories.

The legalistic orientation of Level Four also provides a structural setting for hierarchical dualism. It is based on a felt need for external social regulation to protect people from instances of bad faith, and on fear that lying beneath outward conformity to social expectations there are many who act only out of personal interest. This fear may find expression in dualisms. The world may be divided into the "law abiding citizen" and the "criminal." By naming the "enemy" of the common interest, it may be felt that the common interest can be better protected.

At Level Three the individual sees the self as a good member of a good human community. This belief in the goodness of the self and others is naive. The view that people are basically good and that they almost always mean to treat others well is partially maintained through segregating those who display bad faith as "different" or "strange." Again, the foundation for hierarchical dualism has been laid. Evil can be circumscribed at this level by identifying it with those who are not "like me" or "like my group" in important or trivial respects.

The first two levels can also readily incorporate hierarchical dualisms. Both levels are egocentric. The orientation toward one's own interests and needs easily allows for depreciating the "other." Since one's moral attention is focused inward, the violence done by stereotyping is seldom recognized.

It is fairly easy to see how hierarchical dualism can be incorporated as a part of the structures of moral reasoning up through Level Four. It becomes more difficult to reconcile Level Five moral reasoning with hierarchical dualisms. Most adults, however, are capable of Level Five moral reasoning. Nonetheless, prejudice remains common. While it may be that

Level Five reasoners are more resistant to prejudices than others, everyday observation indicates that few people are exempt.

Ruether has perhaps provided a key for understanding this puzzling phenomenon. She sees sexism in particular, but also other forms of hierarchical dualism, as established very early in psychological development, providing a foundation for one's self-image. In addition, for Ruether, sexual symbolism is closely related to a person's whole sense of order and value. If prejudices are intimately tied to a person's self-understanding and sense of self-worth, then challenges to the person's prejudices are likely to provide stress. Stress is one of the key factors that Haan has identified that can lead to momentary disruptions of optimal functioning. Defensive processes are elicited and the person easily slips back to a lower level of moral reasoning. Thus a person who normally functions at Level Five may respond to such issues as sex roles, race relations, or sexual orientation in uncharacteristically immature fashion. Their reasoning may fall to a level consistent with hierarchical dualisms. This would be a form of illegitimate regression in moral reasoning.

In summary, two sources for hierarchical dualism have been highlighted. One source is the defensive processing of information. Particularly under stress, people may distort or suppress information that is inconsistent with their present self-understanding. Since sexual identity, racial identity, etc., are intimately involved in self-definition, perceived threats to a person's understanding of what it means to be male or female, for example, may result in regression to less mature reasoning. When a minority person rebels against the cultural stereotype of his or her group, the majority person may feel his or her identity is challenged. Maintaining one's identity, when it is based on hierarchical dualisms, requires upholding the stereotype of the other. I cannot belong to the superior group if I accept the claims to equality of persons belonging to the group I have imaged as inferior. Under the stress of challenged stereotypes, I may abandon my ability to reason in a morally mature manner and revert to a lower level in my moral reasoning. This assumes, however, that hierarchical dualism is easily reconcilable with less mature structures of moral reasoning. This is the second source.

As we have seen, hierarchical dualisms are consistent with the less mature structures of moral reasoning. Prior to achieving Level Five, a person's moral reasoning can readily incorporate the cultural ideologies of prejudice. Not only may a person regress to a lower level of morality under stress, prejudice may also reflect the viewpoint of a person whose moral growth arrested at some point in the developmental process prior to reaching full maturity. Hierarchical dualisms may reflect developmental deficiencies. If this is the case, an analysis of the processes that normally lead to moral growth may provide clues for responding to problems of prejudice.

MORAL EDUCATION

Most interesting about a theory of moral development, from an educator's viewpoint, are the processes of moral growth. What causes or stimulates change? It will be helpful to contrast Haan's answer to this questioning with Kohlberg's and his colleagues.

The Kohlberg school has proposed one primary answer: cognitive disequilibrium. Since moral growth is viewed as proceeding through an invariable sequence of cognitive moral stages, moral change occurs when a person becomes aware of the inadequacies associated with his or her current stage of reasoning. Moral education programs have been developed that provide cognitive disequilibrium. The use of hypothetical moral dilemmas has been one of the popular techniques used by educators to stimulate moral growth. In the process of discussing a moral dilemma, it is theorized, participants will be exposed to a variety of viewpoints including some that reflect reasoning at the stage above most participants'. Hearing higher stage reasoning will promote cognitive dissonance; the person will be attracted to the higher stage of reasoning and begin to recognize limitations within his or her current stage.

In contrast to Kohlberg's view of cognitive disequilibrium, Haan highlights *social disequilibrium*. The difference is derived from Haan's orientation to moral action rather than moral thought. Social disequilibrium refers to disruptions that occur within human relationships. Let me offer an example.

Johnny is eight years old and currently uses predominantly Level Two moral reasoning. He is playing with some blocks with a friend named Albert. Because Johnny's reasoning is predominantly egocentric, he is unaware that his selection of the most attractive blocks will not meet with approval by Albert. When an argument ensues, Albert leaves. This disruption, and dozens of similar instances, eventually lead Johnny to re-evaluate the pattern of moral exchange that he imposes on others. It is these social disruptions that lead to moral change. Eventually Johnny will seek a new form of moral balance.

Education that takes moral growth as one of its aims should be "experience-based."[35] The capacities for mature moral exchange develop through experience with others. But not all forms of social interaction will be equally advantageous. In particular, two characteristics stand out as important dynamics of moral education. Interaction that fosters a recognition of interdependence will assist in developing a student's sense of the basic connection among all humans. Such a sense plays a prominent role in moral motivation. We need to recognize that we are not ultimately loners and must find healthy ways to relate to others. Such an awareness can be fostered by tasks that demand cooperation for their successful completion. In addition, education needs to make use of opportunities for moral negotiation arising out of interpersonal dilemmas. This is often difficult for educators to appreciate because it calls for a valuing of controlled conflict. Typically, we wish to help students avoid conflict. In moral education, however, an element of conflict is appropriate, for a conflict of interest engenders dialogue through which common agreement may be established. Negotiation in the context of felt interdependence is at the heart of moral growth. We will return to more specific suggestions for such education in the final chapter.

For Discussion

1. In Table 1 (page 76) six defense mechanisms are listed. Which of these do you think are most often reflected in the thinking of prejudiced people? Defend your selection.

2. Describe an unstated moral balance that you have with a friend. What happens when the friend violates the balance? How do you feel? What do you do?

3. Describe some of the moral agreements that have traditionally characterized the relationships between (a) women and men, and (b) blacks and whites.

4. Do you think prejudices are always irrational?

5. Explain in your own words how prejudices enforce moral imbalance.

6. What critiques do you have of the ideas presented in this chapter?

For Further Reading

Haan, Norma. "An Interactional Morality of Everyday Life." In N. Haan, R. Bellah, P. Rabinow, and W. Sullivan (eds.), *Social Science as Moral Inquiry*. New York: Columbia University Press, 1983.

Haan, Norma, Elaine Aerts, and Bruce Cooper. *On Moral Grounds: The Search for Practical Morality*. New York: New York University Press, 1985.

Kohlberg, Lawrence. *Essays on Moral Development. Vol. 1. The Philosophy of Moral Development*. San Francisco: Harper & Row, 1981.

Kohlberg, Lawrence. *Essays on Moral Development. Vol. 2. The Psychology of Moral Development*. San Francisco: Harper & Row, 1984.

COMPASSION AND JUSTICE: THEOLOGICAL METHOD IN LIBERATION THEOLOGY

The Brazilian educator Paulo Freire contrasts authentic education with what he calls a "banking" model of education.[1] In the banking model, educators view their task as one of "depositing" knowledge into the minds of students. This has often been the model unconsciously adopted by religious educators. Theology is equated with a vast store of truths from which educators draw in order to make deposits into the minds of students. The assumption is that some people (theologians) possess answers while other people (students) possess questions, or if not questions at least a willingness to learn theologians' answers. Educators become faithful servants transmitting the wealth of scholars and theologians to the poverty-stricken minds of students.

If we were to reject this view of education, what alternative role is theology to play? To develop a response, it may be helpful to distinguish between theological content and theological method. Theological content pertains to the specific beliefs, values, and truths held by a theologian or community of believers. Theological method, in contrast, refers to the process of constructing theologies, pointing to such questions as: What are the sources of theology? In what ways does God's self-revelation take place? How trustworthy is experience?

The clue to the appropriate use of theology in religious education may be to focus on theological method.[2] This is the area of theology that will aid the religious educator in understanding how people move from personal and communal experience to theological conviction. Theological method provides the educator with a clue to the relationship between the historical sources of faith, such as the Bible, and contemporary experience. A theological method is a map for the journey toward an understanding of Christian faith.

An explicit focus on theological method was uncommon in theology until very recently. We should not be surprised, then, to find that religious educators have paid little attention to this area. While many religious educators have emphasized the importance of a sound theology, few have placed equal emphasis on the process of theological construction. A self-consciousness about theological method, however, will alter the way we read theology. We will not only examine the theologian's presuppositions and conclusions, but also the life experiences that gave rise to the questions the theologian addresses.

Too often religious educators have approached theology as if it were a packaged product independent of its maker. When theological content is severed from its historical and biographical roots, theology is disjoined from experience and becomes a matter of abstract truth-claims rather than an articulation of living faith. Theology is vital because it is an attempt to make sense of our lived faith so that the gospel of Christ can be more effectively communicated. It is distorted if it is taught or learned simply as a set of truths about God. Unfortunately, this has frequently been the pedagogical reality. Let me offer one brief illustration from my Lutheran heritage.

The theology of Martin Luther developed out of his quest to find peace with God. As a youth, Luther was terrified of God, fearing that God's wrath awaited him. This fear was so overwhelming that once, in the midst of a tumultuous thunderstorm, Luther became so stricken with fright that he cried out in desperation, "Save me, Saint Anne, and I will become a monk!" The storm ended and Luther packed his bags. Once in the monastery, Luther was a tireless worker, spending hours in study, prayer, and confession. But Luther's burning doubts about his own worthiness could not be dampened. It was not until some years later that Luther finally stumbled across the revolutionary key that would unlock his religious reawakening. It is summed up with the insight, "We are saved by grace through faith and not by works of the law." For Luther, the burden was lifted and he experienced the loving embrace of God for the first time. That, in short, was Luther's experience.

Some years later Luther turned to education. In his famous *Small Catechism,* designed for use by parents with their children, he sought to distill the essence of his theological discovery. While offering a powerful, almost poetic summary of Reformation insight, the catechism reveals the difficulty of basing education on theological content. Luther's "answers" are powerful in light of the weighty questions that had troubled him and many of his contemporaries. But teaching the catechism does not reconstruct the process by which Luther arrived at his insights. Most learners have not passed through the hell of Luther's childhood and, consequently, they do not experience Luther's bliss when learning of God's free gift of grace. Lutherans have discovered that teaching the conclusions that someone else reached cannot duplicate that person's faith.

Close attention to theological method will assist the educator in keeping theology tethered to experience. Of course, once the educator decides to focus on theological method, a selection must be made from among various competing approaches. This chapter will be concerned with theological method as discussed by the Uruguayan liberation theologian, Juan Luis Segundo, and its implications for an educational model designed to overcome hierarchical dualism.

I have chosen Latin American liberation theology as my theological frame of reference for a number of reasons. First, like feminist theology, it takes dualism as a major obstacle to be overcome. Jose Miguez Bonino, for example, states: "It seems to me, in fact, that the clue to this theology is the elimination of all and every dualism."[3] Liberation theology is also useful for our purposes because it lifts up the experience of the oppressed. It is concerned with hierarchical social relations and seeks in its methodology to provide a megaphone for the voiceless to speak their words. Further, it is a vehicle not only for speaking, but for acting. Liberation theology is concerned only secondarily with theological concepts; it is concerned primarily with the transformation of reality. Thus, the liberation theologian seeks to overcome hierarchical dualism both as it has been crystalized in theological formulations and as it has structured interpersonal and intergroup relations.

The chapter includes three main sections. The first surveys liberation theology as it has taken shape in Latin America. It is designed as background for an explanation of Segundo's work on theological method, the topic of the second section. In the final section, I will probe how Segundo's work on theological method can be used to expand Dewey's model of inquiry and make it operational for religious educators.

What Is Liberation Theology?

On the world scale, Christianity is undergoing major transformations today. One keen observer and participant in these changes, Walbert Buhlmann, refers to the phenomenon as "the coming of the third church,"[4] a church focused by the reality that humanity is not predominantly white, male, middle-class, and well educated. Most people are poor, hungry, illiterate; many suffer under repressive governments and the prospects for immediate improvement are dim. The reality of the poor is by no means new, of course. What is new is that theologians have emerged from the Third World and are giving voice to the yearnings of the poor for freedom and dignity. This has resulted in major upheavals in religion, for the world and

theology look quite different when viewed through the eyes
of the poor. Nowhere is this new way of doing theology more
apparent than in Latin America. The theological ferment in
Latin America has developed into a multifaceted movement
known as liberation theology.[5]

In a book devoted to presenting Latin American liberation theology to the North American audience, Robert McAfee
Brown offers a characterization of liberation theology in a six-
point contrast with traditional theology.[6] These points form
a useful outline which I will develop for the purposes of this
chapter. In brief, the six points are:

1. a different starting point: the poor
2. a different interlocutor: the nonperson
3. a different set of tools: the social sciences
4. a different analysis: the reality of conflict
5. a different mode of engagement: praxis
6. a different theology: the "second act"

1. A Different Starting Point: The Poor

Where does one turn when one wants to reflect on the
religious dimension of life? Theology begins somewhere. Selecting the starting point for theological reflection is crucial, for
where one begins determines the questions that one asks. Various starting points have been used in the past: nature, the
church, human rationality. Most commonly, however, people
have begun with the Bible. The Bible is accepted as the basic
source and norm of theology.

The difficulties with beginning theological reflection
with the Bible will become more apparent when we discuss
Segundo's hermeneutic, or interpretative, circle. For now, let
me simply point out that the Bible must always be interpreted.
One can interpret either haphazardly or systematically, but one
cannot avoid the necessity to interpret. Furthermore, interpretations will reflect the reader's pre-existing values and assumptions, particularly if these have not been carefully examined.
Let me offer a brief example based on a Bible study that I once
conducted in a typical middle-class congregation. I began by
reading the following text from the Gospel of Luke:

> Blessed are you poor, for yours is the kingdom of
> God.
> Blessed are you that hunger now, for you shall be
> satisfied.
> Blessed are you that weep now, for you shall
> laugh....
> But woe to you that are rich, for you have received
> your consolation.

I asked, "Who are the poor"? It is not a tricky question! But the answers played tricks with the text. "They are those who are humble" was one reply. "The poor are all of us when we recognize our need for God" was another. For this group "the poor" had a variety of meanings. But no one suggested that it might refer to those who live in real, material poverty! While most of the participants held the Bible to be the starting point of theology, the exercise revealed that the true starting point was a variety of theological preconceptions formed out of privileged life experiences.

If the Bible must be interpreted, then some source other than the Bible must inform the theologian. Beginning with the Bible is an illusion. When one tries to begin with the Bible, the Scriptures generally buttress one's previous beliefs. This does not mean that the Bible does not have a central role to play in religious formation. In fact, the Bible can help to expose one's unconscious prejudices, opening one to God's revelation. But for the Scriptures to have this power, a different beginning point must be adopted.

Human experience is the inevitable starting point of theological reflection. But experience itself is not uniform. Is some part of our experience, more than others, an appropriate place to begin? Are some people's experiences more revelatory? To determine an appropriate beginning point, we might ask, "Who were the people best able to hear God's word through Jesus?"

For liberation theology, the normative starting point is the experience of the struggling poor.[7] It was the poor who most readily responded to God's call in the first century and it is the poor today who are still in the most advantageous situation to hear God's word. In the language popularized by libera-

tion theology, Jesus revealed God's "preferential option for
the poor."[8]

God's preference for the poor is a constant theme in
the Bible. The Hebrew prophets, for example, frequently
equated doing justice for the poor with knowing God. The
following passage from Jeremiah 22:15-16 expresses this viewpoint:

> Do you think you are a king because you compete in
>   cedar?
> Did not your father eat and drink
> and do justice and righteousness?
> Then it was well with him.
> He judged the cause of the poor and needy;
> then it was well.
> Is not this to know me?
> says the Lord.

As we move to the New Testament, we find the theme
repeated. Even before Jesus' birth, Mary sang about God's
favorable action on behalf of the oppressed (Luke 1:51-53):

> He has shown strength with his arm, he has scattered
>   the proud in the imagination of their hearts,
> he has put down the mighty from their thrones,
>   and exalted those of low degree;
> he has filled the hungry with good things,
>   and the rich he has sent empty away.

Mary was not disappointed. Jesus did show preferential favor for the outcast. In Luke 4:18-19, for example, the
gospel writer records the beginning of Jesus' ministry by relating
a story about Jesus in the synagogue. Jesus picks up the Old
Testament scriptures and uses them to clearly announce the
purpose and theme of his ministry:

> The Spirit of the Lord is upon me,
> because he has anointed me
> to preach good news to the poor.
> He has sent me to proclaim liberation to the prisoners
> and recovery of sight to the blind,
> to liberate the oppressed,
> to proclaim the year of the Lord's favor.

If God favors the poor, what does this mean for those of us who are not poor? Are we excluded from God's love? Does it mean that we should idealize poverty? Is poverty something God wants for us?

Poverty is an equivocal term. Gustavo Gutierrez offers three primary meanings.[9] Poverty designates in the first place *material poverty*. In this sense of the word, poverty is degrading. Material poverty is a subhuman condition. The Bible, Gutierrez observes, constantly denounces this kind of poverty and those responsible for it. *Spiritual poverty,* on the other hand, is positively valued and designates an interior attitude of unattachment to the goods of this world. Sometimes the Bible uses the term in this way and speaks of the poor person as the "client" of Yahweh. This meaning of poverty has no direct relationship to material wealth.

Gutierrez sees material poverty and spiritual poverty as synthesized in the particular Christian meaning of the word: poverty as a commitment to solidarity and protest. Christian poverty involves learning to emphasize with the materially poor and to protest with them against the structures and individuals responsible for their oppression. This is *poverty in Christ:* "Just as Christ carried out the work of redemption in poverty and under oppression, so the Church is called to follow the same path."[10]

Poverty, of course, should not be romanticized. Gutierrez is well aware that living under the boot of oppression can disfigure one's humanity:

> The world of the poor is not made up simply of victims. The universe of the poor is inhabited by flesh-and-blood human beings, pervaded with the forces of life and death, of grace and sin. In that world we find indifference to others, individualism, abandoned children, people abusing people, pettiness, hearts closed to the action of the Lord.[11]

For liberation theologians, the struggling poor are the people to whom God most clearly speaks. If we wish to know God, identification with the oppressed is the place to begin. Gutierrez writes, "The poor human being, the 'other,' now steps forward as the one who reveals the totally 'Other.' "[12] Hugo Assmann, a Brazilian theologian, refers to the "epistemological privilege of the poor."[13] Assmann, like Gutierrez, is referring not to the poor who have internalized the "oppressor's consciousness" (Freire),[14] but to the "struggling poor," to those who are engaged in action to overcome poverty. It is these people who are free to see the world without the blinders that are inevitable when a person has privileges to protect.

In his thought-provoking study of Christology, John Sobrino also identifies the poor as the privileged beginning point for all authentic theology:

> The privileged meditation of God ever continues to be the real cross of the oppressed, not nature or history as a totality. ...Oppressed persons are the mediation of God because, first of all, they break down the normal self-interest with which human beings approach other human beings. Merely by being there, the oppressed call into question those who approach, challenging their "being human"; and this radical questioning of what it means to be a human being serves as the historical mediation of our questioning of what "being God" means.[15]

2. A Different Interlocutor: The Nonperson

Theology is not done for the sake of providing an occupation for theologians. Theologians seek to develop theologies that respond to the important questions that have surfaced within their social world so that the gospel might be more clearly proclaimed. But whose questions deserve priority? This is a vital issue since the selection of which questions to address is already an ambiguous determination of what kind of answers need to be provided.[16] The cerebral questions that arise from the privileged social situation in which most schooled academics live differ significantly from the wrenching life-and-death questions of "the wretched of the earth." For liberation theology, it is the poor who are asking the crucial questions, and it is the poor as "nonpersons" to whom theology must be accountable.

Liberation theology must be viewed in light of the context that gave it its birth. The recent history of Latin America has been characterized by a growing awareness of the shocking existence of the exploited class. Previously, attention had been focused only on those few who had created a social order for their own benefit. The poor, the majority, lived in silence on the fringes of society. They were simply "nonpersons." But now the oppressed are beginning to make their voice heard, and liberation theology is an attempt to listen and respond to the new questions being asked.

Responding to the concerns of the poor is in striking contrast to the emphasis of most theologians. Ever since the Enlightenment, theologians have usually sought to address the questions of educated skeptics. These questions focus on the meaning of Christian faith in light of contemporary philosophy, science, and psychology. Can one be "reasonable" and still be a believer? However, in *Christology at the Crossroads,* Sobrino identifies a second phase of the Enlightenment that has not been given adequate attention. If the first phase was initiated by Kant and his challenge to the *rationality of faith,* the second phase was begun by Karl Marx and his challenge to the *relevance of faith* to the plight of the oppressed.[17] The second phase does not ask whether Christianity is meaningless, but whether it is alienating. Can religion be more than an opiate of the people? Does religion interfere with needed social change by encouraging the downtrodden to accept their present situation as "God's will" or by focusing their attention away from current problems in favor of "pie in the sky"?

The academic community has tended toward answering the rational questions. Much of contemporary theology has been an attempt to make God intelligible to the modern individual who is steeped in science, demythologized, and existentially bored. Within these circumstances, there is a tendency to deal with God in individual and personal terms. The social ramifications of the gospel are given less attention. In contrast, the questions of "nonpersons" are ones of protest. These questions have been taken up by liberation theologians. Since the issue is not the meaningfulness of Christian dogma, but the relevance of the Christian gospel, answers come through liberating actions more than words. The gospel is the message of liberation, a synonym for salvation. This brings us to the question of the precise meaning of "liberation" for this theology.

Critics of liberation theology have sometimes charged it with reducing the gospel to a message of social-political emancipation. Were this charge true, liberation theology would certainly present an abridged gospel. However, for these theologians, liberation has three closely related spheres of meaning.[18] In the first place, liberation does have a socio-political meaning. Part of God's plan of salvation is for oppressed peoples to gain their freedom from domination and exploitation by the wealthy. Although the gospel is not reducible to its socio-political meaning, it is certainly not less than this. The central event in Old Testament history is the liberation of the slaves from Egypt and the establishment of a new nation. Any faith community that bases its trust in the God of the Exodus cannot ignore the revealed desire of God to liberate the captives, free the oppressed, and work justice for the marginalized.

A second sphere of meaning is the psychological. Oppressed people cooperate in their own oppression because many have internalized beliefs about themselves, the world, and God that are counterproductive to their own interests. Many, for example, believe that their poverty is the "will of God" or that the rich have gained their wealth due to superior personal characteristics. Salvation includes breaking the spell of these ideas. Psychological liberation creates the freedom to criticize beliefs and ideologies that inhibit responsible action to change one's circumstances. This understanding of liberation broadens the horizon of change by combining external and internal liberation.

Finally, liberation in this theology means freedom from sin. Estrangement from God binds one to patterns of behavior that truncate relationships and divide communities. All people need liberation from sin. In Christ, as we accept the grace of God's love, we are set free from our bondage to sin.

These views on liberation are not new. Typically, however, one view is elevated above the others so that "true" liberation means socio-political liberation,[19] or "true" liberation takes place in the heart when one takes charge of one's life,[20] or "true" liberation is forgiveness of sin and freedom from its bondage.[21] Avoiding dualisms, each of these is seen by liberation theologians as necessitating the others. Jose Miguez Bonino notes, "The originality of this theology is not to have discovered these three levels of meaning, but to have started from their *unity* as the fundamental point of departure."[22] The charge that liberation theology represents a reduction of the gospel to the political realm is obviously false. A more appropriate concern might be raised regarding opponents: Have they themselves reduced the gospel by neglecting one or another dimension?

3. *A Different Set of Tools: The Social Sciences*

Philosophy has traditionally been the handmaiden of theology. The concepts and categories of secular philosophers have been employed by traditional theologians to articulate the perspective of faith. Such theologians, wishing to dialogue primarily with fellow scholars, needed to speak their language, primarily the language of philosophy. Liberation theologians, on the other hand, are not seeking to defend their rationality, but are seeking instead to insert the gospel message into the realities of historical change. For them, a theologian's message is a noisy gong or a clanging symbol if it is not embodied in liberating acts of love. The good news of the gospel is a hollow promise if it does not transform the bad news of history. And to turn the bad news of oppression into the good news of liberation, the theologian needs to be aware of the concrete processes of social control and social change. Enter the social sciences. The social sciences help the theologian understand the sources and nature of oppression and, consequently, guide the theologian's choice of strategy for overcoming injustice. Use of the critical social sciences keeps the theologian engaged with life, avoiding any tendency toward a detached idealism. Gutierrez notes in this connection:

> Lyrical but vague statements in defense of the dignity of the human person are completely ineffective insofar as they do not take account of the causative factors underlying the existing social order or the concrete conditions that must be met in fashioning a just society....A scientific line of reasoning is absolutely necessary.[23]

Such analysis of oppressive mechanisms inevitably connects theology with politics, economics, and various aspects of public policy; hence, liberation theologians argue that the political dimension is an intrinsic part of the dynamism of God's word.[24] If the gospel does not speak in political language, then it cannot be salvific for those who suffer under oppressive political systems.

For liberation theologians this creates a problem: Which approach to social science should be employed? A variety of competing schools of thought offer divergent conclusions about the mechanisms of oppression. The theologian must recognize both that no perspective can claim absolute allegiance and that a selection must be made. We are thrust back to our starting point. To select from among the competing schools of social science, the theologian must make a judgment about which ones most clearly articulate the perspective and reality of the struggling poor. Only those approaches and disciplines that have arisen from a concern for the issues raised by the struggling poor can claim priority for the theologian's attention. In the judgment of most Latin American liberation theologians, Marxian sociology seems to address the issues of the poor most clearly.[25]

The very name of Karl Marx raises images of horror in the minds of many North Americans. Liberation theology is often discredited because it is said to be little more than dressed up Marxism. The paranoia around Marx clouds the issue. Liberation theologians are not Marxists or communists; they simply find aspects of Marxist thought helpful in understanding the context of Latin America. Specifically, what many liberation theologians find attractive about Marxist analysis is its forthright treatment of class struggle and its description of how human consciousness reflects the interests of one's social class. Marx did not invent these realities. Anyone, for example, who teaches that it is easier for a camel to get through the eye of a needle than for a rich man to enter the Kingdom of Heaven does not need Marx to recognize that there are natural antagonisms between the haves and the have nots. When liberation theologians borrow selected dimensions of Marxist analysis, that does not transform them into card-carrying communists. Such a claim is as false as the spurious claim that anyone who recognizes the reality of the subconscious is an incestuous Freudian.

4. A Different Analysis: The Reality of Conflict

Marxist analysis is useful for liberation theologians because it is based on the recognition that within the contemporary world, conflict is ubiquitous. In the countries of Latin America, for example, a tiny handful of families hoards vast amounts of wealth, while the majority of the population lives in squalid poverty. The wealthy do not accept social change without a fight. Conflicts of interest are inevitable.

Theology cannot stand outside this reality. It is into a world of conflict that the word of God must come if it is to come at all. The incarnation reveals a God who does not stand above history but enters the human struggle for justice, dignity, and freedom.

Latin American theologians and scholars did not always believe in the necessity of conflict. Liberation theology arose in part as a reaction to the failure of theories and models of development formulated by the United States for Latin America. These were plans to lessen poverty by strengthening indigenous economic structures. Underlying these programs was the assumption that the economic process, without undergoing any structural modification, could turn the "underdeveloped" nations into modern, prosperous societies once they reached a certain "take-off point." Support for development was intense in Latin America during the 1950s, producing high expectations. However, it is now generally conceded that developmentalist policies failed.[26]

Understanding the failure of developmentalism will reveal why Latin Americans now accept conflict as inevitable. Social analysis by Latin American scholars has led to the conclusion that the "underdevelopment" of their countries must be viewed as a by-product of the development of other countries.[27] Wealthy nations, such as the United States, gained their prosperity through exploitation of the Third World. Thus, the Third World cannot follow the same path to development as the United States because there is no Fourth World available for exploitation! Segundo points out that the real distinguishing feature of developmentalist models is that they camouflaged the relational character of "underdevelopment."[28]

While developmentalism assumed that there was no inherent conflict between the development of the Third World and the interests of the prosperous nations, liberation theologians maintain that only a struggle to break the domination of the rich countries will enable Latin Americans to become artisans of their own history. Consequently, the goal has changed from "development" to "liberation."[29]

The dawning awareness of exploitation by foreign powers coincided with a growing recognition of institutionalized violence at home. Many liberation theologians began their work at the local level and found themselves in conflict with the local business and political representatives.[30] Gradually, however, with continual conflict, the circles of oppressive mechanisms were observed to extend outward, in a connected fashion, until the parameters were international. Local authorities had the support of regional authorities who, in turn, were backed by the power of the state; the government, for its part, was propped up by the financial and military support of North America. In their process of struggle, many Latin Americans became aware of the frequent use of torture, imprisonment, controlled presses, assassinations, and other methods of institutional violence by governments committed to protecting the privileges of small minorities. This experience of conflict—at first glance not a theological theme—is central for liberation theology. In Assmann's terminology, Christians have come to see "the world as conflictivity."[31]

The poor exist as a social class. Given the realities of conflict, to be "for" the poor in the concrete means to be "against" the rich. There is no possibility of a "neutral" position. To ignore this basic reality is to move into idealism. Gutierrez notes:

> The proclamation of a God who loves all people
> equally must be fleshed out in history, must become
> history. And that will entail challenge and conflict

insofar as we proclaim that love in a society deeply
marked by inequality and injustice, by the exploitation of one social class for the benefit of another.[32]

Many of us from rich nations may deplore this "sim-
plistic" division of humanity into oppressors and oppressed.
But the division accurately portrays reality as experienced by
most Latin Americans. Further, the poor, the "nonpersons,"
have little trouble in identifying who is doing the oppressing
and who is oppressed. It is not an accident that it is those in
the upper economic classes who have difficulty accepting the
dichotomy.

The reality of conflict is also the concrete situation of
the church. In his book, *The True Church and the Poor,* Jon
Sobrino reflects on this reality.[33] He notes that conflict is
frequently disguised with language about pluralism. True
pluralism demands a non-evaluative stance toward varying and
contrasting forms of Christian commitment. But such neutrality
is neither possible nor desirable. The church is built on the
foundation of the historical Jesus who practiced a preferential
option for the poor. A similar stance on the part of many Christians is creating divisions within the contemporary church.
While such divisions reflect a lack of unity, they may also be
the window through which the light of the gospel is enabled
to shine. Siding with the poor may be divisive, but it is still
the means by which the church participates in constructing the
conditions for the reign of God.

5. *A Different Mode of Engagement: Praxis*

If conflict is inherent in our society, then the people
of God must act within a situation of conflict. Theology is
not an armchair activity. God is not available to the detached
mind contemplating relationships among religious symbols.
Such a view of theology would make God irrelevant to the
needs and aspirations of oppressed people. If God were revealed in the comfort of one's study through contemplation
or meditation, then it would not be so important to participate
in the painful historical struggle for justice. But God is not
loved apart from the love of neighbor. And Jesus told us who
our neighbor is: the person in need, the victim. This places

us squarely on one side in situations of conflict. In Matthew 25:31-40, Jesus offers an almost sacramental view of the oppressed person:

> When the Son of man comes in his glory and all the angels with him, then he will sit on his glorious throne. Before him will be gathered all the nations, and he will separate them one from another as a shepherd separates the sheep from the goats, and he will place the sheep at his right hand, but the goats at the left. Then the King will say to those at his right hand, "Come, O blessed of my Father, inherit the kingdom prepared for you from the foundation of the world; for I was hungry and you gave me food, I was thirsty and you gave me drink, I was a stranger and you welcomed me, I was naked and you clothed me, I was sick and you visited me, I was in prison and you came to me." Then the righteous will answer him, "Lord, when did we see thee hungry and feed thee, or thirsty and give thee drink? And when did we see thee a stranger and welcome thee, or naked and clothe thee? And when did we see thee sick or in prison and visit thee?" And the King will answer them, "Truly, I say to you, as you did it to one of the least of these my breathren, you did it to me."

There is no true theology without engagement. That is to say, theology does not exist by thought alone; it must be nourished in action. Further, action does not simply follow an already finalized theology; rather, theology *arises from* action and *leads to* renewed engagement. The word "praxis" is used to describe this double movement in which action changes theory and theory changes action in an ongoing dialectic.[34]

Praxis begins when the need to transform reality is recognized. In a person's transforming actions, both the world and the person are changed. All true religious knowledge, according to this viewpoint, arises out of these transformations. Gutierrez writes, "Knowledge is not the conformity of the mind to the given, but an immersion in the process of transformation and construction of a new world."[35] To know God is to do justice.

6. A Different Theology: The "Second Act"

We are once again at our beginning point: the poor. One important characteristic of this beginning point, in contrast to most others (e.g., the Bible, church tradition, etc.), is that poverty is not uniquely a theological reality or problem. Compassion for the poor is not confined to theologians. Any sensitive human being can respond to the indecency of letting two-thirds of the human family go to bed hungry each night, or to the atrocity of political imprisonment and other forms of institutional violence, or to the inhumanity of insanitary living conditions that breed disease and despair. One does not need to spend years within the halls of a seminary to feel compassion for the victims of economic slavery, racial prejudice, or sexual exploitation. The very existence of the oppressed is a cry that can be heard by any person, religious or not, who has "ears to hear."

Compassion is a human sensitivity. It is not the property of theologians. The commitment to identify with the struggling poor and to seek justice precedes all authentic theologizing. It is a commitment open to all. Theology is a "second act" which follows this first act of commitment to the oppressed. The most crucial determinant for a sound theology, then, is not familiarity with biblical languages or years of training in philosophy, but a simple compassion for the suffering innocent and a dedicated commitment to justice. The illiterate peasant who has compassion knows God more profoundly than the well-schooled theologian who has forgotten that Jesus came to preach good news to the poor.

Hugo Assmann draws a connection between this "second act" character of liberation theology and its use of the social sciences.[36] He points out that theology comes "second" in two ways: It is the "second act" following the "first act" of commitment, and it is the "second word" after the "first word" of the social sciences. Commitment to the oppressed goes hand-in-hand with a social scientific analysis of their situation. We shall see later, however, that Segundo, while accepting this general description, cautions that it can be misleading when abstracted from the circular nature of theological development. The first and second act are not so much linear as circular.

Even the selection of social scientific tools involves an act of faith and at least an implicit theology.[37]

To conclude this six-point summary, let me quote Gutierrez's definition of liberation theology, for it encompasses much of what has been said and has been extensively quoted and used by other liberation theologians:

> Theology will be a critical reflection from and about the historical praxis of liberation in confrontation with the Word of the Lord lived and accepted in faith. It will be a reflection in and about faith as a liberating praxis: an intellection of faith made from an option; a reflection based on a commitment to create a just, fraternal society, and with a duty to contribute to make that commitment fuller and more radical. The theological discourse become truth is (veri-fied) in its real, fecund insertion in the process of liberation.[38]

Method and Content: A Look at Christology

Gustavo Gutierrez is widely recognized as the leading spokesperson of liberation theology. In his groundbreaking work, *A Theology of Liberation,* he clearly recognized that the major accomplishment of liberation theologians was not in advancing new interpretations of the traditional concepts of theology; rather, it was in the way that theologians work. It is not in theological content, but in method. The six points just reviewed are methodological distinctions between the liberation way of doing theology and "traditional" approaches.

Although liberation theologians have emphasized method over content, it would be a dualistic error to suppose that method and content can be radically separated.[39] Method is formed in and through an analysis of specific content; similarly, content takes its concrete form in response to the method of the theologian. For Latin American liberation theologians, Christological reflection has perhaps been the most fruitful occasion for the development of methodological insight.[40] As an illustration, let us look briefly at the Christological reflections of Gutierrez and Segundo. The development reflected in their work testifies to the evolution that occurs when one moves from the riches of academia to the rags of the slum.

Originally, Gutierrez's ideas were informed by a fairly traditional theological training at Lyon, France, where he no doubt learned to think of Christology in the traditional categories of Nicea.[41] A look at the footnotes of *A Theology of Liberation* shows that Gutierrez was well schooled in European theology and that he drew from it heavily. However, the world of the exploited differs considerably from that of the academician. As Gutierrez tried to articulate his theological concepts in a way that made sense to, and was liberating for, the Latin American community, he found he needed to make significant changes. As he took the situation and questions of the peasants seriously, and adjusted and constructed his thinking accordingly, a new approach to the doing of theology began to emerge.[42]

In Gutierrez's view, Jesus cannot be known directly but only via the neighbor. The uniqueness of Christ is his union with all human beings; thus "our encounter with the Lord occurs in our encounter with people, especially in the encounter with those whose human features have been disfigured by oppression, despoliation, and alienation."[43] Since the poor exist not as isolated individuals but in exploited social classes, the Christian love of neighbor cannot be private or individualized. To love Christ involves one in political struggles to alleviate the misery in which the present incarnate Christ exists.

Gutierrez expands on this theme of Christology when he talks of Jesus' relation to the political structures of his day. He disagrees with those who see in Jesus a prototype of a twentieth-century revolutionary. Gutierrez maintains that while Jesus was sympathetic toward the first-century revolutionaries, the Zealots, he would not identify himself as one. His proclamation of the gospel was universal and not confined to the narrow nationalism of the Zealots. Similarly, his teaching of "spiritual freedom" toward the law contrasted with the Zealots' literal interpretations.

But Jesus was concerned with the structural and political dimensions to the liberation he preached. As evidence that Jesus indeed confronted systems, Gutierrez points out that he took on publicans (Matt. 9:10ff), Sadducees (Matt. 3:7), and the

Roman government itself in the person of Herod. In each instance, Jesus can be seen as attacking not an individual, but a structural arrangement that exploited segments of society. When we join the struggle that Jesus revealed as the will of God, then we come to know who Jesus is.

Juan Luis Segundo has also dealt extensively with the question of Christology and, as we will see, it has been influential in his thinking about theological method. In outlining Segundo's work, it is useful to distinguish an earlier approach embodied in the five-volume series *Theology for Artisans of a New Humanity*,[44] from that of his later works, notably *the Liberation of Theology*[45] and his recent five-volume set, *Jesus of Nazareth Yesterday and Today*.[46] In his earlier work, Segundo uses the traditional Christological controversies as his major reference point and interprets them in light of Latin American realities. His later work reflects a greater freedom from the categories of tradition and a more self-conscious awareness of method.

The book *Our Idea of God* illustrates Segundo's earlier reflections. In this third book of the *Theology for Artisans of a New Humanity* series, Segundo begins by asking, "Why all the fuss over Christology?" In response, he turns to an analysis of the classical Christological controversies and in particular the issue of subordinationism. The subordinationists, as the name implies, taught that Jesus was a lesser God.[47] Jesus was divine, but he was not equal with God the Father. Fortunately, says Segundo, the church condemned subordinationism.

Segundo points out that subordinationism was motivated by a dualistic way of viewing reality. Its argument is based on the assumption that since Jesus was "in the flesh," he could not have been truly God. The dualism is one that denigrates what is of this world: time, history, humanness. Segundo correctly observes that if what is of value can be placed outside this world, then one's responsibility for present reality can also be downplayed. If Christ cannot be fully God, then human concerns are of little significance. According to Segundo, in condemning subordinationism the church was ruling out any form of escapist dualism;[48] it was ruling out any separation of the sacred and the secular.

Segundo also notes that the emperor Constantine favored subordinationism and for very good reason. If there exists a hierarchy in heaven, then it is only logical to expect a hierarchy on earth, thus legitimizing his position as ruler. In rejecting this sort of heavenly hierarchy, the church removed a support from the emperor's throne.

The error of subordinationism was to deny the full divinity of Christ. The opposite error was to deny his humanity. Throughout his works, Segundo not only affirms the divinity of Christ, but also maintains a strong emphasis on his humanity.[49] It may be that it has become more difficult for today's church to accept Christ's full humanity. Segundo believes that a liberation Christology is forced to combat this heresy, a heresy that reflects the same dualistic assumption that divinity and humanity are somehow fundamentally opposed. The underlying presupposition, never stated explicitly, is that Jesus, being God, could not have been completely human.

Segundo amplifies on his earlier Christology in *The Liberation of Theology,* but his emphasis turns to the theological method of Jesus. Segundo contrasts the method of Jesus with that of the Pharisees.[50] The Pharisees, according to Segundo, were well-trained theological experts. To determine God's will, the Pharisees used a deductive process. They began with past revelation and sought to deduce from it the correct course of action in the present situation. This is academic theology *par excellence.*

But Jesus' method was different, Segundo maintains. Jesus rejects the possibility of forming any concrete judgments on the sole basis of past revelation. For example, the laws of the Sabbath do not resolve the question of what can or cannot be done on the Sabbath. Segundo maintains that Jesus interpreted the meaning of divine revelation not in a legalistic way, but from a frame of reference structured by commitment to the liberation of the oppressed. The question is not, "What does the Sabbath allow or disallow?" The question is, "How can the teaching about the Sabbath serve to enhance the lives of the suffering innocent?" Such a change of questions keeps theology open to the newness of history. In contrast, the Pharisees desired to keep their theology pure from the uncertainties of history. These insights about the method of Jesus are formalized by Segundo in his more elaborate discussion of theological method.

Theological Method

We turn now to the creative and thought-provoking work of Juan Luis Segundo on theological method. In particular, three aspects of his thought are highlighted: his hermeneutic circle, his view of the church, and the relationship he discerns between faith and ideology. Throughout this section, I will attempt to represent Segundo's own framing of the issues. In the final section of the chapter, I will make constructive use of Segundo's thought to develop aspects of Dewey's theory of inquiry.

THE HERMENEUTIC CIRCLE

In discussing theological method from the Latin American perspective it is important to keep in mind the "second act" character of theological reflection in the liberation model. Theology is a reflection on praxis. Thus it is a reflection done out of a prior commitment. Juan Luis Segundo has attempted to articulate this perspective in his work, *The Liberation of Theology*. He refers to his theological method as a "hermeneutic circle."[51]

Hermeneutics is the science and art of interpretation. A person uses the principles of hermaneutics to move from the words of a text to a meaningful interpretation. For example, one principle of biblical hermeneutics holds that a text must be viewed in light of the culture and circumstances in which it was written.

Segundo's hermeneutic circle is a way of thinking through theological issues. It leads to a new interpretation of the Bible. Segundo states that there are two preconditions for implementing his method.[52] First, there must be a commitment to raising profound questions about our real situation, and, second, a willingness to let these new questions lead to a new interpretation of the Bible. If a person believes his or her interpretations of the Bible are beyond question, then the hermeneutic circle will collapse and the person will simply "discover" his or her own shadow. A circle represents an open, ongoing process.

The "hermeneutic circle" itself consists of working through four stages of analysis with regard to any theological problem or question:

> First, there is our way of experiencing reality, which leads us to ideological suspicion. Secondly, there is the application of our ideological suspicion to the whole ideological superstructure in general and to theology in particular. Thirdly, there comes a new way of experiencing theological reality that leads us to exegetical suspicion, that is, to the suspicion that the prevailing interpretation of the Bible has not taken important pieces of data into account. Fourthly, we have our new hermeneutic, that is, our new way of interpreting the fountainhead of our faith [i.e. Scripture] with the new elements at our disposal.[53]

Of particular importance to understanding Segundo's thought on theological method is his discussion of the "political option."[54] His argument is that there is "no such thing as Christian theology or a Christian interpretation of the gospel message in the absence of a prior political commitment."[55] Any so-called non-political interpretation of the faith is simply an interpretation from within the status quo; to not make a political option for the poor is to opt for maintaining the privileges of the few. To make a political option is to begin the circle. It creates "our way of experiencing reality."

Segundo, of course, holds that authentic theology is practiced from within a political option in favor of the oppressed. The commitment to liberating change—to the "elimination of all and every dualism"—provides the emotional force that drives the hermeneutic circle. Segundo maintains that once a person begins to work with the struggling poor, that person will have experiences likely to raise profound questions about common beliefs and practices. One begins to wonder, "Are these beliefs and practices reflective of reality or are they reflections of the interests of those who benefit from leaving society undisturbed?" The moment this question is asked, ideological suspicion is born. We have entered the second phase of the circle.

The heart of ideological suspicion is a feeling that "things aren't right," that one's previous experiences have been manipulated to the advantage of the advantaged. This suspicion is sharpened and clarified through the use of social sciences to understand the dynamics perpetuating the status quo.

Among the beliefs and practices that come under scrutiny as ideological suspicion unfolds are the theological interpretations of reality. In Latin America, for example, ideological suspicion has led to a questioning of the theological division of reality into the sacred and the secular. According to this widely held belief, God is concerned with a religious realm that is separate from the secular realm of everyday life. God is concerned with worship and prayer, but not with material well-being and political organization. Ideological suspicion, however, raises a question, "Is this division of reality into two separate realms an actual expression of God's design, or is it an idea propagated because it benefits those in power?" One begins to suspect the latter. The dualism between sacred and secular has encouraged the poor to remain content with their plight because, it is believed, God will reward them in heaven and/or because it is un-Christian to become involved in secular struggles for justice.

Ideological suspicion flows into what Segundo labels "exegetical suspicion." Exegesis is a type of hermeneutics dealing specifically with biblical texts. Consequently, exegetical suspicion leads the person or group to question the prevailing manner in which the Bible has been interpreted and explained. Exegetical suspicion led some in Latin America, for example, to wonder whether the division of reality into sacred and secular is really true to the Bible. A new hermeneutic takes shape as the community begins to discover dimensions of the faith heritage that previously had been ignored or distorted. Thus, the liberation theologian finds that the Bible discourages a dualism between the sacred and the secular, that God, rather than ordaining that some be poor, is on the side of the poor and seeks their liberation.

Segundo's hermeneutic circle aims at providing a means by which the religious experience of an oppressed group can come to theological expression without distortion. A presupposition underlying the method is that all human experience is historically conditioned. Theologies reflect the theologian's location in a particular matrix of class, race, sex, and culture. In the past, many theologians have attempted to write from what was taken to be "universal" human experience.[56] Such an endeavor was doomed to failure from the outset. Generic humanity does not exist. Theological distortion creeps in when theologians ignore or deny the influence of their culture and status on their concepts. When theologians fail to recognize the limitations imposed by their own human particularity, they inevitably support hierarchical dualisms. By failing to recognize how their theology is organically connected to their experience — an experience, no doubt, situated in affluence — they propagate a set of beliefs congruent with their interests as if those beliefs reflected the experience and interests of all.

The result of theological distortion has been a theology that has served the interests and concerns of white North American and European males.[57] As an illustration, let us take the theological concept of "transcendence." The transcendence of God has sometimes been viewed as suggesting a God independent from the human and natural world, a God omnipotent and omniscient, a God "wholly Other," above all our noblest and holiest conceptions. Ideological suspicion grounded in everyday experiences of powerlessness may lead one to question this understanding of God. Perhaps this God is little more than a projection of idealized elements in the experience of the powerful. Those who have viewed themselves (consciously or unconsciously) as powerful and knowledgeable have fashioned a God in their own likeness. Furthermore, such a God serves the interests of the powerful because the concept of transcendence is used figuratively to remove God from the "petty" concerns of everyday life.

This ideological suspicion may lead the inquirer to exegetical suspicion. The biblical interpretations that buttress these images of transcendence may come to be seen as only a partial rendering of the biblical tradition. In the Bible, God is often imaged as having power in powerlessness and wisdom in foolishness. And the Israelite God did not stand high above creation, but entered the struggles of the slaves for freedom.

It is not difficult to understand why theology has usually reflected the perspective of the social elite. Social groups do not have equal access to educational and cultural opportunities.[58] Since theology has traditionally been a specialized discipline of higher education, theologians, inevitably, have been members of society's most advantaged group. On the world scale, theology has been the prerogative of the rich. It has been an insider's game at the rich man's club.

Segundo's hermeneutic circle is designed to provide a means for new questions to be addressed. it is not so much a technical device constructed to offer a normative framework for the development of systematic theologies; rather, it is a distilled description of the actual processes of theological reflection that have emerged in the small religious communities flourishing in Latin America. Segundo's hermeneutic circle is best carried out as a communal reflection. While not technical, it is a demanding process requiring insight, courage, and commitment. This has some important implications for the context of theologizing: the church.

THE CHURCH

When Segundo presents the specific steps of his hermeneutic circle, his terminology is non-specific with regard to the nature of the experience or commitment with which the circle begins. This generality allows a range of people with various experiences and commitments to make use of the theological method. But it would be incorrect to assume that Segundo sees his method as appropriate for everyone. We have noted that an option for the poor is prerequisite to authentic theologizing. For Segundo, such an option is expressed through alliance with a community identified with the struggling poor. Theology is not practiced individually. It is the product of a community.[59] In order to understand Segundo's method, then, it must be seen in the context of his view of the church.

Segundo's ecclesiology is influenced by his training in

social science. Early in his career, Segundo centered on the principle of the "conservation of energy" as a determining factor in much of human life. Each of us has limited energy to accomplish the things we desire. Because energy is limited, most of life tends to be governed by the "law of minimum effort"; we tend to repeat the familiar, the routine, the simple. Occasionally, however, we will seek out more elaborate, more complex ways of responding to life's circumstances. These will be rare in number. Creativity is not possible in most of life because it demands a great commitment of time and energy. Concentrated effort can be expended only in a few chosen areas. These principles hold for groups as well as individuals. The law of minimum effort, stated sociologically, holds that in any given situation the majority of people will follow the path of least resistance; however, there may be a small minority who will seek out and experiment with more complex behaviors.[60]

This analysis raises questions for an institution. Should it be structured to depend primarily on simple, routine behaviors so that participants can follow the law of minimum effort? Or, should it be so structured as to demand the creative energies of devoted members? The first choice opens the institution to a greater number of people because a high expenditure of energy is not required. The latter dictates a comparatively small community that can be engaged in more creative endeavors. The answer, of course, depends on the purpose of the institution.

Before we directly ask about the purpose of the church, however, let us look at a related issue regarding the nature of the church. Segundo suggests that the church must confront two important facts about its existence:[61] (1) the church has been and always will be a minority community; and (2) the church was, is, and will be universal. These paradoxical statements about the church reflect, Segundo observes, two parallel strands in the New Testament with regard to salvation. In some places salvation is said to be contingent upon particular, specific means; at other times it is said to be universal. Typically, the church has emphasized the first line of thought, saying that only confessing Christians are saved. As a result, the church has minimized the demands of membership so that as many people as possible might join.

If the church is required for salvation, then salvation is its purpose. Segundo, however takes the theme of universal salvation as primary. The church is not needed to bring salvation. This does not mean, however, that the church has no role in God's plan. For Segundo, the church has a vital but partial function within the salvific process: it proclaims love as the means of God's salvation and symbolizes the liberating action of God in history. Freed from the necessity of bringing in as many people as possible, the church can concentrate its efforts on effective action on behalf of all humanity. This role requires creativity and hence the church is likely to be a minority community.

In Segundo's view, the church, as a particular community, is the conscious and visible sign of the presence of Christ in the heart of each human being (the church as universal). The church is a "sign-community."[62] It bears witness to the grace that is universal and names it. The implication is that the church exists for those outside it. The church is the salt of the earth, but salt does not exist to turn everything into salt. It has a limited but essential role. The church exists to make the invisible hand of God visible. It works for justice and social change so that God's intention for all people is revealed. "To this end we toil and strive, because we have our hope set on the living God, who is the Savior of all people, especially those who believe" (I Tim. 4:10).

The church is a minority that is involved in reading the "signs of the times" and interpreting them in light of God's plan of liberation. This does not give the church a totally unique position in the world. Grace is universal. The roots of fanaticism lie in the belief that believers only share in God's grace. God is active throughout the world, far beyond the borders of the visible church, but the church has the unique role of becoming the community where this universal activity is raised to consciousness and signified. This takes concentrated effort.

The church is to be a minority community of "gospel-creators," not a crowd of "gospel-consumers." A large crowd in a church can simply listen to the gospel with more or less attention. A community can discuss it together, reflect on it, compare it to real life, and act on it. Only in a community can the hermeneutic circle that creates gospel be completed.

In summary, the church is the conscious part of a salvific process. By struggling against short-term majority solutions, the church functions as a resource for the minority involved in creative solutions that lead to humanization. The church is a community where, under the direction of the Spirit, the biblical message is made contemporary. In its inner structure and in its outer work, the church seeks to be a symbol of the redemptive grace that is at work in the world. Beginning with an identification with the poor and oppressed, the church seeks creative and responsive solutions to poverty and injustice.

Moving through the hermeneutic circle aids a community in translating their particular experience into a theological formulation of that experience. There is always the danger, however, that the process might be viewed as a ladder to ultimate truth rather than a continuing circle of ever expanding awareness. For Segundo, a careful distinction between faith and ideology can help prevent this kind of dogmatism from creeping in.

FAITH AND IDEOLOGY

Segundo uses the word *faith* in a variety of ways. We will misread him, however, if we assume that faith is necessarily connected to religious belief. For Segundo, even the atheist has a faith. Faith is an anthropological constant; all people have faith.

Faith, for Segundo, is that set of meanings and values that give direction and purpose to a person's life. Since everybody must have some sense of life's meaningfulness, everybody has faith. Faith enables us to live and act in a very complex, but more-or-less consistent, manner.[63] The source of this kind of faith—which Segundo designates "anthropological faith" to distinguish it from specifically religious faith—is trust in a person or persons who provide a model or witness to what life lived according to these values is like.

Even very young children have a rudimentary faith; the parents usually serve as the child's first models. The child cannot know with certainty that the parents' lives are really good examples of how life ought to be lived, but the child trusts their witness and develops a rudimentary faith. In adolescence, the choice of concrete witnesses is broadened, but there is still a need to place faith in a particular model (or small number of models). Faith is always based on trust in a witness rather than on proof of a particular perspective. We can never jump ahead to the end of life to see if any one of life's many paths is more meaningful than another. We must place our trust in an available model even though we lack certainties.[64]

One's anthropological faith, based on trust in a particular model, leads to an awareness of values that are only partially realized in present reality. The result is the development of an ideology. Let us see how this works. Suppose a teenager trusts the witness provided by her president. The teenager's faith reflects an internalization of the values represented by the president. Soon, however, the teenager realizes that reality does not completely support those values and the desire to transform reality is born. Efforts to change reality, however, meet resistance and, confronted with this situation, the teenager elaborates an ideology. Segundo writes, "I shall use the term 'ideology' for all systems of means, be they natural or artificial, that are used to attain some end or goal."[65] Ideology does not have a negative connotation here. Every person possesses a faith and an ideology.

Ideologies do not claim our complete loyalty. They are valid only to the extent that they are useful to us. In contrast, faith claims our absolute allegiance. A second distinction between faith and ideology lies in the fact that faith entails a stronger relationship to the goal, while ideology points to the means to achieve the goal. These distinctions hold, however, only for the mature person. For the immature person, faith and ideology are often confused and both are absolutized. Let us say, for example, that a young revolutionary has trusted in the witness of Marx. Mature faith would recognize that the basic Marxian values and insights are not tied to all of Marx's ideas about how to bring about the communist state. For the immature person, however, both the goal and the strategy are absolutized.[66]

According to Segundo, no hermeneutic can escape the necessity of beginning with an already existing anthropological faith. Thus, when Christians read the Bible, they cannot do so with an "open mind." The values and perspectives that constitute the reader's anthropological faith predispose the person to find and accent certain aspects of the biblical corpus. We come to the Bible with presuppositions and prejudices.

But what, more precisely, is the relationship between anthropological faith and religious faith? Typically we assume that when a person is religious, faith is equivalent to religious commitments. Anthropological faith, however, always preceeds religious faith since the child trusts concrete human witnesses long before he or she is able to comprehend what it means to trust God. The result is that one's anthropological faith contours the way one perceives religion. Religious revelation builds on one's pre-existing anthropological faith.[67] Religious faith offers images and symbols to aid in the development of anthropological faith. This may be the meaning of Jesus' oft-repeated words, "for those who have ears to hear..." Those who had "ears to hear" were the people whose anthropological faith predisposed them to accept the good news of the gospel. As we have noted, it is not academic training that predisposes someone to hear the good news. It is nothing esoteric. It is simply compassion for the oppressed and a commitment to justice. When these elements are present within one's anthropological faith, then the person is likely to be open to Christian revelation.

For Christians to enter the hermeneutic circle correctly, Segundo claims, they must already be committed to solidarity with the oppressed. Compassion preceeds theology; revelation follows commitment. It is only after one's human faith leads to action on behalf of the oppressed that biblical religion becomes revelatory and our anthropological faith is deepened and broadened.

The distinction that Segundo draws between faith and ideology is itself an outcome of the hermeneutic circle. It arose from reflection on a problematic experience. Many Latin American Christians discovered in the early years of liberation theology that the church was frequently a foe rather than a friend of the poor. Many theologians and church leaders taught that Christians must remain neutral in politics and be guided only by what is written in the Bible, the book of "divine revelation." Consequently, many Christians wondered whether their faith had anything of value to contribute to the struggle for human dignity and freedom.[68]

These experiences led a few theologians to develop ideological suspicion. Is the attempt to begin theology from "neutral ground" or in a past "divine revelation" really a mask for maintaining the status quo? Ideological suspicion moved to exegetic suspicion. Does the Bible itself represent God as a deity known primarily through neutral reflection on previous revelations? The answer would appear to be no. Segundo notes, for example, that "the people who were best informed about God's revelation in the Old Testament let Jesus pass by and failed to see in him the new and definitive divine revelation."[69] It was the theological illiterates who were most open to the liberative activity of Jesus.

What does this have to say about the Christian contribution to social change? Does the Christian have anything unique to offer? Hugo Assmann answered no, suggesting that the Christian can bring to the revolutionary struggle no *a priori* principles derived from "divine revelation."[70] Any attempt to guide the work of social change by principles derived from events of ancient history, Assmann reasoned, would inevitably lead to backward solutions that rob the future of creativity. Assmann goes so far as to suggest that the less one knows of Christianity prior to commitment to the liberation struggle, the more authentic and whole the commitment is likely to be. For Assmann, only after one commits oneself to the revolutionary struggle can one authentically become a Christian.

Segundo notes, however, that the relationship between revolutionary commitment and faith is not as simple as Assmann seems to imagine. First of all, "dozens of groups, movements, and parties claim to possess the one key that will open the door to real revolution."[71] Therefore commitment to social change necessitates making a choice among differing ideologies. Such a choice must be informed by the very best empirical evidence, but social science is incapable of offering definitive criteria for selecting an ideology. Such a selection is inevitably informed by one's faith. Christian faith can lead one to an openness to the oppressed person and therefore can lead to an authentic struggle for justice.

This response, however, does not resolve the problem of the essentially conservative nature of a Christian contribution, based on faith, to liberation struggles. Rooted in past revelation, does Christianity inevitably lead its adherents to an effort to conform the future to norms derived from the past? Segundo elaborates his response by suggesting that there is a crucial difference between a mature faith that can distinguish itself from ideologies and an immature faith that cannot. Essentially, these reflect two different approaches to the Bible.

For the child and adolescent, as well as for many adults, faith and ideologies are not distinguished. As a result, biblical ideologies are absolutized and said to be eternally valid. For example, this person may argue that Jesus was nonviolent in his approach to political change and, therefore, we must be also. This person fails to appreciate that the Bible has many ideologies, none of which can be normative for all situations. Were the Israelites nonviolent in the book of Judges? For this person, faith will always lean backward in time (no matter how "radical" the person's language) since he or she is attempting to make present reality conform to a norm derived from a past ideology.

For mature Christian faith — faith that is distinguished from ideology — biblical material is relative to its culture and yet, almost paradoxically, is our ultimate norm. The Bible is the record of the ideologies that various communities in different times and circumstances formed to make concrete their faith in the living God. For contemporary Christians, it is through these biblical ideologies that one learns how to create new ideologies in openness to the Spirit. According to Segundo, the hermeneutic circle remains open and responsive when a person recognizes that faith must be incarnated in a specific ideology, but that faith can never be identified with any ideology. For Segundo, faith in Christ does not mean the absolutizing of his concrete techings. Rather, it involves submission to a process of learning to learn. It involves trust in the hidden God who is the educator reflected in the ideologies of Scripture. A crucial passage needs to be quoted in full:

> What, then, does the faith say to me in the concrete? What is its truth content? If I remain logically consistent in deducing conclusions from the above principles, then my only response can be: nothing. Let me repeat that in another way. If someone were to ask me what I have derived from my faith-inspired encounter as a clear-cut, absolute truth that can validly give orientation to my concrete life, then my honest response would be: nothing.
>
> However, we are carrying the balance of faith to an irrational extreme in talking about one encounter with the objective font of absolute truth. If it is in fact a matter of only one encounter, then there is no solution to the problem. The absolute truth would remain totally obscured behind the ideology exhibited in that one historical encounter.
>
> This *reductio ad absurdum* prompts us to rediscover the decisive importance of the (historical) density of the Bible. Over the period of twenty centuries different faith-inspired encounters took place between human beings and the objective font of absolute truth. . . . What came to be known in each of these encounters was an ideology, but that was not what was learned. Through the process people learned how to learn with the help of ideologies. This deutero-learning has its own proper content, and when I say that Jesus had two natures, one human and one divine, I am saying something about the content of this learning process. But these contentual items cannot be translated into one or another specific ideology because they belong to a secondary stage or level of learning. They are essentially methodological symbols. On the one hand they have no direct ideological translation; on the other hand they have no function but to be translated into ideologies.[72]

Living faith cannot be recorded in words. What the Bible contains is a long series of ideologies constructed by a people inspired and led by God. The danger for us today is that we will read a specific ideology and absolutize it as if it were God's intention for eternity. The inevitable result is a conservative faith that keeps one in the past and closes one to the new work of the Spirit.

But, one might ask, how do we discern in the present what is of God and what is not? For a mature faith, the Bible becomes normative only by way of indirection: When one looks to the Bible it points not to itself, but to the "signs of the times." Only as one becomes involved in the present work of liberation will the Bible enlighten faith and give direction to the construction of new ideologies that reflect God's word for today. "Historical sensitivity" to one's present context gives rise to the questions that get the "hermeneutic circle" moving. In essence, we are back to compassion for victims and commitment to justice. Using "ideology" in its pejorative sense, Segundo writes, "A real, effective option on behalf of the oppressed can de-ideologize our minds and free our thinking for the gospel message."[73]

Dewey Revisited

Segundo's reflections on theological method provide a way of thinking about religious issues and problems. It is an approach to inquiry into the relationships among God, humanity, and the world. Let us turn now to briefly look at how these insights might deepen and sharpen Dewey's reflections on inquiry.

COMMITMENT AND INQUIRY

Dewey offered a number of helpful suggestions concerning the conduct of inquiry, but his own reticence about religion led to a relative lack of interest in theological method. In *A Common Faith* Dewey embraces a "religious" attitude while rejecting all definite religious creeds, institutions, and practices. In Dewey's view, "Religions now prevent, because of their weight of historic encumbrances, the religious quality of experience from coming to consciousness."[74] For Dewey, commitment to a particular religious tradition prevented an openness to present experience, particularly the religious dimensions of experience. Dewey associated the quality of being religious with faith in "the unification of the self through allegiance to inclusive ideal ends, which imagination presents to us and to which the human will responds as worthy of controlling our desires and choices."[75]

Dewey's reticence regarding religion is but one instance of a general attitude toward allegiance to any tradition that claims one's *a priori* commitment. As Donald Piatt succinctly observed: "The pragmatist is the least bound by prior commitments of all philosophers."[76] While experience is viewed as enhanced by meanings gained in prior experience, all meaning is provisional and fundamentally projective. It is future-leaning. The necessity of avoiding dogmatisms and dualisms made Dewey suspicious of all commitments that were not subject to empirical investigation.[77]

Religious faith, or at least Christian faith as it is commonly understood, requires commitment to a heritage believed to communicate something of the divine. Loyalty to a tradition plays an indispensable role. Is such a commitment incompatible with Dewey's understanding of experience and inquiry? Does it inevitably lead to "supernaturalistic" dualisms? I believe it does not. Segundo's distinction between faith and ideology suggests a paradigm for a non-dogmatic, future-leaning theological construction.

Segundo's understanding of the development of ideology closely parallels Dewey's understanding of the development of hypotheses. Dewey holds that all inquiry begins with the identification of a "problematic situation." For example, he states: "The two limits of every unit of thinking are a perplexed, troubled, or confused situation at the beginning and a cleared-up, unified, resolved situation at the close."[78] But what is involved in the perception of a problematic situation?

Dewey recognizes that social existence is the context for many of the problematic situations that give rise to reflection.[79] It is this dimension of life with which Segundo is primarily concerned. But Dewey does not adequately address how specific social situations come to be recognized and experienced as problematic.[80] Segundo's discussion of anthropological faith makes concrete the dynamics involved in the recognition of a situation as problematic. Problems are experienced as problems only from a perspective that has a view of the unproblematic. Ruether makes a similar point about the perception of evil: "Consciousness of evil, in fact, originates in the process of conversion itself."[81] Only as one is making a commitment to a particular vision of reality does the "is" of the present become problematic.

SEGUNDO'S VIEW

Anthropological faith from Segundo's viewpoint is the embracing of a meaning-structure witnessed to by a concrete model or models. It is based on a relative witness, but the faith is itself absolute. It cannot be confirmed or denied empirically, for the meaningfulness of life can only be judged from an eschatological viewpoint that always transcends our existential context. The anthropological faith that has been expressed and embodied in specific religious traditions is but one form of anthropological faith, but it provides the believer with a more-or-less coherent symbol system through which to approach questions of ultimate meaning.

Dewey's methods of inquiry are inadequate at the point where the problematic situation is formulated in terms of the existential questions of meaning. To what must I give allegiance? Is life better than death? What do I owe my neighbor? How can I find purpose? Answers to such questions cannot be empirically demonstrated; the hypothesis testing would require more than a lifetime of trying to live out any one of the many options that could be suggested. Segundo, basing himself on observation of how people actually resolve such questions, holds that we must all begin from assumptions based on faith.

Once a faith-stance has developed, it provides the orientation from which specific contexts come to be problematic. Specific ideologies evolve, which are equivalent to Dewey's hypotheses about how the situation can be rendered unproblematic. If the ideology proves unsatisfactory, a new ideology can be formulated.

For Segundo, as for Dewey, inquiry begins and terminates in ordinary experience.[82] The hermeneutic circle begins with an experience of reality and terminates with a new experience of reality. What gives coherence and unity to the thinking in the circle is the commitment that underlies the specific phases of thought. For Dewey, thought is pervaded by aesthetic dimensions that provide it with a unifying quality: "Thinking goes on in trains of ideas, but the ideas form a train only because they are much more than what an analytic psychology calls ideas. They are phases, emotionally and practically distinguished, of a developing underlying quality."[83] For Segundo, that underlying quality is intimately tied to the nature of the commitment that pervades the hermeneutic circle. According to Segundo, commitment to the poor is the perspective that allows the Christian tradition to become revelatory. But it is not a dogmatic tradition; it is itself transformed in response to the living experience of the oppressed.

Related to the issue of commitment is the question of the nature of religious inquiry. What are the procedures available for religious reflection? What form will theologizing take when commitment to the Christian heritage is fused with commitment to human liberation? I have suggested that a false understanding of theology as a process of comprehending "universal" features of the human condition has been one source for hierarchical dualism. Segundo's theological method represents a model for non-distorting theologizing.

Avoiding Theological Distortion

Segundo challenges theologies that purport to be universal but that in reality reflect the interest and concerns of the privileged. Theological distortion occurs when certain aspects of human experience are selected and made absolute. Dualisms result because absolutizing a partial perspective is possible only if, at the same time, other perspectives are denied.

Assume a theologian to assert, "God does not choose sides in human conflicts because God loves everyone equally." The statement may accurately reflect the theologian's experience of the grace of God. But other people's experience might lead to a different conclusion. For someone who lives daily with continuous unjust suffering, the theologian's God is not a loving God. A God who does not take sides is hard to experience as loving if your deepest need is to find the scraps from the master's table. Is God indifferent to injustice? The statement that God loves everybody equally eventually leads to a dualism between eternity and history or the sacred and the secular. Only a God disconnected from the realities of life in the here and now can stand "above it all" and not take sides. Such dualisms, of course, support the status quo by intimating that God has no interest in seeing things change.

The transformation of a limited perspective into a universal theology parallels the process of "vicious abstractionism" discussed by Dewey. As noted in Chapter Two, vicious abstractionism involves not only selection but also denial. Denial in theology has been evidenced not only by the suppression of aspects of the theologizing party's own experience, but also by the frequently stated claim that theological concepts are unrelated to political and socio-economic structures.

In contrast to "traditional" modes of doing theology, the thrust of Segundo's work on theological method can be summarized in three points. First, theology begins with a prior human commitment to liberate the oppressed. This commitment itself may have a variety of sources, including religious tradition. The commitment fosters "ideological suspicion" of cultural beliefs, practices, attitudes, and institutions.

Second, the ideological suspicion leads by way of a series of dialectics through a hermeneutic circle. Thus, ideological suspicion, in interaction with the received religious tradition, leads to theological suspicion. Theological suspicion, in interaction with established exegetical material, leads to exegetical suspicion. Exegetical suspicion, in interaction with the present understanding of hermeneutics, leads to a new hermeneutic. Basing one's action on the new heremeneutic creates new experiences which renew the circle. The circle is continually stimulated by use of the social sciences to clarify the suspicion that dominant cultural ideologies function to perpetuate the status quo.

Third, the whole process is dependent upon a mature faith. A mature faith is one which can separate faith from ideology while recognizing that the former exists only in and through embodiments of the latter.

Segundo's work begins with a determined experience — commitment to the oppressed — and proceeds by way of constructing all values in light of that commitment. By starting with a commitment to overthrow cultural hierarchy and to understand theology within the single history of a liberation commitment, Segundo has designed a theological method that works to overcome hierarchical dualism.

For Discussion

1. What do you think and feel about the claim of liberation theologians that God favors the poor?

2. What part of this chapter disturbed you the most? Why?

3. Explain the meaning of "praxis" in your own words. When have you engaged in praxis?

4. Use Segundo's "hermeneutic circle" to think through the meaning of the Lord's Supper. Begin from the experience of victims of prejudice.

5. Are prejudiced beliefs part of a person's faith or ideology? Explain your response.

For Further Reading

Brown, Robert McAfee. *Theology in a New Key: Responding to Liberation Themes.* Philadelphia: The Westminster Press, 1978.

Gutierrez, Gustavo. *A Theology of Liberation*. Maryknoll, N.Y.: Orbis Books, 1973.

Segundo, Juan Luis. *Faith and Ideologies*. Vol. 1 of *Jesus of Nazareth Yesterday and Today*. Maryknoll, N.Y.: Orbis Books, 1984.

Segundo, Juan Luis. *The Liberation of Theology*. Maryknoll, N.Y.: Orbis Books, 1976.

THE NATURE OF PREJUDICE AND THE STRUCTURE OF CHANGE

Each of the previous chapters has provided a comprehensive perspective from which to examine the problem of prejudice. By viewing the dynamics of hierarchical dualism through the lenses of educational philosophy, moral psychology, and theological method, the reader has been invited to develop a complex and nuanced perspective on prejudice. An underlying assumption has been that no single analysis is adequate. Prejudice is not simply an outgrowth of male sexual repression, immature morality, or authoritarian theologies. As Gordon Allport notes, "It is a serious error to ascribe prejudice to any single taproot."[1] The causes of prejudice are multiple and extend into the socio-economic structure, human sexuality, cultural ideology, and ego identity. Prejudice can be motivated by fear, a desire to exploit, a need for self-esteem, or by any number of other factors. In spite of this diversity of causes and the multiple ways prejudice finds expression, I have also suggested that hierarchical dualism is common to all forms of prejudice.

The present chapter is transitional, an interlude in the progress of the book. Each of the preceding chapters moved in an orbit of concepts and categories related to the discipline under review; each had its own language and preferred form of analysis. Now it is time to synthesize, to consolidate in a common language the insights offered by each perspective. In the next chapter, I will build on these insights for the purpose of providing practical guidance for educating against prejudice.

The chapter is organized into two major sections. In the first, I offer twelve summary statements about the nature of prejudice. I hope that such a review will not only facilitate the organization of knowledge, but will contribute to the reader's self-awareness. In the second section, I return to the key concepts of experience, democracy, and inquiry, elaborating on how Dewey, Haan, and Segundo contribute to our understanding of them. These themes are key to any educational effort designed to move participants from prejudice to pluralism.

Through the Looking Glass

Not a person among us stands on holy ground and views the social world free from the distortions of personal and social history. No one is without prejudice. Even an analysis of prejudice such as that undertaken in the present work reflects numerous prejudices on the part of the author—prejudices that went unnamed and unchallenged during the writing. Prejudicial attitudes, values, beliefs, and actions are deeply rooted in each of us, but this does not mean that it is pointless to reflect on our lives in an effort to confront and reorient the prejudices we can name. I hope this book has provided one way for the reader to examine the historical, social, and psychological conditions that have given rise to and perpetuated various forms of prejudice. I hope too that the concept of hierarchical dualism will help readers identify their own prejudices.

In the next chapter, I offer a model for addressing problems of prejudice. Before engaging in an educational task, however, it is important that the educator integrate the subject matter. To design anti-prejudice programs with integrity, one must be committed to challenging personal prejudices. In the following pages, therefore, I invite the reader to participate in a process of self-examination.

Listed below are 12 summary statements about the nature of prejudice derived from the interdisciplinary analysis of the previous chapters. Readers are invited to reflect on each statement and try to identify concrete ways in which the statement is true of their own experience. The 12 statements are:

1. Prejudices are based on a pattern of experience that is hierarchical and dualistic.
2. Prejudices reflect a desire to control the uncertainties of life.
3. Prejudices buttress the self-esteem of the prejudiced person.
4. Prejudices reinforce current distributions of social power.
5. Sexism is foundational for other forms of prejudice.
6. Different prejudices are related.
7. Prejudices are buttressed by adaptable stereotypes.
8. Prejudices reflect moral distortions.
9. Prejudices achieve stability through irrational psychodynamics.
10. Prejudices are justified by appeal to ultimate criteria.
11. Prejudices have negative psychological consequences for both "oppressor" and the "oppressed."
12. Prejudices have physical consequences.

Each of these summary statements can be demonstrated within our own experience. Let us look at each one in turn.

1. *Prejudices are based on a pattern of experience that is hierarchical and dualistic.*
    The theme of hierarchical dualism has been the unifying thread tying together the various analyses of this book. To say that prejudice is based on a pattern of hierarchical and dualistic experience implies that prejudice has both value and cognitive dimensions. Hierarchies attribute value; dualisms cog-

nitively organize experience. Underlying prejudices are the fundamental value hierarchies of good and bad, true and false, strong and weak. Prejudiced people believe their own group is good, true, and strong, and that other groups are basically evil, wrong, and weak.

We all have tendencies to think dualistically. We all want to reduce our world to hierarchies of simple values. Do you view Americans as good and the Soviets as bad (or vice versa)? Do law-abiding citizens tell the truth and criminals tell lies? Are males strong and females weak? If none of these are characteristic of your thinking, what hierarchical dualisms do you succumb to?

2. *Prejudices reflect a desire to control the uncertainties of life.*

Life is characterized by uncertainty; there is no way to guarantee that valued experiences and things will last. The precariousness of life creates a craving for control over the fluctuations of fortune. This craving promotes dualisms by encouraging a belief in imaginary certainties that stand against the real, observable world.

This "quest for certainty" operates on many levels. On a philosophical level, the enemy of certainty may be chance, and reality is correspondingly reduced to immutable law. On a societal level, change may be perceived as the enemy and security is sought through stable institutions and robust leadership. As Gordon Allport prophetically noted: "The prejudiced person looks for hierarchy in society. Power arrangements are definite, something he can count on.... What America needs is a strong leader—a man on horseback!"[2] On a personal level, ambiguity may be perceived as a threat, leading to a desire for clearly defined relationships and roles.

All of us, of course, prefer security to meaningless or haphazard fluctuations. The question becomes one of how we respond to life's inevitable uncertainties. How is the "quest for certainty" manifest in your life? To answer, it will be helpful to identify your deep fears. Often we are not even aware of these, but some may be named as likely candidates. Death? Social upheaval? Financial ruin? Nuclear destruction?

Whatever your fears, it is likely that you have developed psychological means for diminishing them. One such technique, or defensive process, is to give greater truth-value to what is comforting and to deny or ignore counter evidence. Can you name ways this is the case?

For example, you may have a deep fear of nuclear war. Many of us resolve this fear by clinging to a hope that runs something like this: "Our government's policy of nuclear deterrence has kept us out of war so far, so if we keep our defenses strong we will be safe." Such reasoning can be identified as a faulty "quest for certainty" because it reflects an attempt to resolve the fear by grasping an isolated truth apart from other relevant truths (for example, the fact that every weapons build-up in history has terminated in war). Rather than resolving our fear through constructive, but tenuous, actions to end the arms race, we resolve the tension through selective beliefs.

3. *Prejudices buttress the self-esteem of the prejudiced person.*

Prejudices not only serve to reduce ambiguity, they also buttress the self-esteem of the prejudiced person. It is one of the unfortunate realities of current human existence that people often feel good about themselves when they feel "better" than someone else. Prejudices provide ready means for this kind of ego support.

The relationship between self-esteem and prejudice indicates that a person's view of others is closely tied to that person's self-image. People who have a poor image of themselves will likely develop negative images of others. Prejudice works to buttress people's poor self-images by enabling them to say to themselves, "At least I'm less despicable than _____," with the blank filled in by a derogatory epithet for a minority group.[3]

When you're feeling low, do you generally look to find some means for comparing yourself to another so that the comparison is favorable to you? Do you ever think in terms of groups for this purpose? It is important to spend a few moments thinking about your own self-image. What makes you feel good about yourself? Make a list. Are some of the items on the list intrinsically tied to being better than someone else?

In addition to allowing for a distorted but comforting

comparison, prejudices buttress self-esteem in another way, by allowing one to escape dealing with one's own shortcomings. This works by the well-known process of scapegoating. Rather than face my own failings, I repress awareness of them and project my inner anxieties onto victims of my prejudice. My own submerged feelings of intellectual incompetence are translated into a belief that blacks have lower IQ's than whites. My own repressed fears of intimacy are translated into an exaggerated emphasis on the sexuality of women.

The reader is again invited to reflect on how this process may operate in his or her life. What insecurities would you rather not face? What sorts of people do you generally have difficulty relating to? Answers to such questions may provide clues to latent prejudices.

4.   *Prejudices reinforce current distributions of social power.*
The utility of prejudice for maintaining self-esteem is one reason why prejudices persist. Another reason is that they perpetuate current distributions of social power. Some people are highly advantaged by patterns of discrimination and prejudice.

The group with the greatest power to define social reality will define it to its own advantage. Through institutional and interpersonal power, the advantaged group is able to create and enforce discriminatory arrangements that represent "rigid moral imbalances." Institutional structures and practices are constructed to reinforce the status quo.

This description of the development of discriminatory practices and institutions may sound conspiratorial. Sometimes it is. More frequently, discrimination is a by-product of unquestioned assumptions and values. For example, to most middle-class Americans it seems perfectly natural that acceptance into college should be based on entrance exams. Most people fail to realize that previous inequities in education (among other factors) have resulted in a situation where minorities are often in a poor position to score well on such exams, regardless of ability. It is as if two people, person A and person B, are competing for a grade, but person A has stolen person B's books.

We have noted that prejudice reduces uncertainty, buttresses self-esteem, and perpetuates social inequality. For those who benefit from prejudice because of its anxiety-reducing and esteem-enhancing functions, obvious discriminatory behavior offers little additional gain. However, those who benefit in terms of social power are more likely to actively promote discrimination. The sociologists Levin and Levin note that different segments of society are likely to gain in different ways:

> We believe that there is a strong tendency for those in the lower segment of the majority group to benefit from discrimination and prejudice at the level of the personality. Prejudice makes them "feel better" about their difficulties. It allows them to displace aggression, protect self-esteem, and reduce uncertainty. In contrast, the upper segment of the majority group is much more likely to benefit at the level of the social structure. They reap economic benefits in the form of paying lower wages, controlling production costs, protecting their advantaged power position, acquiring land, and so on.[4]

The upper segments of society have the most to gain from discriminatory practices, but all of us share in social power and gain to some degree from the status quo. Unless you are a lower-class, minority, non-Christian, lesbian woman, you probably have been, in part, empowered by current social arrangements. It is important to reflect on concrete experiences of power.

Power is not an evil, but the misuse of power is the source of most human misery. Empowerment that comes as a birthright—because we were born male or white or North American—represents power that is particularly subject to misuse. Because we did not consciously seek it, we often do not recognize that this kind of power is intrinsically power *over* those who are not male, white, or North American. It is an illusion to claim that we have not been privileged by circumstances of birth. Similarly, an appropriate response to our empowered condition is not to repudiate it (as if we could!), but to turn it 180 degrees so that, rather than continue to support the status quo, it can be used to facilitate the construction of more just social arrangements.

In what ways are you a beneficiary of unjust human relations? As a white, middle-class male, it is very easy for me to name ways I have benefited from the privileges accorded whites, the middle class, and males. I have had a good education, more than adequate housing, sound nutrition, relative freedom from harassment, to name only a few. These are reflected in my relative optimism, my belief that I can contribute in some small way to a better world, and my trust in my own employability. My attitudes are not completely self-made; they reflect the status of my social position. Can you trace dimensions of your personality back to advantages you have received by current social arrangements?

5.   *Sexism is foundational for other forms of prejudice.*

In all human groups there are males and females. The intimate and sustained association between the sexes has provided a setting in which hierarchical dualisms have become stable and enduring. Because male-female relations are foundational for social existence and social order, it is not surprising that the relationship between elite males and other human groups came to be modeled on that of the gender relation. Thus, women's oppression became the historical model on which the domination of other human groups was based.

The process of individual development parallels the historical path. Sexual identity is the earliest group identification that the young child learns. In a sexist culture, the growing individual learns that male-female relations exhibit a structure of hierarchical dualism. This early learning contours the child's expectations about the relationships among other human groups. As the child learns additional group identifications, he or she will seek to apply the structure of hierarchical dualism. Thus, gender prejudice paves the way for other prejudices.

Although sexism provides a foundation for other forms of prejudice, this is not to say all prejudices are reducible to sexism. Every form of prejudice has its own unique historical development and psychodynamics; each must be carefully studied on its own. If sexism could miraculously be eliminated, this would not bring an end to the problem of prejudice. But sexism does play a unique role. The relation between man and woman has been and continues to be the source for the psychological structure of hierarchical dualism, though this structure can be manifest in a variety of ways. It is important, therefore, to reflect on this most intimate of relationships.

How do you relate to the other sex? Do you expect baby boys to be dressed in blue and girls in pink? Do you prefer that little boys play with guns and balls and little girls with dolls and aprons? Do you expect the women of the parish to put on the dinners and the men to build the new addition? Do you expect spiritual or political leadership from one sex more than the other? Do you expect women but not men to give up their names when they marry? If you are married, are occupational and household labors shared in accordance with interests and abilities rather than divided by tradition? If you hear a story about a child left at home because both parents have careers, do you accuse the working mother before the working father of neglecting the family? A yes to any one of these questions points to gender prejudice. Of course, the list could be extended. To what similar question would you answer yes?

6. *Prejudices are related.*

Prejudiced people are generally not prejudiced against just one group. Ideologies of sex, race, class, etc., are interwoven in a way that consolidate the privilege of the dominant group (e.g. white males) while often dividing the subordinate groups, divisions that do not allow victims to consolidate.

It is tragic that victims of social injustice find it difficult to cooperate. In the heat of political struggle, the recognition that one's oppressions are linked with those of others often melts away. Thus, blacks and Jews, feminists and labor, find themselves at odds with one another.

Researchers have told us that victims of prejudice generally follow one of two paths:[5] They either become even more prejudiced than the average member of society, or they become passionate advocates of equality. If the first, the victim amplifies in his or her own psychology the set of prejudices present in society. This may even include a prejudice against other members of one's own group. On the other hand, experience of prejudice can lead to a commitment to eradicate this evil wherever it is found.

In an attempt to recognize our own misplaced anger, it is important to reflect on personal experiences of victimization. The sharing of stories will inevitably lead to recognition that the enemy is not one another, but a system of injustice that locks numerous groups into inferior positions.

Other readers, like myself, will have more difficulty naming experiences of victimization. Because I am close to the pinnacle in the pyramid of power, it is more difficult for me to name specific experiences of victimization. But it is not impossible! I have been victimized by corporate advertising designed to create and manipulate artificial needs. I have been denied accurate, undistorted news information that would allow me to make more informed decisions. The fruits of my labor have been drafted through the Internal Revenue Service to pay for covert Latin American wars without my consent or approval.

The stereotypic images available to me are paradoxically broad and yet rigid. I have not been channeled into low paying service occupations, leaving me with a multitude of paths to follow. I have been free to claim a self-image that incorporates power, freedom, and dignity. But the benefits accrued have a price; they come at the expense of other people who I have been told (subtly, of course) not to be like. Thus, for example, there are rigid stereotypes against acting "effeminate," lest I be identfied with that sub-species called women. I am to be strong, but not to exhibit "brute force," lest I be identified with the black man. (Note, for example, that football quarterbacks who need "smarts" are usually white, but boxers who need only "muscle" are black.) I am to be industrious, but not zealously so, lest I be identified as a Jap or Jew. On the other hand, I am to be leisurely, but not too leisurely, lest I be identified with the "lazy" who occupy the Third World.

It is important for those of us with advantaged positions to reflect carefully on our own experiences of victimization. It is only through drinking deeply from the springs of personal experiences of oppression that we can begin to identify with those who experience life primarily as victims. Guilt is not a good motive for working for social justice. Only when we recognize common experiences can sound coalition-building occur.

Prejudices are not isolated phenomena, but are linked in a massive, though often subtle, system of exploitation for the benefit of a relative few; they serve to maintain a system of privilege. When we reflect on our experiences of exploitation, we can begin to see the common features that bridge one prejudice to another, thereby exposing a system of oppression that has personal, interpersonal, societal, and international dimensions. Keeping the whole web of connections in mind will help to create networks of cooperation among oppressed peoples.

7. *Prejudices are buttressed by adaptable stereotypes.*

I have had numerous occasions to allude to the central role that stereotypes play in the formation and perpetuation of prejudice. Stereotypic thinking is not equivalent to prejudice, but is an important dimension of it. Stereotypes are the cognitive content that joins with a value-laden emotional antipathy to form a prejudice.

Stereotypes are rooted in normal processes of cognition. Every moment we sift through the thousands of stimuli that enter our brains through our senses and distill them into a few meaningful impressions. We form categories to simplify the job of recognizing meaningful patterns of stimuli. The process of categorizing our experience necessitates unconscious choices about where to focus attention. The result is that we tend to overestimate the similarities between the objects that are included in a single category and also underestimate the similarity between objects that we have placed in different categories. When the same process is applied to human groups, stereotyping often results.

Stereotypes themselves may be erroneous, but they are not necessarily prejudicial. They are prejudicial when they function to reinforce negative attitudes toward a group. Stereotypes efficiently support negative attitudes because they can readily be assimilated to the basic positive-negative polarities of hierarchical dualism. Thus, stereotypes about some groups being dirty and others clean reinforce and reflect pre-existing judgments about good and evil.

Stereotypes are quite adaptable. If enough evidence is accumulated so that I must abandon a negative stereotype of a particular group, this does not eliminate the prejudice. Another stereotype can quickly develop to fulfill the same role. It will be remembered how Ruether documented fundamental shifts in the stereotypes used to characterize women, yet the prejudice against women remained unscathed.

What stereotypes are operative in your thinking? What images come to mind with the following words: lesbian, politician, boxer, corporate executive, Latin American peasant? People can be stereotyped because of innate characteristics, such as nationality, race, and sex, or because of functions or occupations. The source of the stereotype is not as important as the implications for stereotyping. Stereotypes reduce people to our restricted images of them. It is important to become sensitive to stereotypes in our thinking so that we are better able to meet and talk with the people behind the masks we project on them.

8. *Prejudices reflect moral distortions.*

The dialogue between members of elite groups and members of subordinate groups does not represent an equal sharing of information, feelings, perspectives, and values. In more or less subtle ways, the dialogue is dominated by members of the group with greater social power. This domination leads to conclusions and actions that are morally imbalanced, even if "paternalistic" resolutions are adopted that seem to be just.

Moral dialogue occurs on two fundamental levels: between individuals and between groups. On the interpersonal level, informal customs allow the advantaged member to interrupt more frequently, to have the final word, to speak more forcefully, and numerous other fairly subtle regulators of social exchange. The cumulative result of such patterns of exchange over a period of time and across many situations is that preference is given to the concerns and values of the dominant party.

Moral dialogue among groups often occurs in more formal ways. In a representative democracy, political dialogue (which is inevitably a form of moral dialogue) is often carried on through one's representative. This creates serious difficulties if one is unrepresented or underrepresented. Is it fair to have the fate of the Equal Rights Amendment, for example, decided by a dialogue among predominately male state legislatures? Should the question of the ordination of women be put before an all-male tribunal? Are poor persons adequately represented when votes are taken about welfare?

Can you identify ways you participate in distorted patterns of communication? In your work place, are the views and perspectives of those at the bottom end of the pay scale given equal attention to those at the top end? Do the places you turn to for news and information offer perspectives informed by a variety of viewpoints? For example, are socialist interpretations as readily available as capitalist ones? If not, who is making the decison for you about what is true?

9. *Prejudices achieve stability through irrational psychodynamics.*

Prejudices involve an irrational dimension that distorts human experience. Dewey speaks of a "hidden value choice." Haan and Ruether talk in terms of defensive psychological processes. Segundo refers to "ideologies" in the pejorative sense, meaning irrational biases passed as "common sense." All are referring to an irrational element that usually accompanies prejudice.

It is difficult to become aware of the irrational dimensions of our own thinking. By its very nature, irrationality poses as rational. Have you ever thought about how illogical dreams are and yet how believable they seem at the time? The attitudes, beliefs, and actions of prejudice are often just as irrational and equally difficult to recognize as such.

It is natural that each of us will find ways to shield ourselves from confronting our prejudices. Our own sense of self-worth and self-identity may partly reside in holding a self-image that is dualistically contrasted to images of some "other."

We need to learn to spot the mental tricks we use to avoid recognizing our own prejudices. Escape to blindness is often found through one of two doors.

The first door opens outward toward the macroworld of politics, economics, and major social institutions. The people who take this door limit the problem of prejudice to the psychological realm. These people may have a keen awareness of the way prejudicial patterns of thought and action have profoundly affected their personality and relations with others. They carefully search the intimacies of human relationships for stereotypic images and distortions. People who use this defense of focusing attention on the depths of their psyche, may fail to attend with equal vigor to the problem as it is manifested in the major institutions of our day. They may fail to see, for example, that sitting comfortably in one's living room, reflecting on sexual stereotyping, may itself require class privileges rooted in a system of exploitation of Third World countries. Delving endlessly into the nuanced cycles of prejudice as revealed in psychological imagery does not necessarily expose the connections that link these images to starving children in far away lands, nuclear threats, or banking practices in South Africa.

The second door of escape opens inward toward the microworld of interpersonal relations. Those who choose this door may possess a keen sense of justice and a sharp awareness of the socio-political mechanisms used in the oppression of numerous social groups. What they fail to see is the daily, personal forms of prejudice. By focusing exclusively on the political, the connection between socio-economic exploitation and speech habits, for example, may be missed.

This group is particularly vulnerable to what might be called *subversion by the subtle.* Many, perhaps most, of the devastating oppressions are no longer maintained through brute force in the United States or other "modern democracies." Many people fail to recognize the extent to which prejudice permeates the social fabric because they want to name something as oppressive only when it consists of such gross violations of human rights as legal segregation, torture, or imprisonment without due process. Many of today's most powerful means for maintaining social advantage are not so blatant. The successes of the civil rights movement and the feminist movement have been counterbalanced by a refinement of the means through which power and prejudice are maintained. Thus, for example, women are oppressed by media images that caricature feminists; poor blacks are exploited when the powerful steal their language and label affirmative action programs "reverse discrimination."

Each single mechanism of oppression may appear insignificant. It may appear trivial that women are reduced to linguistic invisibility by masculine "generic" language. It may simply appear a matter of convenience that naming customs dictate that women give up their name and become "Mrs. _____" upon marriage. It often seems like an innocent cultural trapping that many of our social manners reflect an image of women as powerless and in need of a caretaker. Women who voice objections to such practices are often labelled radical feminists who blow things way out of proportion. Taken together, however, the subtle mechanisms culminate in a culture in which there is epidemic wife-beating, a "feminization of poverty," and an image of "masculinity" that is enhanced when others, whether individuals or nations, are forced into submission.

10. *Prejudices are justified by appeal to ultimate criteria.*

People have a variety of ways of explaining the group differences that they believe exist.[6] Inevitably, prejudice is explained not in terms of one's negative attitudes and beliefs but in terms of some ultimate source for the "failings" of the outgroup. Some people will hold up nature as their ultimate recourse and attribute the lower status of the outgroup to inferior genes. Other people will attribute the outgroup's supposed inferiority to environmental or cultural factors that are believed to be the ultimate human determinants. Of greatest concern to the present work are those people who justify their prejudice by appeal to religious beliefs.

It is disturbing to note that researchers have frequently found a connection between religiousness and prejudice.[7] In general, those who attend church are more prejudiced than the non-religious person. Although debate continues over the meaning and validity of these findings, even the hint that religiousness might encourage prejudice is reason for considerable alarm if not surprise. For the religious educator, a major obstacle to be overcome is the belief that God has ordained that some groups be disadvantaged.

The reader is invited to reflect on her or his image of God. In what ways is the image a buttress for prejudice? Is God a "Father"? Does God divide people into "the saved" and "the damned"? Does God ordain that some will be poor? Is God a mighty ruler? Even an image of God as "above" the petty struggles of humanity, or an image of God as equally loving all people and thereby unable to "take sides," places God in a psychological role that is ill suited to actively challenge prejudicial patterns of thought.

11. *Prejudices have negative psychological consequences for both "oppressor" and "oppressed."*

The divisions of persons or groups into the categories of "oppressor" and "oppressed" can be useful to characterize situations in which one group has greater power to influence the options and conditions of another group. Both groups, however, suffer psychologically from this situation. As the oppressors oppress, they are dehumanized. As the oppressed internalize the perspective of the oppressor, they participate in their own oppression.

One of the most dehumanizing consequences of prejudicial thought for the oppressor is the tendency to become desensitized to human suffering. This is often evidenced in an overly rationalistic approach to problems. Commenting on a protest against apartheid in South Africa, for example, I heard one government official remark, "The protesters mean well, but you have to be reasonable." Translation: "Don't get emotional." There is a subtle equation of emotion with distorted thinking. Indeed, emotion can lead to distorted thinking, but it can equally well lead to constructive action. Rational thinking that is done apart from emotional engagement often leads to false armchair solutions.

The victims of oppression are in double jeopardy. To a large extent, they internalize the negative stereotypes by which the dominant group defines them. Thus, for example, while most men feel capable of (though not desirous of) doing jobs normally performed by women, many women do not feel capable of doing the jobs normally performed by men. In addition to internalizing negative self-images, oppressed people also internalize the values of the dominant group. Thus, many disadvantaged people may feel that the only way to get ahead is to mimic the compulsive, rationalistic, consumptive style of the dominant managerial class.

Oppressed people are often slow to name themselves as victims of oppression. In part, this reflects their internalization of the perspective of the dominant group. Rather than blame the oppressor, they blame themselves for their plight, thus becoming enslaved by their own debased self-images. Another reason why oppressed people fail to see their situation as oppressive is that such recognition might call into question the limited sense of value and security afforded them. Women, for example, have been taught to find value and security in terms of their relationships with men. They are valued as sisters, wives, and mothers. If a woman rebels against the patriarchal culture, she threatens the very ties that have been her main source of meaningfulness. When the culture offers highly restricted images of meaningful life, the victims of these restricted images are likely to cling to them strongly. This is particularly true in the case of white, middle-class women who, because they are integrated into elite culture, share in the privileges of dominant males.

12. *Prejudices have physical consequences.*

We have noted that prejudice has negative psychological consequences for both the oppressed and the oppressor. Prejudices also lead to physical consequences, but unlike the psychological ones, the oppressors enjoy positive physical consequences while the oppressed suffer negative ones. Let us look first at the most evident negative consequences. Children starve. The poor are homeless. Women are raped. Gays are beaten. Disadvantaged people, as Mary Hunt once said, "feel it in their bodies."

The physical consequences that plague the oppressed

can have their source in either institutional arrangements that deny them fair access to goods and services or in explicit acts of violence against them. It has been estimated that the money required to provide adequate food, water, education, health and housing for everyone in the world for one year is equivalent to the amount of money currently spent in a two week period on weapons.[8] When so much is devoted to protecting the privileges of so few, it is fair to speak of corrupt social structures and dehumanizing institutional arrangements.

Many outgroups—particularly racial minorities, women, and gays—are also frequent victims of physical assault. People with mild prejudices would certainly not condone such acts of violence. In fact, one of the most frequent techniques used to deny personal prejudice is to point the accusing finger at those who are more extreme and say, in effect, "I don't do that, so I'm not prejudiced." While it is true that most white people would not condone the attacks of the KKK, that does not mean that the members of the KKK are the only ones responsible for their brutalizing attacks. When a majority disparage a particular group through derogatory language, for example, a minority will act out the disparagement through physical acts of violence.

The relationship between the prejudices of the majority and the acts of violence by a small element within the privileged group can be stated in *the pyramid principle:* The latent antipathies of the many will be amplified in the overt actions of a few. Most people accept minor insulting remarks or humor that builds on negative stereotypes as simply harmless talk, but would not condone outright discrimination against the targeted group. However, when such talk is prevalent, a portion of the majority group will carry the prejudice beyond languages into overt acts of violence which the majority will condemn. Each step up on the pyramid of violence is supported by the broader levels below it.

The relationship between the various manifestations of prejudice can be seen in the case of women. In today's society, few people profess that women are inherently inferior beings without full moral worth. But most people acquiesce to a language structure that evolved during strongly patriarchal periods. The exclusive use of male pronouns to refer "generically" to all people reduces women to linguistic invisibility. It would be inappropriate to designate someone who talks about "the family of man" as necessarily a dehumanizing sexist. But with such use of language many people move up a further step on the pyramid. When women become the brunt of stereotypic jokes, the object of whistles and stares, the recipients of patronizing admonishments, a few more will confine women to prescribed roles and routines, actively discriminate against them in jobs, debase them in pornography. Finally, a few will brutalize women through rape or wife-beating. While the level of intensity varies considerably, these acts build on each other. The broader the base of mildly prejudiced people, the higher the rate of atrocities of a minority. It does little good for the majority to condemn the acts of the few, for it is their less intense actions that form the base of the pyramid.

In contrast to the physical sufferings of victims of prejudice, the benefactors of prejudice and discrimination often enjoy certain physical consequences. The rich have large houses, health clubs, and swimming pools. Thus, the phrase "everybody is oppressed" is both true and trite. While the upper classes may see their analysts weekly, the physical consequences of oppression make it obvious who is oppressed and who is oppressing. One doesn't have to be a follower of Abraham Maslow to recognize that suffering physical deprivations is worse than having to make psychological adjustments.

Toward a Common Language

It is time to turn our attention to the positive concepts of an educational model designed to reduce prejudice by looking again at the themes of experience, democracy, and inquiry that we first encountered in Dewey. Now able to expand on the meaning of these terms, we can take advantage of the insights provided by Haan and Segundo. In the following chapter, an educational model will be proposed that builds on these key ideas.

EXPERIENCE

With his philosophy of experience, Dewey sought to challenge prevailing sociological and philosophical dualisms. For Dewey, experience is characterized by a blend between doing and undergoing — between our actions and the corresponding acts of the environment. In Dewey's philosophy, things or concepts that we often view as separable and opposite are revealed as inseparable and related. Thus, such distinctions as humanity-nature, theory-practice, mind-body, fact-value, individual-community do not really refer to fundamentally different kinds of realities. The fact-value distinction, for example, when viewed in relation to activity oriented toward achieving a goal, represents connected phases of experience. Facts orient our doing, which in turn is directed toward a valued consummation.

For Haan, like Dewey, experience is a "doing and undergoing." Focusing on the social environment, Haan maintains that people try to create moral balances between their giving and their receiving. In mature experience, there is a balance between these. When moral exchange is less than fully mature, however, the giving and receiving are out of balance. In early development, there is often a desire to receive disproportionately more than one gives; the reverse is true during the next phase of development. Even mature people, however, can use immature levels of reasoning when their sense of integrity and coherence is threatened.

Haan's description of moral experience provides a means for analyzing how morality can be distorted to conform to prejudice. In everyday life, our moral awareness makes us sensitive to the feelings and needs of others. But when we feel threatened by something or someone around us, defensive psychological processes reduce our sensitivity. This is often what happens with prejudice. For many people who gain self-esteem by identifying themselves as members of a superior group, prejudices are integrated with their view of themselves. Confronted with a member of an outgroup, such a person experiences the other not as a unique human being, but as a reflection of the experiencer's stereotypes. This is really a special instance of what Dewey called "vicious abstractionism." A stereotype is an abstraction that hides a value choice.

Segundo reminds us that any philosophy of experience is inadequate so long as it treats experience "in general." He makes clear that human experience as it has evolved under the impact of class [and race and sex, etc.] divisions is not only one-sided, as Dewey maintained, but also conflictive. Segundo suggests that Christian religious experience is most authentic when it reflects the questions of meaning and value that arise from the underside of exploitation. The biblical narrative, for Segundo, provides the normative story through which the concerns of the struggling poor come to be seen in their full significance. Thus, it is the experience of the struggling poor that provides the necessary vantage point to dissolve such religious dualisms as God-human, eternity-history, saved-damned.

DEMOCRACY

Dewey's vision of ideal social life was clearly rooted in his American experience, but it would be a mistake to equate his meaning of democracy with the political system of the United States or any other country. For Dewey, democracy is a form of social interaction. A society is democratic to the extent that citizens hold interests in common and there exists equitable opportunity among all people to participate in the social process.

Dewey saw democracy as the form of social organization that prevented people from having artificially limited experiences based on impenetrable boundaries of sex, race and class. When social boundaries are relatively rigid, different groups have different types of experiences. Eventually, these differing experiences are reflected in dualisms. Thus, for example, the laborer has a different life experience from a college professor. When intellectuals and workers are clearly divided, theory becomes disconnected from practice and a host of dualisms, such as mind-body, thought-action, intellect-emotion, are fostered.

Haan's theory of a "truth-identifying dialogue" is a description of democracy at the interpersonal level. Mature moral exchange is democratic in the sense that all parties' desires and needs are given equal consideration. Haan goes beyond Dewey, however, by providing a developmental analysis of the path by which children come to understand and adopt democratizing procedures. In essence, Haan provides a model for the development of democratic thought.

Segundo's work reflects the ideal of democracy but views the means for obtaining this end from the vantage point of the poor. Segundo holds a view of reality as conflictive, requiring a dialectic of "taking-sides" in order to achieve justice. This has important implications for his view of the church. Segundo's prescription of a "minority" church may at first appear to run counter to the theme of democracy. This, however, would be a misreading. For Segundo, "mass" and "minority" tendencies are a part of each of us, and his view closely parallels Dewey's view of the relation of habit to thought. Thought is a specialized and "minority" form of habit that has the purpose of meeting new challenges. A society that "not only changes but which has the ideal of such change as will improve it"[9] will of necessity allow for the functional separation and coordination of mass and minority tendencies.

INQUIRY

Inquiry is the final concept that will serve as background for the model of education to be presented in the next chapter. The process of inquiry involves systematic thinking about the connections of experience. The goal of inquiry is to move the person from a relationship with the social world that is uncritical, non-cognitive, and imitative to one that is critical, intentional, and reconstructive. In the context of the present work, the goal is to move from a way of thinking that is hierarchical and dualistic to one that embraces egalitarian pluralism.

The meaning that inquiry has for this model can be drawn out by diagramming the processes involved in moving from prejudice to pluralism as these have been illuminated by Dewey, Haan, and Segundo. These theorists nicely complement each other in their emphases. Dewey's analysis of the process of change rests in a psychosocial perspective, with an emphasis on the individual and his or her intellect. Haan also develops a psychosocial analysis but puts a greater emphasis on social and moral relationships. Segundo undertakes a theological analysis of the movement. Together the theorists offer a textured and nuanced description of the movement from hierarchical dualism to egalitarian pluralism. The diagram below parallels the phases of change as each theorist understands them:

	Dewey	*Haan*	*Segundo*
Phase A:	Habit	Imbalance	Naive Faith
Phase B:	Indeterminate Situation	Interpersonal Disruption	Commitment to Oppressed
Phase C1:	Reflective Thought	Moral Dialogue	Ideological Suspicion
Phase C2:	Reconstructed Experience	New Balance	New Hermeneutic

Each of these theorists has provided a framework for thinking about critical issues for educational design. In Phase A, each theorist sets the problem of hierarchical dualism in an anthropological context by isolating a fundamental aspect of human nature that contributes to the problem of prejudice. In Phase B, each theorist has isolated a precondition that allows for the possibility of change and growth. Each theorist has identified processes by which change occurs in Phase C1; and, in Phase C2, the process of change is connected with an image of the human potential that contrasts with hierarchical dualism. Phase C2 relates to Phase C1 as end to means; the continuity between the two is indicated by designating them both with "C."

1. *Phase A: The Anthropological Setting*

Phase A in the diagram reflects each theorist's view of a dimension of the human situation that allows for prejudice. For Dewey the person is profoundly an organism of habit. Habits constitute the will; they are what define character. Habits, as non-cognitive tendencies to respond in similar ways to similar stimuli, are what conserve and perpetuate the thrust of past actions into the present.

Habits represent both the problem and the potential of the human. On the one hand, habits conserve and generalize tendencies that may be detrimental. Habits may promote a false sense of security in response to the compelling "quest for certainty." From this perspective prejudice can be viewed as a collection of habituated responses. Habits, however, are also our source of hope. No change for the better can be stabilized unless it becomes a part of our habits.

For Haan, the fundamental fact of human existence is that we live in interdependent balances with one another. However, the mutual expectations that structure human life are not always morally legitimate. While all humans have a compelling need to view themselves in moral terms, the moral relationships we are party to may be fundamentally distorted. Haan speaks of these as imbalances. When Dewey's and Haan's views are set side by side, we see that prejudice is made up of reciprocal expectations existing within habituated social processes that can be described as morally imbalanced.

Segundo frames the question in terms of his two anthropological constants: faith and ideology. In order to experience life as coherent and meaningful, Segundo maintains, each person constructs an ideology. This ideology is formed from within a commitment to a particular witness to meaningful existence. When faith is mature, it can relativize its ideological commitments. Problems arise, however, when faith is not distinguished from ideology. Ideologies are then given absolute value. Prejudices are ideologies; they reflect beliefs and values that have their source, at least in part, in some witness to meaningful life. As ideologies, they should be open to correction from experience. But prejudices by their nature are not open to revision; they reflect the influence of a naive faith that has not been distinguished from ideology. For Segundo, hierarchical dualisms reflect a naive faith in which ideology is confused with revelation. Naive faith uncritically accepts beliefs and values from a tradition without testing them in the fires of real life.

2. *Phase B: The Condition for Change*

Habits operate efficiently, according to Dewey, when the actions demanded by environmental stimuli are clear. The harmonious exchange between organism and environment, however, is frequently interrupted, creating a continuous alternation of balance and imbalance between an organism and its environment. When imbalances occur, habits are rendered ineffective and the appropriate response to the environment becomes ambiguous. For Dewey, when an indeterminate situation interrupts the smooth functioning of habit, the possibility for something new to happen has been created. Phase B in the diagram represents that moment when there exists a disharmony, an indeterminate siutation. At this point, impulse is liberated and provides the psychodynamic impetus for imagination and reflection to find ways to reorganize habit.

Focusing on the social dimension, Haan specifies interpersonal disruption as the precondition for change. Moral balances are complex and reflect informal norms that are based on imperfect information about ourselves, others, and the nature of our joint situation. Consequently, interpersonal disruptions are frequent and expected. Thus, the potential for change is often present. Nonetheless, some moral imbalances go unnoticed for long periods because they are based on false information that is culturally accepted as true. Many forms of discrimination are moral imbalances of this type. Such moral understandings continue to structure social exchange until someone perceives that the balance is not based on informed consensual agreement. The perception of such an arrangement constitutes an imbalance, a disruption of interpersonal harmony, creating the potential for change.

For Segundo, the fusion of ideology and faith characteristic of Phase A is interrupted in Phase B by a commitment to the oppressed. This commitment involves both discerning the relational character of social circumstances (for example, poverty is functionally related to wealth) and a commitment to change the circumstance of the disadvantaged. A commitment to the oppressed reveals the moral imbalance of the social situation and makes possible the relativizing of ideologies tied to the status quo.

3. *Phase C1: The Process of Change*

Dewey is a believer in intellect. Although he acknowledges the origin of inquiry in the non-cognitive, he places his trust in the rational phase of inquiry. The operation of intellect has the power to transform or reconstruct experience. Reconstruction occurs primarily through a process of logically related symbols that are abstracted and generalizable. Dewey consequently spends considerable energy detailing the logical difficulties of dualism and elaborating a pluralistic philosophy of experience.

There is much to be said for Dewey's view. He offers a coherent account of the process of inquiry and does not fall into a dualistic error of separating the intellect from non-cognitive functions. Any program designed to challenge prejudice will eventually need to raise the issue for cognitive consideration if gains that are made are to be permanent. However, Dewey may have underestimated the contribution of non-cognitive processes to the transformation of experience.

Although Haan recognizes that logical analysis plays an indispensable role in human functioning, she also emphasizes the importance of non-cognitive factors. Moral reasoning involves much more than reasoning in a formal, deductive sense. Moral relationship involves intimate attention to non-generalizable information. The experience of hierarchical dualism will not be reconstructed purely through rational analysis. It will require that those who have been affected by or acted on prejudices participate in sincere truth-seeking dialogues aimed at constructing a new moral balance.

Ideological suspicion is the primary vehicle for change in Segundo's analysis. It originates in a commitment to the oppressed and advances through a process of unveiling the interests and motives that lie beneath the ideologies of the status quo. In partnership with Dewey, Segundo sees reflective thought (in the form of social scientific analysis) as the vehicle through which suspicion is developed. But Segundo does not share Dewey's optimism regarding intellect. Ideological suspicion reveals that all inquiries are partial and biased. The task from Segundo's standpoint is to begin from within a particular commitment and use the resources of intellect to comprehend the world from that standpoint. In particular, Segundo maintains that the task of the Christian is to systematically work through the questions that arise from within a partiality for the oppressed.

4. *Phase C2: The Human Potential*

For Dewey, the goal of inquiry is to reconstruct experience so that the connections present in the environment are more evident. Making previously unperceived connections salient leads to the collapse of dualisms. The expansion of meaningful experience is what Dewey means by growth, the word he most frequently uses to talk about the human potential. For Dewey, growth away from hierarchical dualism leads to reconstructed experiences in which the pluralism of experience is recognized.

For Haan, the human potential is characterized by a "truth-identifying dialogue." Such dialogue, based on an egalitarian process of construction, creates a moral balance that is particularized and meets everyone's needs and interests as well as the situation will allow.

Segundo emphasizes the interpretive element involved in a reconstructed experience and points to both the continuity and disjunction with received tradition. He refers to "a new hermeneutic" as the end toward which ideological suspicion points. What is "new" about the new hermeneutic is not the content to which it is applied. Rather, it is the incorporation of newly perceived connections within the received tradition that were not previously taken into account. The previous ideology is revealed as a biased, selective interpretation. The new hermeneutic breaks the hold of enforced social hierarchies by undercutting their transcendent justification. The narratives and symbols of the religious tradition are reinterpreted in light of the suffering created by the unjust system, a system that was buttressed by the earlier hermeneutic.

In summary, the concepts of experience, democracy, and inquiry can serve as pivotal concepts for comprehending the problems engendered by prejudice; they also point toward the goal of liberative education. We seek an education that expands an appreciation for pluralistic experience, under democratic conditions, that has been refined by inquiry. In the next chapter, I will suggest a model for educational practice that builds on these insights.

For Discussion

1. What stereotypes do you frequently use?
2. Do you feel better about yourself when you find that you are better at something than someone else?
3. How might self-esteem be affirmed without putting others in an unfavorable light?
4. Do you agree with the statement, "The group with the greatest power to define social reality will define it in such a way as to advantage itself." Explain your response.
5. Where do you see "subversion by the subtle" occurring?
6. In what ways are you an oppressor and in what ways have you been oppressed?

For Further Reading

Allport, Gordon. *The Nature of Prejudice.* Reading, Mass.: Addison-Wesley Publications, 1954/1979.

Bagley, Christopher, Gajendra Verma, *et al. Personality, Self-Esteem and Prejudice.* Westmead, England: Saxon House, 1979.

Jones, James. *Prejudice and Racism.* Reading, Mass.: Addison-Wesley Publications, 1972.

Levin, Jack and Levin, William. *The Function of Discrimination and Prejudice,* 2nd ed. New York: Harper & Row, 1982.

Pettigrew, Thomas, George Fredrickson, *et al. Prejudice.* Cambridge, Mass.: Harvard University Press, 1982.

Shields, David L. "The Psychology of Prejudice." *PACE/ Professional Approaches for Christian Educators* 16, 1986.

REDUCING AND
PREVENTING PREJUDICE:
A MODEL FOR TEACHING

In the last chapter I outlined the phases of change as depicted by Dewey, Haan, and Segundo. These phases provide a foundation for describing an educational model for challenging patterns of prejudice. The dynamics of change were stated abstractly and a few readers may have been frustrated by the generality and theoretical nature of the description. It is certainly the case that no amount of theory, by itself, will bring about change. But change in itself is not the goal. Rather, the goal is constructive change—change that opens participants to fuller, broader, and more complete experience. Such change cannot be brought about through educational activism that results in a flurry of activity with little guidance. Theory and action must be coordinated.

There is no simple recipe for creating open attitudes. It does not work to take a cup of whites, add a tablespoon of Latinos, blend in a half cup of blacks, sprinkle with dialogue, and bake to pluralism. The procedures and recommendations shared in this chapter will not be effective if they are mechanically implemented. The sensitive teacher will need to reflect on the variety of resources presented and employ them creatively, adapting them to the particular needs arising out of a concrete situation.

Having said this, however, I believe the basic structure of an educational practice that will contribute to overcoming prejudice can be specified. I have divided such a model of education into four phases:[1]

1. The teacher elicits an experience of prejudice (common experience).

2. The participants are invited to envision the social context through the eyes of the disadvantaged (development of partiality and commitment).

3. The participants use their capacities for critical thought to analyze the sources of prejudice and its embodiment in discriminatory action (application of ideological suspicion).

4. There is an opportunity for confronting and appropriating the normative sources of one's tradition (dialectical exchange with tradition).

These four phases follow the path of inquiry developed earlier. There is certainly nothing magical about dividing the process into four phases. Dewey, in fact, numbered the steps of inquiry differently in different places in order to discourage an overly-routine interpretation of the process. However, I have found the four phases to be a useful guide for the development of specific educational procedures.

Before detailing each phase, a few preliminary remarks are in order. All people are not equally engulfed by prejudice. We differ in the tenacity to which we hold to prejudicial attitudes and dehumanizing stereotypes; we vary in the degree that prejudices are central to our self-image and buttress our self-esteem. Some people readily act out their prejudices, others do not. And the targets of prejudice differ in the severity to which they have been victimized. Because of this diversity, no single educational effort will be equally effective for all people. Some will respond readily to prejudice-reduction efforts, others will not.

For people who have deep emotional commitments to racial, sexual, ethnic, or other antipathies, a direct challenge to their beliefs and attitudes will be ineffective. While there are times to put the educational goals aside and speak out directly against bigotry, such denunciations are for purposes other than changing the bigot's attitudes. It does little good to protest to the white racist, "You ignorant worm! You're as rational as a crazy person and as moral as a tyrant." A certain amount of discretion and indirection may be necessary. The most effective prejudice-reduction program may be one that is not about prejudice. The educational phases that I am about to outline can be incorporated as underlying currents into educational programs that have other primary goals.

Prejudice may be most effectively undermined through indirect approaches, but education cannot end there. An effort should be made to move from the indirect to the direct. What is originally only implicit must eventually be made explicit. Only when a person has consciously and systematically reflected on the nature of prejudice and its sources and consequences can the person begin to forumulate a clear commitment to pluralism that will remain stable in the face of new challenges.

With these remarks in mind, let us look at the phases of an educational model designed to reduce prejudice.

1. COMMON EXPERIENCE

The first task of the teacher is to create a common experience of prejudice, but not any experience will suffice. The goal is to create an experience in which prejudice is viewed as a problem. In Paulo Freire's language, the goal is to problematize the situation.[2] In many respects this is the most difficult phase of the model. While it is relatively easy to elicit hierarchical dualistic patterns, it can be quite difficult to create an experience in which prejudice is felt to be a problem.

It is simple to state formally the necessary components of such an experience. To problematize prejudice it is necessary to do two things: (a) elicit habituated responses that reflect hierarchical dualism, and (b) reorganize the environment in such a way that the habitual response can no longer function without reflection. Let us try to make these more concrete.

Eliciting Habits

The first problem the teacher will have is finding a way to elicit an habitual response that reflects prejudice. This is not accomplished quickly, for we are looking for a *pattern* of thought and action. A habit is a tendency to respond in similar ways to similar stimuli; it becomes evident only with time. Because habits are not immediately evident, it will be advantageous for the teacher to spend some time getting to know his or her co-learners. The better the teacher understands the worldview of the students, the better position the teacher is in to know what prejudices are likely to arise.

Knowledge of one's co-learners is probably most effectively gained through informal sharing outside the classroom context where students are more likely to "be themselves." In such settings, there are several things that can serve as indicators of prejudice. Humor is always a good clue to the particular prejudices of a group, especially humor of a teasing sort. A fourth-grade boy who teases a lower status classmate for being a sissy is likely wrestling with masculine-feminine stereotypes. Favorable judgments made about certain groups or people may also provide an indirect clue about prejudicial attitudes. Perhaps Mary thinks President Reagan is great. Why? Because he isn't soft on the commies. Often we idealize people who show strength against those we despise. It will not take a great deal of listening to begin to perceive the prejudices operative in any group.

Unfortunately, many teachers will find themselves in situations where informal sharing outside the classroom is difficult or impossible. While helpful, such sharing is only one path to the goal. With one high school class, I accomplished the same end by playing a couple rounds of *The Ungame,* a game in which participants are invited to answer questions about themselves. By using the light-hearted questions dictated by the game, students quickly began to reveal a great deal about their values, ideals, fears, and prejudices.

The selection of curricular materials is critical. In evaluating curricular resources, the teacher should keep *the difference principle* in mind. This principle indicates that for prejudice to be overcome, people of different groups with different life experiences should be represented. The teacher should seek materials that include diverse ethnic and racial groups, both sexes, and other national groups (particularly non-Europeans). The focus of the curriculum need not be on prejudice or stereotyping. In fact, during this first phase of the model it is probably better if prejudice-reduction is not the explicit aim.

There is a variety of reasons for choosing curricula that avoid stereotypes and present human diversity. Obviously such materials discourage students from thinking of "their" group as the model for normative humanity. During this phase of the educational model, however, such material can serve another important function. The teacher can use the human diversity that is graphically presented on the pages in a way that is analogous to a Rorschach inkblot! The teacher can elicit patterns of prejudice by allowing students to project their interpretations onto the images. For example, I asked a class of third graders to tell a short story about a black boy pictured in their textbook. The children made up stories that were liberally sprinkled with references to ghettos, fatherless families, laziness, and stupidity. Since we hadn't done the lesson that corresponded to the picture, the stories built only on the students' own impressions of black life.

In eliciting responses, three key points will help to create an appropriate experience. The first is that this phase is necessarily "student oriented." The teacher cannot lecture students into an experience of prejudice. If the teacher is to allow students to express their prejudices, the teacher must focus attention on what "comes naturally" to the students. It is better not to rush in with evaluations when prejudices are expressed. Attentive and non-evaluative listening will facilitate the development of the experience. Initially the teacher might even allow those participants with greater social power to dominate the exchange. This itself will provide a mild experience of hierarchical dualism.

A second point is that we are looking for habitual action that is experientially relevant. To be most effective, the prejudice should be demonstrable, given the participants in the class. That is, members of both the ingroup and outgroup should be present. This may not always be possible. It sometimes may be necessary to work with racism, for example, with an all white class. But the most profound education will occur when members of both the dominating and dominated groups are present. it is therefore important that the educational group itself be heterogeneous. Again, the difference principle is important. The educator should seek to bring into relationship people whose life experiences are likely to be divergent at crucial points.

Educators will not need to strain their creativity to implement the difference principle. One of the most profound human differences is that of sex. Fortunately, almost all educational settings can bring together males and females. Of course, it is advantageous to expand the circle of diversity beyond gender. Depending on the context and other educational objectives, numerous other differences might be used: race, ethnic background, sexual orientation, religious beliefs. Even people from different schools, friendship groups, or academic orientations may provide significant and sufficient differences.

The third point is that the experience should tie in with student's faith-ideology. The habitual patterns of interpretation and action should reflect students' tendencies to substantiate their viewpoint through appeal to a transcendent or ultimate value. Common in religious education contexts will be an appeal to a person's religious heritage and to its source documents. "Women should stay in the home because God made them to be mothers." The educational experience should provide an opportunity for students to share their faith commitments as these are presently understood and as they currently influence action.

Altering the Environment

The second part of the first phase involves interrupting the operation of habits through modifying the environment. Here we are concerned primarily with the social environment. Facets of social life that went largely unnoticed in the habitual experience need to be brought to awareness in such a way that moral imbalance is perceived.

One effective way to alter the environment is to simply change the focus of attention. Up to this point the class has probably revolved around those students who enjoy center stage. Often these more extroverted students are unaware that they have dominated the exchange. There is nothing wrong, of course, with being extroverted and no attempt should be made to make these students feel guilty. But it may be time to hear from the less vocal members who may or may not share the prejudices of the more outspoken. This phase will be particularly effective if there are students in the class who have been mildly victimized by the prejudices uncovered. This is not uncommon.

The teacher may need to use a variety of techniques to help the less vocal students express themselves. It is certainly inappropriate to force people to talk who would prefer not to. Some students may simply be intimidated by large groups and will do fine if the class is broken into small groups. Less direct techniques also may be employed. For example, students could draw pictures or make collages on the topic under consideration and the teacher could highlight for discussion some of the themes present in their work.

Another method that has been successfully employed to disrupt the habitual patterns of prejudice is called "counterattitudinal advocacy."[3] This technique is based on having a student espouse a position that is opposite from the position that he or she actually holds. Thus, with a person who believes that mandatory retirement at age 65 is appropriate, a situation is created in which the student becomes an advocate of no mandatory retirement age.

Counter-attitudinal advocacy is most effective when the participant does not feel coerced into adopting the opposite stance. The teacher would be ill advised to say, "Oh, so you think blacks ought to stay in their own neighborhoods. Well, I want you to write an essay advocating fair housing." There are many ways to get students to take the perspective of a perceived opponent without coercion. Role plays and simulation games can be effectively employed. Taking the perspective of a historical character can be useful. Mock debates, position papers, group projects, and numerous other techniques can be arranged so that a person willingly adopts a counter position. Even though the person feels that he or she is "role playing" or taking a different perspective "for fun," counter-attitudinal advocacy can effectively disrupt the flow of habit.

Since prejudices are related and the psychological structure that underlies them is basically the same, it is not necessary that the teacher focus immediately on the more salient or severe prejudices. There are times when such a direct approach would not be advisable. For example, dealing directly with a prejudice against overweight people may engender considerable anguish among some members of the class. Perhaps it would be better to begin with a prejudice against kids from other schools or younger grades, or some other prejudice that would be less anxiety-producing. Students can draw the parallels later.

2. DEVELOPMENT OF PARTIALITY AND COMMITMENT

This second phase is intended to root the process in a concrete perspective that is conditioned by a particular struggle for human liberation. This phase flows naturally from the previous. The disruption of habit reveals (albeit, often obscurely) the victims of prejudice. The development of partiality and commitment arises naturally from empathy with those who were and remain hurt or disadvantaged by the prejudice. As Segundo states: "A hermeneutic circle always supposes a profound human commitment, that is, a consciously accepted partiality, based certainly not on theological criteria but on human ones."[4]

The task of the teacher at this point is to focus attention on the *invitational dynamic* of the social situation. If the situation has been successfully rendered problematic, if moral imbalance has been perceived, then there now exists the possibility for change. The teacher has an opportunity to elicit a response to an invitation. Students are invited to convert to the perspective of the oppressed. For the invitation to be effective, the teacher must redirect the attention away from expressed beliefs and ideas to concrete experiences of pain. The invitation does not come from "on high"—from the teacher, but "from below"—from those who suffer. As Matthew Lamb put it, "The cries of victims are the voice of God."[5]

During this phase, identification with a concrete person is helpful, particularly for students below the senior high level. Various "isms" must be removed from the abstract and made quite specific. Racism *per se* is not the focus, but the plight of Andrew, a black janitor in a film. The teacher must be cautious lest this identification become paternalistic or patronizing. The appropriate response is not, "Oh, poor Andrew," but "We can learn from and with Andrew about what it means to be black in America." If paternalism begins to emerge, it may be helpful to role play the situation and see how the person in the disadvantaged position feels about these patronizing responses to his or her condition. The teacher must be sensitive at this point not to move forward (returning to the first phase if necessary) until there is a commitment to raise questions and pursue responses from the perspective of the disadvantaged.

The teacher can focus directly on prejudices that have impact on members of the class or the teacher can focus on more removed prejudices. Focusing on a prejudice that is relevant within the class (e.g. sexism) is the most powerful way to proceed, but may arouse defensiveness on the part of the advantaged, and the disadvantaged are often reluctant to name their own oppression. Focusing on a more remote prejudice carries less capacity for personal transformation; nonetheless, the insights gained through examining the prejudices of others can become the catalyst for opening oneself to critical self-awareness.

A number of procedures can be used to help make the invitation clear. If the focus is on immediate prejudices, then sensitive listening to the feelings and thoughts of the disadvantaged members can aid the process. The teacher needs to highlight the human pain that results from prejudice. One way is to encourage direct expression of thoughts and feelings by disadvantaged students. Such skills as "active listening,"[6] in which the teacher feeds back what he or she perceives the emotion of the speaker to be, can be helpful. The teacher should be a model of attentive, sympathetic listening and help all participants to identify with the situation of the disadvantaged.

If the focus is on a prejudice removed from the immediate class situation (e.g. racism in an all white class), various techniques requiring empathy can be employed. Movies, autobiographies, novels, interviews, and other techniques can be used to encourage identification with concrete individuals who have been victimized by prejudice and discrimination. In one successful prejudice-reduction program, a series of dramatic plays were used in an elementary school to develop empathy for minorities.[7]

Literature is a rich resource for developing an identification with a person representing a minority group. The stories of Robin Hood or Pancho Villa could be used with children to develop an awareness of and an identification with groups suffering systematic exploitation. With adults, Steinbeck's moving novel *Of Mice and Men* could provide insight into the emotionally and mentally retarded. May Sarton's short novel *As We Are Now* begins with the line, "I am not mad, only old." It is a powerful beginning to a harrowing novel about the problems of old age. The possibilities are endless. Whenever these "second-hand" accounts are used, it is helpful to conclude with open-ended questions that help participants to identify ways in which their own experience parallels that of the disadvantaged group or how their experience, while not the same, is also disadvantaged as a result of the impoverishment of others.

Before turning to a description of the third phase, a word of encouragement is in order. Given the number of prejudices that people hold and the tenacity with which they often hold them, the teacher may feel at this point that the task of overcoming prejudice is almost impossible. It is true that reducing prejudice is one of the most challenging tasks facing the educator, but the task is by no means impossible. In fact, if the teacher succeeds in promoting identification with just one outgroup, then he or she may be surprised at how quickly other prejudices may fall. People tend to be consistent and are generally prejudiced against a whole range of groups or have very few significant prejudices. Once a person has identified with one victim, it becomes much easier to hear the voices of other victims. The first leap is the most difficult and the teacher should not be discouraged if it is necessary to repeat the first two phases a couple times before moving to the next phase.

3. APPLICATION OF IDEOLOGICAL SUSPICION

The third phase of the model involves the intellectualization of the commitment to the oppressed through the elicitation, development, and research of critical questions about the social reality that has been constructed or re-presented. The phase is most effective when it evolves hand-in-hand with some form of action against prejudice or discrimination.

There are several key concepts that will inevitably need to be discussed during this phase: dualism, stereotyping, prejudice, discrimination, and scapegoating are certainly among the most important.[8] The role that discrimination and prejudice play in perpetuating current distributions of status and power will need to be analyzed and criticized. The particular way that hierarchical dualism is expressed in racism, sexism, antisemitism, and ageism, among others, will need to be explored in an age-appropriate manner.

At this phase, the teacher becomes a prober and helps students, by means of open-ended questions, to think critically about the connections between, on the one hand, the attitudes, beliefs, and attributions made during the first phase and, on the other hand, the psychological needs and social benefits that such attitudes, beliefs, and attributions may reflect. The teacher initiates this process, but he or she should encourage the students to carry it forward through questioning and challenging each other. Moral dialogue among the students, particularly if the prejudice is demonstrable within the class, is an effective method for developing critical insight. The teacher's role becomes that of a monitor who seeks to maintain conditions favorable to open dialogue free from domination.

Case studies can be a very effective means to develop critical insight. Students can be provided with brief details of a particular historical event or a recent news item and use their questioning and research skills to probe the event, tracing its roots back to psychosocial, political, and economic dynamics. With an older class, for example, a newspaper article on the killing of a black man by an angry mob of blacks in South Africa might be distributed. Students could brainstorm on what information they need to know to thoroughly understand this event and then organize themselves to try to develop appropriate analyses. In their search they will probably discover not only the ugly racism of apartheid, but the divisions that develop within oppressed groups between those who collaborate with those in power, the social reformers, and the revolutionaries. The ties between racism and economics, politics, and religion will likely surface, as will the role of American corporations.

This third phase is the heart of the process and students should be encouraged to extend their analysis as far as their capacities allow. The leader should be aware, however, that if the prejudice highlighted in the first phase is an immediate one relevant to the class, this phase may create excessive stress. Stress is not necessarily negative; it can be a positive motivator for optimal awareness and growth. But when the analysis and discussion puts too great a strain on definitions of self, defensive processing will interrupt the educational process. If the teacher feels that the discussion is becoming too heated or that some individuals are exceptionally uncomfortable, the focus needs to be temporarily shifted and emotional support provided. It is pointless to debate a point or push for insight when a person consistently responds defensively. Only after the person's sense of self-worth has been affirmed can more threatening material gradually be introduced. Optimally, the situation should tax the participants' coping processes but not become so stressful as to elicit defensive reasoning.

To be most effective, this phase is best carried out in an action-reflection mode. As Allport noted, "The student seems to gain more when he loses himself in community projects."[9] Having identified with a victim, a real, even if small, effort at correcting the injustice provides the most effective setting for deepening participants' appreciation for the dynamics of prejudice. A class using the case study described above might decide to write letters to Congress or spend one afternoon picketing a corporation that conducts business in South Africa, passing out information sheets devised by members of the class.

Another form of action that might profitably be employed are studies into the prejudices of the local community. Ideas for these studies can be gained from published social scientific investigations, or students can devise their own. For example, one junior high class took a street corner survey asking passersby who they would vote for among a hypothetical slate of candidates for president. Half of the passersby were given a list of three men together with a description of their qualifications. A second half were given the same list of names and qualifications except one male name was changed to a female name. It was found that the man who had the same qualifications as the woman was selected more frequently than the woman. Results from such studies might be published in the local newspaper or be included in a letter to the editor.

Prejudices are often reinforced by simple ignorance. The third phase is an appropriate time for cross-cultural education in which the emphasis is placed upon acquainting the participants with different cultures and traditions. Numerous resources are available for this purpose. We will return later to this topic.

Education is most effective when it remains close to the general life experience of the students. Participants are better equipped to make critical judgments about information with which they have had some experience than with information distant from their lives. Thus, with a first grade class, focusing on salary discrepancies between men and women is not likely to move the process forward. A first grade alternative might be a case study involving a lemonade stand where boys get away with charging more for their product than girls. The children could be asked to guess why the children's parents let the boys charge more. Even young children may suggest that "It's just natural" for the little homemaker girls to make lemonade, whereas boys "need to learn to be breadwinners."

4. DIALECTICAL EXCHANGE WITH TRADITION

The fourth phase roots the process in a significant tradition. Depending on the class, a variety of traditions might be used. In public education, for example, a teacher might encourage a junior high class to read and criticize the Declaration of Independence or the Constitution in light of the previous phase. Are there contradictions between the ideals and beliefs professed in these foundational documents and the realities of American life? If the students could rewrite sections, how would they change them?

The dialectical exchange with tradition should not focus exclusively or even predominantly on negative criticism. The exchange should seek to embody the prophetic dialectics of promise and judgment, appreciation and critique. It should seek to give positive expression to the dreams and visions of the participants and recover the promise and hope of the tradition. A new moral balance should be sought that enhances the possibility of fulfilling these visions.

Students will be ready for a dialectical exchange with tradition to the extent that the previous step was successful in developing independence and the critical skills necessary to maintain it. Dialectical exchange implies that each side in the dialogue is able to maintain distance without collapsing into the other side. Students must not simply conform to the tradition; nor can they simply remake the tradition to conform to their interests and needs. An equilibrium must be reached in which the student is challenged, yet maintains sufficient distance so as to be able to criticize the tradition in light of present experience. When equilibrium is reached, a reconstructed experience has been achieved.

Among Christian educators, the fourth phase provides an opportunity for the Christian Story to be shared.[10] This will usually mean Bible study. The presentation of the Christian

Story can be done through group study, dramatic reading, simulation or role play, lecture, or almost any other technique. The central criterion is that the tradition be presented in a challenging but non-authoritarian manner.

By "dialectical exchange" I mean a process in which the Christian Story is not only presented but also criticized. The ideological suspicion, rooted in present life experience, should be applied to the biblical narrative and prevailing interpretations of it. As Thomas Groome puts it, "If our pilgrimage is to unfold the Vision rather than merely repeat the past, then the present cannot passively inherit and repeat the Story."[11] Just as the Story is used to challenge and sustain the stories of participants, so also must their stories challenge and develop the tradition. As their stories challenge the tradition, a new way to interpret the Bible is developed.

Some readers may be troubled by the idea of criticizing the Bible. It is beyond the scope of this book to provide a detailed discussion of the normative role of the Bible for the life and faith of the church. The Bible is, of course, the wellspring of Christian hope and vision. But the Bible was written by human beings conditioned by their time and place and the inspiration of the Spirit did not remove the historical and human limitations of the writers. Furthermore, the Bible itself reflects the kind of process I am suggesting. The Bible developed over many centuries as later generations reflected on the teachings of earlier generations and sought to continually discern what is of God and what is of human fraility. The most obvious example is Jesus' numerous sayings of the form, "You have heard it said. . . ,but I say onto you. . . ." God's revelation continues today as the Spirit enlightens the present church to the path of human liberation, freedom, and dignity.

There are numerous biblical passages that can serve as a basis for a study of prejudice. The book of Jonah, for example, is a tale about a prophet whose prejudice against the people of Nineveh led him to flee from the Lord; his animosity led to anger against God when the people of Nineveh repented. We can easily imagine the stereotypic, over-generalized thinking that Jonah entertained to denigrate these foreigners.

The New Testament is replete with stories that might be used to study intergroup relations. John 4:7-9, for example, might be used:

> There came a woman of Samaria to draw water. Jesus said to her, "Give me a drink." For his disciples had gone away into the city to buy food. The Samaritan woman said to him, "How is it that you, a Jew, ask a drink of me, a woman of Samaria?" For Jews have no dealings with Samaritans.

In this brief passage, ethnic, religious, and gender prejudice are all in evidence and are forthrightly challenged by Jesus. The background of these deep-seated prejudices, including Old Testament writings against women (e.g. Ex. 20:19; Judg. 19:22-24, Lev. 12:1-5; Deut. 21:10-14) and the breech between Jews and Samaritans makes interesting study material.

The parable of Jesus about the vineyard workers who receive equal pay for unequal work (Matt. 20:1-16) provides an unsettling story about grace and justice. Are we from the wealthy nations similar to those who were "first" hired? Do we think our standard of living is based on our hard work and is consequently deserved? Were those who were hired last in the parable hired at the end of the day because they had been discriminated against? Perhaps this is the meaning of verse 7 where the workers say they haven't been working because "no one has hired us." Victims, but not victimizers, will hear Jesus' concluding words as good news: "So the last will be first, and the first last."

Many other passages are relevant. The story of the woman caught in adultery (Jn. 8:3-11) could be used to discuss the double standard for sexual exploitation. Prejudice against the physically challenged could be discussed with reference to Jesus' healing of the man born blind (Jn. 9:1-3). The narrative of the criminals crucified with Jesus (Lk. 23:39-43) could be used to surface prejudices against the imprisoned. Among the many passages that could be used to open a discussion on prejudice among students are the parables of the Great Feast (Lk. 14:16-24) and the Rich Man and Lazarus (Lk. 16:19-31).

The teacher may find it helpful to briefly recapitulate

the earlier phases when conducting a Bible study. Students may be asked to investigate how a parable of Jesus, for example, contradicted the habitual ways of thinking of his listeners (phase one). In exploring why Jesus turned the tables on his audience, students can discover ways to identify with the individuals or groups who were the outcasts (phase two); the students can move on to criticize the prevailing social practices from the perspective of the outgroup (phase three). Such a process will enable students not only to understand the biblical text in its socio-historical context, but to use it as a resource for their own faith and critical thinking.

The fourth phase, if successfully implemented, will re-create in participants the biblical vision of human wholeness. The Christian Story will be appreciated as the narrative of a God who sides with the downtrodden, who became flesh and dwelt among the poor and suffered the death of a subjugated outlaw. This same God invites disciples to walk the dusty road of solidarity with victims until the dawning of a new day of justice and peace. Armed with a faith rooted in this liberating tradition, participants are prepared to resist the onslaughts of those cultural prejudices that would poison the mind and entomb the soul. The journey from prejudice to pluralism is a resurrection journey toward the ultimate victory of freedom over enslavement, of love over hate, of life over death.

Action, Attitudes and Beliefs

In planning educational programs designed to challenge prejudice, it will be helpful to remember that prejudice has cognitive, affective, and behavioral dimensions. Prejudice involves false beliefs buttressed by overgeneralizations (stereotypes); it reflects an attitude of disparagement; and it often (but not always) manifests itself through oppressive actions. Frequently, educators feel best equipped to deal with the cognitive dimension of prejudice. It is relatively easy to construct a program of cross-cultural studies, for example, that undercuts false ideas about foreign peoples. Proponents of a cognitive approach hope that better understanding will lead to more accepting attitudes and that more open attitudes will eventuate in fewer oppressive actions. Unfortunately, this approach to the problem is like having the caboose lead the train. Dewey, Haan, and Segundo are united in their emphasis that action is the source for change in attitudes and beliefs.

The phases of the educational model just described reflect an action-becoming-thought process. The first phase seeks to elicit habitual action. A common experience is created that forms the basis for later reflection. In the second phase the focus is on attitudes. Participants are led into an identification with the victims of oppression; such an identification has both emotional and cognitive dimensions. During these first two phases, there is no specific attempt to challenge false beliefs. Only in the third phase is a direct discussion of beliefs appropriate. During this phase, a cognitive analysis of the mechanisms of prejudice is undertaken that elaborates and consolidates the information that was *felt* during the previous phase. Finally, during the fourth phase, behaviors, attitudes, and beliefs are wedded together in the context of loyalty to a broader covenant.

USING THE MODEL

A teacher who plans to adopt the teaching approach offered in this chapter is bound to have numerous questions. I cannot anticipate them all, but I would like to offer a few reflections on some of the ones that I think are likely to be asked.

Must I follow the same order of phases?
The sequencing of the phases is important, but not essential. The inventive teacher will inevitably come across situations where a different order is more appropriate. Some teachers, for example, will prefer to begin with the final phase and open with Bible study. Segundo reminds us that the phases are a circle. In a circular process, it is difficult to enter at "the wrong point."

The phases are designed as a guide to an effective implementation of a prejudice-reduction program. I have tried to spell out the logic behind the order suggested. Nonetheless, not only may a phase occasionally be taken out of the usual sequence, but it often may be the case that a teacher will return to an earlier phase rather than proceed to the next. For example, a teacher may begin with a fairly removed prejudice (perhaps a prejudice against immigrants) and after moving through the first two phases, decide to repeat these phases with a prejudice that hits closer to home.

How old must students be to profit from this model?

Any age group that is old enough to participate in educational programs is old enough for the type of education I have described. Prejudices begin early. Even preschool children have rudimentary prejudices, though such prejudices are probably not as fixed in early childhood as psychologists have often maintained; a degree of cognitive sophistication is required for prejudices to solidify and generalize. On the other hand, even greater cognitive sophistication is required for the child to develop a healthy appreciation for human pluralism. Consequently, prejudice-reduction efforts are probably most critical at a time when students are able to replace negative attitudes with informed judgments about human differences and social values. Such cognitive sophistication is probably available beginning at about the third grade, though it is not until early adolescence that pluralistic values can be formulated at an abstract level.

The teacher of young children will probably want to use only abbreviated dimensions of this model. The second phase in particular can be used at any age if the teacher recognizes that there are limits to children's ability to empathize with the feelings and thoughts of another. Rather than working through the four phases, the teacher of younger children will probably want to emphasize a program that discourages the development of prejudice, a goal I will comment on shortly.

What kinds of experiences are most effective?

Direct experience is more powerful than indirect experience. This principle was clearly articulated by Dewey who often recommended that the school be a miniature society and that pupils learn constructive social processes by engaging in social construction. In parallel manner, the best experience for this program is one in which a real prejudice that actually affects the students is brought to awareness. The next best thing to real life is to imitate real life through simulation games, role plays or other dramatic techniques. These, too, can be quite powerful in their impact. Films, stories, pictures, or other media presentations may also be useful. The key in using any technique is Dewey's reminder that a situation is *felt* as problematic before it is formulated into a problem. The pedagogical technique, whether providing direct or indirect experience, should help all participants feel the problematic situation.

What prejudice shall I target?

Since personal experience is preferable to second-hand experience, a prejudice that is evident within the class is probably more powerful than one that is directed against an outgroup not in the class, although dealing with both are important. In deciding where to direct the students' efforts, the teacher will need to decide about the level of trust and openness within the class. It is important not to embarrass or exploit the disadvantaged students for educational gain, but given the opportunity and a climate of trust they will often readily share their feelings of hurt and anger. Generally, the higher the level of trust, the higher the tolerance for stress.

Many factors will influence the amount of stress that a student experiences. Two critical factors in a prejudice-reduction program are (1) whether prejudice is the explicit focus of the lesson, and (2) whether the prejudice under consideration disadvantages some within the class or only unrepresented outgroups. In the following table these two factors are combined to suggest the relative amount of stress the teacher might anticipate from various approaches.

ANTICIPATED STRESS

Teaching Focus:	Prejudice Is Demonstrable:	
	Within Class	*Outside Class Only*
On Prejudice	high	moderate
Not on Prejudice	moderate	low

No one approach is intrinsically better than another but varies with circumstances. As a general guide the following rule can be adopted: Use the approach that produces the most stress without producing defensiveness on the part of participants.

Can I use the model outside the formal classroom?
The model is designed for a wide range of educational settings. It is suitable for public and private school settings, church Sunday School programs, retreats, and other special educational contexts. For example, the model can be used in a parenting class to develop an awareness of sexism; parents can be encouraged to adopt behavioral patterns that discourage gender-role indoctrination.

Should I keep my opinion to myself?
The style of education that has been described emphasizes a discovery approach to teaching. The teacher is not the primary source of information. This approach may cause some difficulties. If the role of the teacher is not to lecture, what should the teacher do when students utter racist remarks or come to conclusions that the teacher finds unconscionable. Teachers may experience a tension between their personal feelings and perceived obligations based on their role. If a student makes a racist comment, the first inclination of the teacher is probably to scold the speaker. Unfortunately, calling a bigot a bigot will not create a warm, accepting human being.

There are sound educational reasons for not correcting or lashing out at every uninformed or biased remark that someone makes. I have outlined an educational process that I believe will promote humanitarian values more effectively than didactic monologues. Nonetheless, silence in the face of open prejudice is also inadvisable. Not to say anything may communicate tacit approval to other listeners. This is a thorny issue that needs careful consideration.

The question is really part of a larger issue. Priests, pastors, ministers, teachers, and other leaders are often reluctant to speak out forthrightly on social issues. For example, at the time when the Reagan administration was seeking further military aid for the "contras" in Nicaragua, many church leaders were fervently opposed to the aid but were reluctant to express their opinion because it would create a rift within their congregation. Such reasoning often reflects an implicit paternalism. It is true that the pulpit is not a soapbox for pastors or priests to express their latest political ideology, but neither should church leadership be a gag that silences dialogue before it begins.

Many church leaders have accepted a definition of ministry that treats the laity as children. In dealing with biblical criticism or with theological, social, or political issues, they are very cautious about offending or disturbing the faith of members. One hears considerable talk about "meeting people where they're at," a phrase borrowed from the field of education where it is used in reference to the need to adapt oneself to the cognitive limitations of children. It may be that in dealing with a highly complex topic, a step-by-step procedure is required to explain one's perspective. Often, however, meeting people where they're at has little to do with complexity and much to do with fundamental values and attitudes. It becomes an excuse for a relationship based on dishonesty and deception.

Dialogue is a key dynamic in education and throughout the structures of the church. But dialogue is profoundly distorted if one participant feels compelled to camouflage his or her true feelings and perspective. One cannot enter dialogue with integrity while "protecting" the other from one's views. The appropriate response to the fact that the other may be offended by your viewpoint is not to "descend to their level" (which is always implied if you cannot trust them to "handle" your view like you believe you can handle theirs), but to open your ears and heart to the pain of their struggle. Genuine dialogue risks pain and struggle, but it carries with it the chance for a healing and growth that is unavailable through distorted exchange.

Back to the classroom. During the first phase of the educational process described above, the teacher is seeking to create an environment where prejudices can be expressed. At such a juncture it is inappropriate to jump in with both feet when prejudices are revealed. However, during the third phase it is entirely appropriate for the teacher to share his or her own feelings, experiences, thoughts, and beliefs. Extreme care should be exercised not to dominate the exchange or to use the natural power that accompanies the teacher's role in a coercive manner, but neither should these considerations exclude the teacher from the partnership of mutual dialogue.

Can I reduce prejudice without reducing pride?

It is sometimes thought that prejudice is the flip side of racial, ethnic, national or religious pride. Pride in one's own group, it is suggested, is premised on believing that one's group is superior to others. If someone is proud to be a Minnesotan, is it because that person is glad not to be a Californian? If I am proud to be white, does that imply that I harbor negative attitudes toward people of color? Sometimes yes, but not necessarily.

All people have a variety of loyalties. We may be loyal to our family, neighborhood, state, nation, race, political party, or any number of other groups. Each group is defined around some common property, whether it be kinship, geography, inherited characteristics, religious beliefs, or ideology.

Prejudices reflect distorted loyalties. When prejudices arise, they represent conflicts or imagined conflicts between the same general type of group. Thus, whites are prejudiced against people of color, Americans against Russians, Christians against Jews. The conflict is not between loyalties to different kinds of groups — a Minnesota chauvinist is prejudiced against members of other states, not against Hindus.

Loyalty to one's city is probably not in conflict with loyalty to one's state or nation. One can experience loyalty toward increasingly broader and more inclusive groups. This broadening of the focus of loyalty is, in essence, what prejudice-reduction is about. When reducing prejudice, the focus is changed to a larger circle of loyalty: humanity. This does not diminish group pride or other loyalties but places them within a more encompassing loyalty that includes those who were previously defined as outside the scope of one's concern. By promoting an identification with the victims of oppression, the common humanity of oneself and the victim is highlighted. Loyalty to the whole human family can place pride in one's various group identifications within a pluralistic vision that appreciates the diversity of human groups.

How can I integrate prejudice-reduction into my curriculum?
The reduction of prejudice frequently will not be the primary curricular goal. Consequently, it is often necessary for the teacher to integrate the model presented here into an already existing curriculum. This is not particularly difficult, but will require some planning and foresight. The phases that have been described concern the process of teaching as much as the specific content. Prejudice-reduction will require that close attention be paid to class structure and teaching style. The model does not work well in highly structured, authority-oriented settings. Students need to accept an active role in their own learning and acceptance of this role may itself take time. If students have not experienced the kind of social interaction, challenging dialogue, and self-motivated inquiry on which the model depends, it may take some preliminary group work before the program can function smoothly.[12]

Let us say the curriculum centers on a study of the Holy Spirit. The first phase, "eliciting a common experience of prejudice," might be accomplished in several ways. As noted before, the most appropriate way may be totally outside the classroom in informal discussions. But the phase can be worked into the lesson as well. Perhaps pictures of a black man, a native American, a white priest, an oriental in yoga position, and an elderly white woman could be placed in front of the class. Students are asked, "If I were to ask each of these people who the Holy Spirit is, how do you think they would answer?" Listen for stereotypic responses that may belie latent or blatant prejudices. Attentive "active listening" may help to uncover these. After eliciting the habitual patterns, it is time to disrupt their smooth functioning. The teacher might begin the next session by placing the pictures back with the introductory remark, "Here are members of St. Anthony's Parish. Today we will talk about ways the Holy Spirit might be experienced in this congregation." By placing these individuals who were probably imagined to reflect quite different groups together under one roof, the habitual way of thinking has been disrupted. Time for the second phase.

The development of self-conscious partiality and commitment might be integrated into a historical study of those groups who have centered their theology on the Holy Spirit. Frequently such sects developed in the context of oppressive social and religious situations. Students could study one such group, for example the movement around Thomas Müntzer in the sixteenth century, to discover why human authority was abandoned in favor of the direct inspiration of the Spirit. Inductive questioning could be used to elaborate how students may feel oppression just as the peasants did who were attracted to Müntzer's program.

The third phase begins when social reality is examined from the perspective of the disadvantaged. Students might seek to explore dynamics within the contemporary church that continue to lead people to avoid the authority of the church in favor of guidance by the Spirit when they perceive a conflict between the two. Many women, for example, may consider the patriarchal structure of the church oppressive and move to various forms of spiritualism. The process must extend beyond a listing of the means by which some are oppressed to critical analysis of why such means are favored by those in power.

Finally, the class could return to the scriptural witness concerning the Holy Spirit and investigate how the early Christians coordinated the need for corporate authority with individual inspiration. Are there dimensions of the biblical testimony that seem oppressive? Are there dimensions that are liberating?

Later in the course the teacher might wish to add several units directly on the topic of prejudice with an action program that will unite the class participants behind a goal to be achieved. Having laid the groundwork through the earlier sessions, the students will likely be ready to deal directly with the topic and possess a base of experience for the meaning of stereotyping, scapegoating, dualism, and other important concepts.

Preventing Prejudice

The four-phase educational model presented at the beginning of this chapter is designed for reducing prejudice. Its thrust is remedial. It would, of course, be better to prevent prejudices from developing in the first place. This noble goal is undoubtably beyond the reach of the teacher and probably even of the educational system as a whole, but striving toward the elimination of the conditions that foster prejudices can still reduce the likelihood that prejudices will become firmly entrenched in the students' personalities. Below are several specific procedures for vaccinating class members against this social disease.

TEACH IN A NON-AUTHORITARIAN MANNER.

If hierarchical dualisms are to be avoided, then the classroom itself must not reflect a rigid hierarchical structure. Models of teaching must be selected that reflect assumptions about human equality and the need for democratic process.[13] Models that emphasize inductive teaching strategies, group work, discussion, role playing or simulation, and joint activity are congruent with these emphases. The reader might wish to review the section on Dewey's approach to education that was presented in Chapter 2 to gain further guidance for democratizing the classroom.

HELP STUDENTS LEARN TO TOLERATE AMBIGUITY.

The "quest for certainty" can be an enemy to tolerant attitudes toward others. It does not affect everyone in the same way, however. People differ in their willingness to live with ambiguity. Unfortunately, we know little about what causes people to have different degrees of tolerance for ambiguity. It may even be a biologically based dimension of personality. Thus the goal of the teacher is not to make everyone highly tolerant, but to increase their level of acceptance of ambiguity.

Appreciation for ambiguity might be encouraged in several ways.[14] The teacher must be careful not to teach with a style that implies that there are always "right" answers. An "appropriate analysis" of an issue is the aim, not achieving the "right solution." Pointing to the diversity of opinions of scholars on a particular issue can also highlight ambiguity. The reality of ambiguity might even be discussed directly, emphasizing its positive contribution to the joy of life.

TEACH FOR MORAL GROWTH.

The morally mature person is less likely to harbor prejudices.[15] An educational program that seeks to deter the development of prejudices will consequently be concerned with the moral growth of participants. At the conclusion of Chapter 3, a brief introduction to moral education from a Haanian perspective was outlined. In summary, an educational approach that seeks to encourage moral growth can be guided by the following three features.[16]

First, it should be interpersonal. The focus of the educational process should be on relationships among people, not on facts, data, or theory except as these help students to understand human relationships. Second, the process should require interdependence. Participants must not only be interacting with one another, but the form this takes should highlight the interdependent nature of human existence. The educational process can foster an awareness of mutual dependence if actions required of students are such that there will be a need to take into account both their interests and needs as well as those of others.

The third principle implied in Haan's model is that dialogue and negotiation must be at the center of the process. An implication of this requirement is that the experience must involve an element of conflict that needs resolution. The emphasis on dialogue must not be mistaken for constant talking. Thomas Groome offers a relevant warning:

> To be dialogical does not mean that the participants are to talk back and forth 'at' each other constantly; such a situation might not be dialogical at all. Paradoxical as it may seem, dialogue begins with one's self. At bedrock it is a conversation with our own biographies, with our own stories and visions. Of course, to be truly known by us, our self-dialogue must be externalized and shared with others, and they, too, must be heard if we are to know more clearly our own stories and visions. Thus dialogue is a subject-to-subject encounter (I/You), in which

two or more people share and hear their reflective stories and visions. By such human dialogue the world can be named and common consciousness created for its transformation.[17]

SUPPORT PARTICIPANTS' SELF-ESTEEM.

Self-esteem has become a major topic in educational circles. A positive view of oneself is important for a multitude of reasons. A child's self-concept influences his or her learning ability, social interaction skills, and many other important facets of experience. For our purposes, promoting high self-esteem is important because those who feel good about themselves have less need to define others in a negative light.

It is actually inappropriate to talk about self-esteem in the abstract as if it were a single dimension. Within each child there is a collection of self-images based on the child's perceptions of competence in a variety of areas. The child who has high self-esteem in sports, for example, will not necessarily feel competent in social relationships or in the classroom. The child who feels secure and competent with peers may not feel so with adults. It is important, therefore, to try to encourage a positive view of self in a variety of tasks and contexts.

Common sense can serve as a fairly reliable guide to promoting self-esteem in class participants. Most of us know what it is that makes others feel good about themselves. The problem is that we tend to get more involved with classroom control or the teaching of subject matter and overlook this vital dimension of learning. Children will develop a positive self-image if they are given encouragement, support, and love; the opposite will be the case if they are treated as a nuisance or subjected to indifference, neglect, and depersonalizing reprimands.

A couple of specific suggestions might spark additional ideas for incorporating self-esteem goals into the curriculum.[18] The positive effect of complimenting a student is multiplied if the child's success can be linked to a pattern of successful behavior. For example, rather than simply noting, "John, you really did a nice job on that drawing," the teacher could elaborate and say, "John, I really like your drawing. I've noticed you often do things well with your hands." In addition, the teacher can strive to bridge different areas: "John, I'm impressed! You're good at drawing, just like you're good at math. You learn things quickly." Most importantly, the teacher needs to create a classroom environment of trust, caring, and openness.

PROMOTE CROSS-CULTURAL UNDERSTANDING.

Knowledge, by itself, does not prevent prejudice. But ignorance will certainly feed the flames of group animosity. To deter prejudice, the teacher should help students gain information about and appreciation for the diverse traditions, practices, and beliefs of various ethnic and cultural groups. Cross-cultural awareness is important because it promotes understanding both of other cultures and of our own. Through cross-cultural studies, cultural differences may come to be seen as a basis for social solidarity, not a sign of division.

The curriculum the teacher employs is an important variable that can influence learners' respect for diversity. Does the curriculum reflect in its graphics and written material a range of human groups? Is it free of stereotyping? Does it highlight the contributions of various groups to the development of church and society? A key question to ask is: "If I were a _____, would this curriculum help me to feel proud of my heritage?"

There are many activities that can supplement the formal curriculum and broaden students' appreciation of cultural diversity. Among the most common are various forms of field trips. A city-rural exchange could be arranged, for instance, in which city youth visit and stay with families in the country one weekend and play host the following. Traveling far, however, is not required. Almost any community has numerous cultural groups and the teacher might seek these out. With a mature class, students could try to investigate the various cultures represented in their own community.

Irving Siegel and James Johnson have proposed an interesting technique for teaching about human diversity that is rooted in Piaget's psychology.[19] These authors suggest a "classification" strategy in which children are encouraged to discover ways groups of people are alike and different from one another. For example, a grade school teacher might write the names of three fictitious European children on the board: Jack Lucido, Mary Smith, and Jack Kommarowski. The children in the class then try to guess what countries these three are from. Following this, the children are asked in what way any two of these children are alike. Suppose Jack Lucido and Jack Kommarowski are said to be alike. The children are then instructed to try to discover all the ways they think they are probably alike. They have the same first name; they probably both go to school; both are boys. Such a brief exercise already communicates to the participants that though these two children may be from different countries they are alike in some respects.

The teacher could then lead the children in an exploration of the significance of the similarities that have been uncovered. The fact that we know both are boys tells us something about naming customs. That they both go to school indicates something of the importance of education in the two cultures. The teacher can then profitably change the focus and ask the children to discover things that Mary Smith and Jack Lucido have in common that are not shared by the two Jacks. Perhaps from their names we might guess that Jack Kommarowski lives in Poland and is the only one who lives under a communist government. Obviously, the exercise could be extended in many ways.

Through exercises of this kind, children learn about the relativity of relationships where all people share some things in common and also have some important differences. Since people can be grouped together in different ways for different purposes, identifying a person with a single group will begin to make less sense. While a diversity of cultures can be appreciated, the individuality of the members of cultural groups will also be recognized.

Cross-cultural education may be particularly difficult for many Christian educators. It is hard for the church to communicate the importance of cultural pluralism when the church itself does not reflect pluralism in its membership and leadership. While the task may be challenging, it is vital since celebration of diversity cuts to the heart of the gospel message. To help broaden the church's cultural base, the Christian educator might want to become involved in decision-making bodies that decide on the nature of the music, art, liturgy, and other visible means of communicating the cultural cast of the parish. Singing Hispanic hymns will not flood the church with new Hispanic members, but the congregation will learn to appreciate other traditions and, with time and the ministry of the Spirit, a climate will be created that will welcome others to participate.

For Discussion

1. Imagine you are working with a group of teenagers who you know have nationalistic prejudices. In addition to the examples offered in this chapter, how might you implement each phase of the teaching model?

2. In the middle section of this chapter, eight questions address the implementation of the teaching model. What additional questions do you have?

3. What suggestions in this chapter did you find most helpful? Why?

4. In what specific ways do you plan to incorporate prejudice prevention as a goal of your teaching?

For Further Reading

Gabelko, Nina Hersch and John U. Michaelis. *Reducing Adolescent Prejudice: A Handbook.* New York: Columbia Teachers College, 1981.

Katz, Judy. *White Awareness: Handbook for Anti-Racism Training.* Norman, Okla.: University of Oklahoma Press, 1978.

Shields, David L. "The Church and the Challenge of Prejudice." *PACE/Professional Approaches for Christian Educators* 16, March 1986.

Shiman, David A. *The Prejudice Book: Activities for the Classroom.* New York: The Anti-Defamation League of B'nai B'rith, 1979.

Notes

CHAPTER ONE_____

1. Jennifer Foote, "Viet 'Outsider' Dies at Hands of a Schoolmate," *San Francisco Examiner,* May 5, 1983.

2. The quote is from a 1983 draft report for the Heritage Foundation.

3. See Lee Hancock, "Fear and Healing in the AIDS Crisis," *Christianity and Crisis,* Vol. 45, No. 11 (June 24, 1985).

4. See Susan Hill Lindley, "Feminist Theology in a Global Perspective," *The Christian Century,* 25 April 1979, 465-469; and Sheila Collins, "Toward a Feminist Theology," *The Christian Century,* 2 August 1972, 796-799.

5. Rosemary Radford Ruether, "The Becoming of Women in Church and Society," *Cross Currents,* Vol. 17 (Fall 1967), 420. For a classic statement of the kind which Ruether is critiquing, see Evelyn Reed, *Woman's Evolution* (New York: Pathfinder Press, 1975). Reed affirms that "the maternal clan system was the original form of social organization," xiii. A similar conclusion is reached by David Bakan who contends that the Hebrew scriptures themselves point to a matriarchal period predating patriarchy, Cf. *And They Took Wives: The Emergence of Patriarchy in Western Civilization* (San Francisco: Harper & Row, 1979). Ruether, however, maintains that "the myth of primitive matriarchy was compounded from two culturally disparate sources: (a) matrilineal and matrilocal culture among primitives, and (b) the predominance of mother-goddess figures in the nonbiblical religions of Mediterranean and Near Eastern peoples," *New Woman/New Earth: Sexist Ideologies and Human Liberation* (New York: The Seabury Press, 1975), 6. For a response to Ruether, see Carol P. Christ, "A Response to Rosemary Ruether, Part II," in *Womanspirit,* Vol. 7, No. 25 (Fall 1980), 11-14. See also, Marymay Downing, "Prehistoric Goddesses: The Cretan Challenge," *Journal of Feminist Studies in Religion,* Vol. I, No. 1 (Spring 1985), 7-22.

6. Ruether, *New Woman/New Earth,* 3-36.

7. Ruether, personal correspondence, September 10, 1982.

8. Ruether, *Sexism and God-Talk: Toward a Feminist Theology* (Boston: Beacon Press, 1983) 161.

9. *Ibid.,* 161.

10. The presence of ethnocentric attitudes in tribal cultures is a commonplace anthropological observation. See Franz Boas, *The Mind of Primitive Man,* (New York: Collier Books, 1938), and Philip Mason, *Patterns of Dominance* (New York: Oxford University Press, 1970).

11. See Carter Heyward, "Ruether and Daly: Theologians Speaking, Sparking, Building and Burning," *Christianity and Crisis,* Vol. 39, No. 5 (2 April 1979), 66-72.

12. Ruether, *Sexism and God-Talk,* 162.

13. *Ibid.,* 161-162.

14. Ruether's analysis is clearly abbreviated and ignores the diversity of male and female roles in early human history. Cf. Frances Dahlberg (ed.), *Woman the Gatherer* (New Haven: Yale University Press, 1981) for a contemporary anthropological treatment of the diversity of gender-roles in early human evolution with an emphasis on the roles of women. An earlier, but still useful treatment, can be found in Elise Boulding's *The Underside of History: A View of Women Through Time* (Boulder, Colorado: Westview Press, 1976).

15. Ruether, *New Woman/New Earth,* 7.

16. See Ruether, "Male Clericalism and the Dread of Women," *The Ecumenist,* Vol. 11, No. 5 (July-August 1973), 65-59. Also, "Home and Work: Women's Roles and the Transformation of Values," *Theological Studies,* Vol. 36 (December 1975), 647-659.

17. Ruether, "The Cult of True Womanhood," *Commonweal* (9 November 1973), 129-130.

18. See Ruether, "Home and Work: Women's Roles and the Transformation of Values," 651. Ruether is here relying on Ann Gordon, et al., "Women in American Society: A Historical Contribution," *Radical America,* Vol. 5, No. 4, (July-August 1971, 25-30.

19. Ruether, "Outlines for a Theology of Liberation," *Dialogue,* Vol. 11 (Autumn 1972), 256-257.

20. Ruether, *New Woman/New Earth,* 108.

21. Ruether, *New Woman/New Earth,* 15.

22. See Ruether, "Feminist Theology in the Academy," *Christianity and Crisis,* Vol. 45, No. 3 (4 March 1985).

23. Ruether, *New Woman/New Earth,* 18.

24. See Ruether, *Faith and Fratricide: The Theological Roots of Anti-Semitism* (New York: The Seabury Press, 1974, 1979).

25. *Ibid.,* 231.

26. See Ruether, "Outlines for a Theology of Liberation," and, "Male Chauvinist Theology and the Anger of Women," *Cross Currents,* Vol. 21 (Spring 1971), 173-185.

27. Ruether, "Male Clericalism and the Dread of Women," 66.

28. See Ruether, "Rich Nations/Poor Nations and the Exploitation of the Earth," *Dialogue,* Vol. 13 (Summer 1974), 201-207.

29. Ruether, "Better Red Than Dead," *The Ecumenist* (November-December 1973), 11.

30. Ruether, *Liberation Theology: Human Hope Confronts Christian History and American Power* (New York: Paulist Press, 1972), 180.

31. Ruether, *New Woman/New Earth,* 119.

32. See Ruether, "Crisis in Sex and Race: Black Theology vs. Feminist Theology," *Christianity and Crisis,* Vol. 34 (15 April 1974), 67-73.

33. Ruether, "Male Chauvinist Theology and the Anger of Women," 183.

34. Lynn White, "The Religious Roots of Our Ecological Crisis," *Science,* Vol. 155 (1967), 1203-1207.

35. See Ruether, "Women, Ecology and the Domination of Nature," *The Ecumenist,* Vol. 14, No. 1 (November-December 1975), 1-5.

36. *Ibid.,* 2.

37. Ruether, "Women, Ecology and the Domination of Nature," 2.

38. *Ibid.,* 4.

39. Ruether, *New Woman/New Earth,* 137.

40. *Ibid.,* 148.

41. See Ruether, "The Personalization of Sexuality," *Christianity and Crisis,* Vol. 33 (16 April 1973), 59-62. An expanded version of the same work is reprinted in *From Machismo to Mutuality: Essays on Sexism and Woman-Man Liberation,* edited by Eugene Bianchi and Rosemary Ruether (New York: Paulist Press, 1976). In *New Woman/New Earth* Ruether spends

a chapter describing the views of Freud, Adler, Horney, Reik and Jung on feminine development. Given Ruether's familiarity with Freud and the post-Freudian psychoanalytic tradition, it is disappointing that she does not isolate repression and projection for specific analysis. Her view of these mechanisms, while unstated, appears to be consistent with the traditional view that they are pervasive and stable personality functions which are difficult to reverse. This view will be challenged in Chapter Three where Haan is shown to argue for a more dynamic and flexible view of defense machanisms. For Freud's view, see the following works: "Repression," in *Collected Works,* Vol. XIV (London: The Hogarth Press, 1946) 141-159; *The Interpretation of Dreams* (London: The Hogarth Press, 1958), Chapter Seven; and, "Introductory Lectures on Psycho-Analysis," *Collected Works,* Vol. XV, 286-303.

42. The term "projection" was introduced by Freud as early as 1894 in his paper, "How Anxiety Originates," *Collected Works,* Vol. I, 189-195. In this early work Freud writes, "The psyche develops the neurosis of anxiety when it feels itself unequal to the task of mastering [sexual] excitation arising endogenously. That is to say, it acts as if it had projected this excitation into the outer world." Two years later Freud elaborated on this view by making clear that projection is a defensive process by which one's own undesirable drives, feelings and sentiments are attributed to the outside world (cf. "On the Defense Neuropsychoses," *Collected Works,* Vol. III, 174-189). The complex coordinations of projection with other defense mechanisms was first clearly discussed by Freud in 1911 in his case history of Schreber, "Psycho-analytic Notes on an Autobiographical Account of a Case of Paronoia," *Collected Works,* Vol. XII, 3-85, especially 59-80. From this case, Freud concluded that the paranoid person has homosexual tendencies that he represses and transforms under the pressure of his superego from "I love him" to "I hate him" (a reaction formation). This hatred he then projects onto the former love object who becomes the persecutor. Ruether emphasizes the coordination between repression and projection, but her analyses of such phenomena as witch hunts and anti-Semitic paranoia would also point to reaction formations. The love object is transformed into a hate object.

43. Ruether, *Sexism and God-Talk,* 162.

44. See R. Terry, *For Whites Only* (Grand Rapids, Mich.: Eerdmans, 1970).

45. Ruether, "Women's Liberation in Historical and Theological Perspective," *Soundings,* Vol. 53 (Winter 1970), 376.

46. Ruether, "Sexism and the Theology of Liberation: Nature, Fall and Salvation as Seen from the Experience of Women," *The Christian Century,* Vol. 90 (12 December 1973), 1226.

47. See Jo Freeman, *Women: A Feminist Perspective* (Palo Alto, California: Mayfield Publishing Co., 2nd ed., 1979). Note especially parts 3 and 4.

48. Ruether, *New Woman/New Earth,* xiii.

49. Mary Daly, *Beyond God the Father, Toward a Philosophy of Women's Liberation* (Boston: Beacon Press, 1973).

50. Carol Christ, "The New Feminist Theology: A Review of the Literature," *Religious Studies Review,* Vol. 3, No. 4 (October 1977), 205.

51. Tertullian, *Woman's Dress.* (PL 1, 1418 b, 19a. *De cultu feminarum, libri duo* 1, 1.).

52. Winnie Davis, *Fantastic Womanhood* (Plano, Tex.: Winone Publishing Guild, 1974), 39, quoting Augustine.

53. Thomas Aquinas, *Summa Theologica,* IQ. 92, A.2 13th Century.

54. Martin Luther, *Table Talk,* No. 727.

55. See Ruether, *New Woman/New Earth,* 111.

56. Ruether, "Ruether on Ruether," *Christianity and Crisis,* Vol. 39, No. 8 (14 May 1979), 126. Ruether elaborated on this view in her article, "Feminism and Patriarchal Religion: Principles of Ideological Critique of the Bible," *Journal For the Study of the Old Testament,"* Issue 22 (February 1982), 54-66. In this work, Ruether contrasts the religion of the "sacred canopy" with prophetic religion. The religion of the sacred canopy is described as a religion which "models religious law and symbols, including the symbols for God, after a patriarchal, hierarchical, ethnocentric and slaveholding society" (55). It is a religion which uses religious symbols to validate the status quo. In contrast, prophetic religion is an evolving religion that combines critique of sacralizing tendencies with historical discernment of contemporary forms of oppression. Ruether admits that both religious tendencies are found in the scriptures, but holds prophetic religion as normative. For Ruether's view on the relationship between women's contemporary experience and their biblical interpretation, see her essay, "Feminist Interpretation: A Method of Correlation," in Letty M. Russell (ed.), *Feminist Interpretation of the Bible* (Philadelphia: The Westminster Press, 1985), 111-124.

57. Ruether, of course, affirms the centrality of Jesus Christ as the liberating core of the Christian tradition. Her most complete reflections on Christology are contained in her book *To Change the World: Christology and Cultural Criticism* (New York: The Crossroad Publishing Company, 1981).

58. Ruether, "Male Clericalism and the Dread of Women," 69. In a later article, Ruether returned to this theme and evaluated the impact of women entering the ministry, (Cf. Ruether, "Women in Ministry: Where Are They Heading," *Christianity and Crisis,* Vol. 43, No. 5 [4 April 1983], 111-116). In this later work, Ruether is less optimistic about the potential

for women to change the patriarchal structures of the institutional church. She suggests the model of "base communities" as an alternative form of spiritual nourishment and worship for women and men with feminist persuasions. These non-clerically oriented communities, which would exist independently of the formal structures of the Church, would still be in interaction with more traditional churches. Ruether writes, "A dialectical relationship between base communities and historical institutions is also necessary if one is serious about the communication and historical transmission of the liberating option of base communities," (114). In anticipation of Segundo's sociology, what Ruether seems to recommend is a specific community for the "minority" church which slowly but progressively transforms the "majority" church. For a careful treatment of the idea of basic communities for Christian women, see Sharon D. Welch, *Communities of Resistance and Solidarity: A Feminist Theology of Liberation* (Maryknoll, N.Y.: Orbis Books, 1985).

59. *Ibid.,* 182-183.

60. Ruether, *New Woman/New Earth,* Chapter One.

61. Ruether, "Sexism and the Theology of Liberation," 1226.

62. Ruether, *New Woman/New Earth,* 31.

63. Ruether advocates a system of economic and political organization designated "communitarian socialism." It is based on the idea that ownership should be socially based, but avoid state control. Cf. "Why Socialism Needs Feminism, & Vice Versa," in *Christianity and Crisis,* Vol. 40, No. 7 (28 April 1980), 103-108. The interested reader should also consult Ruether's two-part series entitled "An American Socialism: A Just Economic Order," *Religious Socialism,* Vol. VII, Nos. 3 & 4 (Summer & Fall, 1983), and Vol. III, Nos. 2 & 3 (Spring & Summer, 1984).

64. It would be difficult to precisely date the historical development of awareness concerning sexual, racial and other forms of human difference. The argument that awareness of sexual differentiation developed earlier than awareness of other forms of human differentiation rests on a logical rather than anthropological argument. The necessity of making sexual distinctions for the very continuation of the species, in addition to the obvious universality of sexual differentiation in all cultures, points toward a very early awareness of sexual distinction. The historical development of prejudice is equally difficult to chronicle. While there is virtually unanimous agreement that sexual asymmetry developed very early, similar evidence for specific racial prejudice is difficult to find (See Frank Snowden Jr., *Before Color Prejudice: The Ancient View of Blacks.* Cambridge: Harvard University Press, 1983).

65. Children develop gender awareness around the age of two or three, depending on the criteria used (see J. Money and A. Ehrhardt, *Man and*

Woman, Boy and Girl: The Differentiation and Dimorphism of Gender Identity from Conception to Maturity. Baltimore: John Hopkins Press, 1972). In contrast, racial awareness does not develop until about age four (for a literature review, see I. Pushkin, et al., "The Development of Racial Awareness and Prejudice in Children," in M.B. Smith (ed.), *Psychology and Race.* Chicago: Aldine Publishing Co., 1973). Once the child learns to discriminate between two classes of objects (or people), the next task is to learn how the classes relate. Children often learn to relate the classes "male" and "female" through the use of hierarchical dualistic stereotypes (see I. Frieze, et al., *Women and Sex Roles: A Social Psychological Perspective.* New York: W.W. Norton and Co., 1978, particularly Chapter Seven). While no empirical confirmation is yet available, on theoretical grounds it might be anticipated that once a hierarchical dualism has been usefully employed to define the relationship between two salient categories of social experience, in this case to comprehend the relation between the sexes, that the same principle of category relation will be generalized as suitable for understanding the relation between other categories of people.

66. See Ruether, *New Woman/New Earth,* 3-4, 182.

67. Ruether, "Women's Liberation in Historical and Theological Perspective," 363.

68. *Ibid.,* 363.

CHAPTER TWO_____

1. John Dewey, *The Quest for Certainty: A Study of the Relation of Knowledge and Action* (New York: G. P. Putnam's Sons, 1929), 3.

2. *Ibid.,* 11-15, and Dewey, *Experience and Nature* (New York: Dover Publications, Inc., 1958), 53.

3. Dewey, *Reconstruction in Philosophy* (Boston: Beacon Press, 1948, 1957), 12-13.

4. Dewey, *Experience and Nature,* 44.

5. For a careful treatment of this dimension of Dewey's thought see chapter one of Dorothy Dunn, *The Problem of Dualism in John Dewey,* unpublished doctoral dissertation, St. Louis University, 1966.

6. Dewey, *Experience and Nature,* 29.

7. Dewey, *Reconstruction in Philosophy,* 150.

8. The term "hypostatization" is used by Dewey to refer to results of inquiry which neglect the context within which the inquiry occurred; the

results then become deceptively independent and falsely self-sufficient. See Dewey, *Experience and Nature,* 167, 184, 195; and *The Quest for Certainty,* 217-219, 238.

9. Dewey, *Experience and Nature,* 24-25, 29.

10. Ruether also points to a hidden value choice when she discusses how dualistic pairs are positively and negatively valued. In her view, the "unchosen" side of these dualisms are not denied "real" existence; rather they are "projected" as the nature of an "other."

11. When this happens, the process of distinguishing aspects within reality is mistaken as a process of differentiating kinds or levels of reality. What is selected for emphasis is seen as discontinuous with the unemphasized elements that are also present in concrete experience. Dewey sees this happening largely as a result of specialization which "breeds familiarity" and tends to "create an illusion." See *The Quest for Certainty,* p. 217. Ruether would add that this is common not only in the process of specialization, but also in the process of coming to self-understanding. For an analysis of how this happened in the process of arriving at a Christian self-understanding, see Ruether, "Anti-Judaism is the Left Hand of Christology," *New Catholic World,* Vol. 217 (January-February 1974), 12-16.

12. See Dewey, *Logic: The Theory of Inquiry,* (New York: Henry Holt and Company, 1938), 105-108.

13. Dewey, *Art as Experience* (New York: Minton, Balch & Company, 1934), 58.

14. Dewey, *Art as Experience,* 147.

15. See Dewey, *Experience and Nature,* 8.

16. Dewey, "The Need for a Recovery of Philosophy," in *Creative Intelligence, Essays in the Pragmatic Attitude.* Reprinted in Richard Bernstein (ed.), *John Dewey: On Experience, Nature and Freedom* (New York: The Liberal Arts Press, 1960).

17. See John Dewey, "Epistemological Realism: The Alleged Ubiquity of the Knowledge Relation," in *Essays in Experimental Logic* (New York: Dover Publications, 1916), 266, 275-276.

18. The definitions of empiricism and rationalism are quite oversimplified and are to some extent inaccurate. They are used only to clarify Dewey's position.

19. Dewey, *Art as Experience,* 124. For an elaboration on this point, see Richard Bernstein, *Praxis and Action: Contemporary Philosophies of Human Activity* (Philadelphia: University of Pennsylvania Press, 1971).

20. Dewey, *Human Nature and Conduct: An Introduction to Social*

Psychology (New York: Henry Holt and Company, 1922. Reprinted with a new introduction, New York: Modern Library, 1930), 63-68.

21. For Dewey, the future is open and cannot be finally determined. This protects Dewey's philosophy against dogmatism. Another implication, which Dewey clearly recognized, is that truth in an absolute or ultimate sense is beyond human reach. Nonetheless, the concept of truth is not thereby meaningless. While ultimate truth cannot be ascertained, a reflective consensus about the meaning of experience points the direction toward truth. Dewey quotes with approval the definition of truth offered by Peirce: "The opinion which is fated to be ultimately agreed to by all who investigate is what we mean by the truth, and the object represented by this opinion is the real." See Dewey, *Logic: The Theory of Inquiry,* 245, n. 6.

22. Dewey, *Human Nature and Conduct,* 196-207.

23. Dewey, *Art as Experience,* 217.

24. Dewey's well-known definition of inquiry is "the controlled or directed transformation of an indeterminate situation into one that is so determinate in its constituent distinctions and relations as to convert the elements of the original situation into a unified whole." See Dewey, *Logic: The Theory of Inquiry,* 104-105.

25. See Dewey, *Human Nature and Conduct,* 55-69.

26. See Dewey, *Art as Experience,* Chapter One.

27. *Ibid.,* 326.

28. *Ibid.,* 326.

29. John Dewey, "Theory of Valuation," *International Encyclopedia of United Science,* Volume 2, No. 4 (Chicago: University of Chicago Press, 1939), 16-17, 22. Dewey's view that values are experimentally verifiable is problematic. While it may be the case that the future consequences of operating by a particular value may be more or less predicted, the value of those consequences cannot be established except with reference to consequences of the consequences. Dewey is faced with an infinite regress unless he can establish a criterion by which one consequence can be said to be better than another, apart from an appeal to further consequences. Dewey did not face this issue squarely because he felt that there was common agreement about what is desirable; the problem, in his view, was in implementing agreed upon values, not in reaching a consensus about what is to be valued.

Related to this issue is the question of commitment. Dewey was committed to harnessing the capacity of intelligence for the reconstruction of the world in keeping with human values. His whole instrumentalist philosophy can be viewed as an attempt to delineate why intelligence functions properly when it systematically directs action in the process of transforming the environment to create a more desirable world. This commitment raises two questions. The first question is whether Dewey's faith in intelligence is founded. The hypothesis that the systematized use of intelligence can create an environment that is more human and humane than before can itself be evaluated by Dewey's instrumental view of truth. Applying this test, many people today, living in the nuclear shadow and on the precipice of environmental destruction, may conclude Dewey's hypothesis has failed.

The second question relates to the earlier observation. Dewey's commitment to intelligence-guided action in pursuit of social transformation rests on a value-assumption that in final analysis lies outside his philosophical theory. As Frederick Copleston noted: "In the long run Dewey's philosophy rests on a judgment of value, the value of action. One can, of course, base a philosophy on a judgment or on judgments of value. But it is desirable that in this case the judgments should be brought into the open. Otherwise one may think, for example, that the instrumentalist theory of truth is simply the result of a dispassionate analysis." *A History of Philosophy,* Volume Eight, Part II. (Garden City, New York: Doubleday & Company, Image Books, 1967), 138. While I accept Dewey's value of action, I do not accept it as self-evident. In Chapter Four I present the theological framework which grounds this value in a historical tradition that witnesses a path toward meaningful existence.

30. Dewey, *Reconstruction in Philosophy,* 183.

31. Dewey, *Democracy and Education,* 141.

32. *Ibid.,* 287-288.

33. *Ibid.,* 274.

34. *Ibid.,* 76.

35. *Ibid.,* 19-20.

36. *Ibid.,* 83, 86.

37. *Ibid.,* 333.

38. *Ibid.,* 250ff.

39. *Ibid.,* 155.

40. *Ibid.,* 232.

41. See *How We Think,* 106-118; and *Logic: The Theory of Inquiry,* 104-118. The numbering of the stages varies in the writings of Dewey. One reason why Dewey may have been inconsistent in his numbering of the stages was to intentionally highlight their continuity and integration and discourage a wooden, lifeless application.

CHAPTER THREE_____

1. See Albert Bandura, *Social Learning Theory* (Englewood Cliffs, N.J.: Prentice-Hall, 1977). Bandura's clear preference for environmental factors over the innate structuring capacities of the individual can be seen in the following quote in which Bandura explains the social learning approach to self-directed activity: "Another distinguishing feature of social learning theory is the prominent role it assigns to self-regulatory capacities. By arranging environmental inducements, generating cognitive supports, and producing consequences for their own actions, people are able to exercise some measure of control over their own behavior. To be sure, the self-regulatory functions are created and occasionally supported by external influences" (p. 13).

2. See H. Gruber and J. Voneche, *The Essential Piaget* (New York: Basic Books, 1977) for an excellent collection of the works by the foremost structural developmental theorist.

3. Jean Piaget, *The Moral Judgment of the Child* (New York: Free Press, 1932).

4. See Lawrence Kohlberg, *Essays on Moral Development. Vol. II. The Psychology of Moral Development* (San Francisco: Harper & Row, 1984).

5. See Norma Haan, *Coping and Defending: Processes of Self-Environment Organization* (San Francisco: Academic Press, 1977) 10-12.

6. See the following works by Jean Piaget: *The Psychology of Intelligence* (London: Routledge & Kegan Paul, 1950); *The Child's Conception of Physical Causality* (Paterson, New Jersey: Littlefield, Adams, 1960); *The Moral Judgment of the Child, Structuralism* (New York: Basic Books, 1970); and *The Child and Reality* (New York: Grossman, 1973).

7. Haan, "Proposed Model of Ego Functioning: Coping and Defense Mechanisms in Relationship to I.Q. Change," *Psychological Monographs,* Vol. 77, No. 8 (Whole No. 571), 1963, 1.

8. See T. C. Kroeber, "The Coping Functions of Ego Mechanisms," in R. White (ed.), *The Study of Lives* (New York: Atherton, 1963).

9. Haan, "A Tripartite Model of Ego Functioning, Values and Clinical and Research Applications," *Journal of Nervous and Mental Disease,* Vol. 148, No. 1 (1969), 14-30.

10. Haan, *Coping and Defending,* 34.

11. Of course other reasons for discrepancy between competence and performance could be identified; for example, forced compliance. These

other reasons, however, belong more to the domains of sociology or politics than psychological theory.

12. See Kohlberg, "Stage and Sequence: The Cognitive-Developmental Approach to Socialization," in D. A. Goslin (ed.), *Handbook of Socialization Theory and Research* (New York: Rand McNally, 1969); and, Kohlberg, *The Philosophy of Moral Development: Moral Stages and the Idea of Justice* (San Francisco: Harper & Row, 1981).

13. For a description of the characteristics of a stage, see Kohlberg, *The Philosophy of Moral Development,* 57-58. Kohlberg is indebted to Piaget for his understanding of stage. See Piaget, "The General Problem of the Psychological Development of the Child," in J.M. Tanner and B. Inhelder, (eds.), *Discussions on Child Development: A Consideration of the Biological, Psychological, and Cultural Approaches to the Understanding of Human Development and Behavior,* Vol. 4 (New York: International Universities Press, 1960), especially 13-15.

14. Kohlberg, "From Is to Ought: How to Commit the Naturalistic Fallacy and Get Away with it in the Study of Moral Development," in T. Michel (ed.), *Cognitive Development and Epistemology,* (New York: Academic Press, 1971). Kohlberg relies heavily on the moral philosopher John Rawls for the philosophical justification of justice as the ultimate ethical criterion. To explain his view, Rawls develops the heuristic notion of an "original position" of equality prior to society. According to Rawls, "among the essential features of this situation is that no one knows his place in society, his class position or social status, nor does anyone know his fortune in the distribution of natural assets," (Rawls, *A Theory of Justice.* Cambridge, Mass.: Harvard University Press, 1971), 12. Behind this "veil of ignorance," Rawls suggests, all rational individuals would choose to order society in accordance with the principles of justice that Rawls explicates. Kohlberg (See *The Philosophy of Moral Development,* Chapter Five) extends Rawls' heuristic device of the "original position" into the similar idea of "ideal role-taking" and claims that it can be empirically found in Stage Six individuals. Kohlberg thus claims the support of Rawls' moral theory for his empirical, psychological theory of moral development. This, however, is inconsistent with Rawls' own disclaimer that his theory, "may not work for the rules and practices of private associations or for those of less comprehensive social groups," (p. 8). This is precisely Haan's point—that the moral reasoning of everyday life is not the same as the formal deductive reasoning used to analyze the distribution of goods and services in society. In everyday morality, it is more appropriate to wear a "cloak of knowledge" than a "veil of ignorance." The more information about the interests, needs, concerns, hopes, and fears of the individuals involved in moral exchange the better.

15. Kohlberg, "Education for Justice: A Modern Statement of the Platonic View," in T. Sizer (ed.), *Moral Education: Five Lectures* (Cambridge, Mass.: Harvard University Press, 1970). This article is reprinted in

Kohlberg's book, *The Philosophy of Moral Development* with the title changed to "Education for Justice: A Modern Statement of the Socratic View." The change from "Platonic View" to "Socratic View" was made to indicate that it draws on Socrates' views as portrayed by Plato.

16. R. L. Krebs, "Some Relationships Between Moral Judgment, Attention, and Resistance to Temptation," unpublished doctoral dissertation, University of Chicago, 1967; and A. L. Lockwood, "Stages of Moral Development and Students' Reasoning about Public Policy Issues," in L. Kohlberg (ed.), *Recent Research in Moral Development,* unpublished.

17. N. Haan, B. Smith and J. Block, "Moral Reasoning of Young Adults," *Journal of Personality and Social Psychology,* Vol. 10 (1968), 183-201; and C. B. Holstein, "Parental Determinants of the Development of Moral Judgment," unpublished doctoral dissertation, University of California at Berkeley, 1968.

18. Kohlberg and Elliot Turiel, "Moral Development and Moral Education," in G. S. Lesser (ed.), *Psychology and Educational Practice* (Glenview, Ill.: Scott Foresman, 1971), 410-465.

19. Carol Gilligan and Mary Belenky, "A Naturalistic Study of Abortion Decisions," in R. Selman and R. Yando (eds.), *Clinical-Developmental Psychology,* (San Francisco: Jossey-Bass, 1980).

20. Carol Gilligan, *In a Different Voice: Psychological Theory and Women's Development* (Cambridge, Mass.: Harvard University Press, 1982).

21. Haan, "Two Moralities in Action Contexts: Relationship to Thought, Ego Regulation and Development," *Journal of Personality and Social Psychology,* Vol. 36 (1978), 286-305.

22. Haan, "A Manual of Interpersonal Morality," unpublished document, Institute of Human Development, Berkeley, 1977, 6-11.

23. Haan, "An Interactional Morality of Everyday Life," in N. Haan, R. Bellah, P. Rabinow, and W. Sullivan (eds.), *Social Science as Moral Inquiry* (New York: Columbia University press, 1983), 234.

24. A similar point is made by Craig Dykstra in the context of his penetrating critique of Kohlberg's theory. See Dykstra, *Vision and Character: A Christian Educator's Alternative to Kohlberg* (New York: Paulist Press, 1981).

25. Haan, "A Manual of Interpersonal Morality," 6-11. For her understanding of moral "truth," Haan is indebted to Habermas' work on discursive justification which forms part of his broader theory of communicative competence (See Jurgen Habermas, "Toward a Theory of Communicative Competence," *Inquiry,* Vol. 13 (1970), 360-375). According to this model, every utterance makes implicit "validity claims" which can

ultimately be justified only in an "ideal speech situation." This consensus theory of truth holds that rational agreement can be reached only when there is opportunity in the assumption of dialogue roles.

26. *Ibid.,* 9-10.

27. The interested reader is referred to the following works: David Shields and Brenda Bredemeier, "Sport and Moral Growth: A Structural Developmental Perspective," in W. Straub and J. Williams, *Cognitive Sport Psychology* (Lansing, N.Y.: Sport Science Associates, 1984); and Bredemeier and Shields, "Values and Violence in Sports," *Psychology Today,* October 1985.

28. Mary Daly, *Beyond God the Father: Toward a Philosophy of Women's Liberation* (Boston: Beacon Press, 1973), 2.

29. Sheila Collins, *A Different Heaven and Earth* (Valley Forge, Pa.: The Judson Press, 1974).

30. D. Zimmerman and C. West, "Sex Roles, Interruptions and Silences in Conversation," in B. Thorne and N. Henley (eds.), *Language and Sex* (Rowley, Mass.: Newbury House, 1975).

31. Elizabeth Aries, "Interaction Patterns and Themes of Males, Females, and Mixed Groups," *Small Group Behavior,* Vol. 7, No. 1 (1976), 1-8.

32. Lynette Hirschman, "Analysis of Support and Assertive Behavior in Conversation," paper presented at the Linguistic Society of America, July 1974; and P. Fishman, "Interactional Shitword," *Heresies,* Vol. 2 (1977), 99-101.

33. Haan, "A Manual of Interpersonal Morality," 14-19.

34. *Ibid.,* 19-22.

35. Shields, "Education for Moral Action," *Religious Education,* Vol. 75, No. 2 (March-April 1980), 129-141.

CHAPTER FOUR_____

1. Paulo Freire, *Pedagogy of the Oppressed* (New York: Seabury Press, 1970).

2. By suggesting theological method as a central resource for religious educators, I seek a middle ground between those who advocate the theological and social science viewpoints. A sound theological method coordinates the contributions that various disciplines offer to the development of religious commitment and is itself rooted in a comprehensive understand-

ing of relevant epistemological issues. The classic statement of the "theological position" in religious education is Randolph Crump Muller's, *The Clue to Christian Education* (New York: Charles Scribner's Sons, 1952). The idea that theology provides the clue to Christian Education has been challenged by James Michael Lee and others who argue for a "social science" approach to religious education. See J.M. Lee, "The Authentic Source of Religious Instruction," In N. Thompson, ed., *Religious Education and Theology* (Birmingham Ala.: Religious Education Press, 1982).

3. Jose Miguez Bonino, *Doing Theology in a Revolutionary Situation* (Philadelphia: Fortress Press, 1975), 70.

4. Walbert Buhlmann, *The Coming of the Third Church: An Analysis of the Present and Future of the Church* (Maryknoll, N.Y.: Orbis Books, 1977).

5. The roots of liberation theology can be traced to Vatican II. This council affirmed the need to insert the church more directly into the modern world. Post-conciliar documents like Pope Paul VI's *Popolorum Progressio* (especially paras. 49 and 54) contain strong statements about the relationship between the rich and the poor, a central theme in liberation theology. Also influential were political theologians such as Moltmann and Metz. Joseph Powers has traced the roots of Gutierrez' work in the theology of Karl Rahner and Edward Schillebeeckx via the theology of Metz with whom Gutierrez studied. ("Some Roots of Gutierrez' Liberation Theology in Recent Roman Catholic Theology," presented to the Pacific Coast Theological Society, April 10, 1974). Neely Preston has also traced roots of liberation thought to Protestant sources, including Bonhoeffer, Moltmann, Pannenberg, and von Rad. ("Protestant Antecedents of the Latin American Theology of Liberation," unpublished doctoral dissertation, The American University, 1977).

The beginning point of an indigenous Latin American liberation theology can be dated at least back to the second conference of Latin American bishops (CELAM), held at Medellin, Colombia, during the summer of 1968. Many themes which are central to liberation theology—such as the preferential option for the poor, the reality of class conflict, the theory of dependency, and the recognition of institutional violence—are present in the sixteen documents which form the conclusions of Medellin. See *The Church in the Present-Day Transformation of Latin America in the Light of the Council: Second General Conference of Latin American Bishops* (Washington, D.C.: National Conference of Catholic Bishops, 1979).

The designation "liberation theology" has many meanings. It is sometimes interpreted to mean any theology in which justice and human freedom are central concerns. In this book I focus on Latin American liberation theology and I am emphasizing areas of general agreement. Specific theologians may take exception to one or more of the points that I present. Nonetheless, I have developed the six-point characterization in a manner that I believe is consistent with Segundo's work on theological method.

6. Robert McAfee Brown, *Theology in a New Key: Responding to Liberation Themes* (Philadelphia: The Westminster Press, 1978). The designation "traditional" theology does not refer to any particular theologian or even any specifiable school of theology. Frequently, my comments regarding traditional theology are guilty of oversimplification. The purpose of the phrase "traditional theology" is to bring out the distinctive elements of liberation theology.

7. Gutierrez writes: "It is time to open the Bible and read it from the perspective of 'those who are persecuted in the cause of right' (Matt. 5:10), from the perspective of the condemned human beings of this earth—for, after all, theirs is the kingdom of heaven. It is for them that the gospel is destined, it is to them that the gospel is preferentially addressed," in *The Power of the Poor in History* (Maryknoll, N.Y.: Orbis Books, 1983), 4.
The "oppressed" would be a better designation if I were discussing liberation theology in global perspective. Black liberation theologians begin from the experience of blacks suffering under white racism; feminist theologians start with the experience of women in sexist society. Other starting points might also be identified. Each beginning point, while unique, would have certain things in common with the other beginning points. The interstructured nature of oppression makes cooperative effort among the oppressed "nonpersons" of the world possible.

8. The phrase "preferential option for the poor" is contained both in the documents of Medellin and Puebla. This option, however, does not imply exclusivity as Gutierrez explains: "Solidarity with the poor, with their struggles and their hopes, is the condition of an authentic solidarity with everyone—the condition of a universal love that makes no attempt to gloss over the social oppositions that obtain in the concrete history of peoples," *The Power of the Poor in History,* 129.

9. Gustavo Gutierrez, *A Theology of Liberation* (Maryknoll, N.Y.: Orbis Books, 1973), particularly Chapter Thirteen.

10. *Ibid.,* 300.

11. Gutierrez, *We Drink From our own Wells: The Spiritual Journey of a People* (Maryknoll, N.Y.: Orbis Books, 1984), 125.

12. Gutierrez, "Liberation Praxis and Christian Faith," in Rosino Gibellini (ed.), *Frontiers of Theology in Latin America* (Maryknoll, N.Y.: Orbis Books, 1979), 16.

13. Quoted in Brown, *Theology in a New Key,* 61.

14. See Paulo Freire, *Education for Critical Consciousness* (New York: The Seabury Press, 1973).

15. Jon Sobrino, *Christology at the Crossroads* (Maryknoll, N.Y.: Orbis Books, 1978), 223.

16. See Susan Langer, *Philosophy in a New Key: A Study in the Symbolism of Reason, Rite, and Art,* third edition, (Cambridge: Harvard University Press, 1957), 4.

17. Sobrino, *Christology at the Crossroads,* Chapter Two.

18. Gutierrez, *A Theology of Liberation,* 25-43.

19. This position has not been frequent in Christian theology, though it was sometimes evident in the Social Gospel movement of American Protestantism in the late nineteenth and early twentieth centuries; see Robert White, Jr. and C. Howard Hopkins, *The Social Gospel: Religion and Reform in Changing America* (Philadelphia: Temple University, 1976). The "theology of revolution" also adopted political change as its primary metaphor for salvation; see Harvey Cox (ed.), *The Church Amid Revolution* (New York: Association Press, 1967).

20. Many popular preachers have adopted psychological liberation as their basic model of salvation. See, for example, Robert Schuller, *Move Ahead With Possibility Thinking* (New York: Jove Publications, 1984).

21. This, of course, has been the most frequent Christian interpretation of salvation. Its dangers lie in excessive individualism and spiritualism.

22. Miguez Bonino, *Doing Theology in a Revolutionary Situation,* 70.

23. In Gibellini (ed.), *Frontiers of Theology in Latin America,* 10.

24. *Ibid.,* 27. A degree of political maturity is thus prerequisite for an adequate understanding of the gospel. As Gutierrez notes, "Only an appreciable degree of political maturity will enable us to get a real grasp on the political dimension of the gospel, and keep us from reducing it to a system of social service, however sophisticated, or to a simple task of 'human advocacy.'" *The Power of the Poor in History,* 68.

25. This is not to suggest that Latin American liberation theologians have accepted Marxist analysis uncritically. See Jose Miguez Bonino, *Christians and Marxists: The Mutual Challenge to Revolution* (Grand Rapids, Mich.: William B. Eerdmans Publishing Co., 1976). Also, Juan Luis Segundo, *The Liberation of Theology* (Maryknoll, N.Y.: Orbis Books, 1976) 57-82.

26. See *To Break the Chains of Oppression: Results of an Ecumenical Study Process on Domination and Dependence,* World Council of Churches, Geneva, 1975. Also, Richard Dickinson, *To Set at Liberty the Oppressed: Towards an Understanding of Christian Responsibilities for Development/Liberation,* Commission on the Churches' Participation in Development, World Council of Churches, Geneva, 1975, especially Chapter Three.

27. See Gutierrez, *A Theology of Liberation,* 38, n. 14. Elsewhere Gutierrez elaborates: "The poor person does not exist as an inescapable fact of destiny. His or her existence is not politically neutral, and it is not ethically

innocent. The poor are a by-product of the system in which we live, and for which we are responsible.....Hence the poverty of the poor is not a call to generous relief action, but a demand that we go and build a different social order....Hence we speak of social revolution, not reform; of liberation, not development; of socialism, not modernization of the prevailing system." *The Power of the Poor in History,* 44-45. For an elaboration on the role that the concept of "dependency" plays in liberation thought, see Vitor Westhelle, "Dependency Theory: Some Implications for Liberation Theology," *Dialog,* Vol. 20 (Fall 1981), 293-299.

28. Segundo, *The Liberation of Theology,* 37, n. 37.

29. *Ibid.,* 22-25. This critique of "development" theories might be adapted to apply to Dewey's theory of experience and growth. Dewey, like the developmentalists, tended to underplay the conflictive nature of reality. This is evident in Dewey's inconsistent view regarding the distortions brought about in experience as a result of class divisions. At times Dewey seems clear that class divisions produce distorted and one-sided experiences (See *Democracy and Education,* 84-86; *Experience and Nature,* 165; and *Art as Experience,* 20-21, 247-248). Most of the time, however, Dewey glosses over the differences in experience in favor of describing experience in generic terms as if his analysis is equally appropriate and adequate for all people. The norm of "growth" is viewed, from this latter perspective, as a process open to all people equally. Dewey displays more commonality with the North American Social Gospel movement, which was contemporaneous with his work, than with Latin American liberation thought. For a comparison of liberation theology and the Social Gospel movement, see "Liberation Theology and the Social Gospel: Variations on a Theme," *Theological Studies,* Vol. 41, no. 4 (December 1980), 668-683.

30. Phillip Berryman, "Latin American Liberation Theology," *Theological Studies,* Vol. 34 (1973), 365.

31. Quoted in Berryman, *ibid.,* 366. Gutierrez elaborates this point by suggesting the need for a rewriting of history from this perspective: "We have indicated that this history in conflictual. But it is not enough to say this. One must insist on the necessity of a rereading of history. History, where God reveals himself and where we proclaim him, must be reread from the side of the poor. The history of humanity has been written 'with a white hand,' from the side of dominators. History's losers have another outlook." *The Power of the Poor in History,* 201.

32. Gutierrez, "Liberation Praxis and Christian Faith," 27.

33. Jon Sobrino, *The True Church and the Poor* (Maryknoll, N.Y.: Orbis Books, 1984), especially Chapter Seven.

34. This is one of the most frequent points made in the writings of liberation theologians. See Hugo Assmann, *Theology for a Nomad Church*

(Maryknoll, N.Y.: Orbis Books, 1975), 74-86 and Gutierrez, *A Theology of Liberation*, 6-11. The focus on praxis has led some critics to charge that liberation theologians pay inadequate attention to sophisticated metaphysical speculation. Schubert Ogden, for example, suggests that liberation theology deals with the "existential meaning of God for us without dealing at all adequately with the metaphysical being of God in himself. *Faith and Freedom: Toward a Theology of Liberation* (Nashville: Abingdon, 1979), 34. The validity of Ogden's critique, however, rests on acceptance of the classical view that theology is "faith seeking understanding." It is just such a claim that is being challenged.

35. Quoted in Brown, *Theology in a New Key*, 71.

36. Assmann, *Theology for a Nomad Church*, 62-63.

37. Segundo, *The Liberation of Theology*, 98-101.

38. Gutierrez, "Liberation, Theology and Proclamation," in Geffre and Gutierrez, *The Political and Mystical Dimensions of Christian Faith*, 70.

39. See Raul Vidales, "Methodological Issues in Liberation Theology," in Gibellini (ed.), *Frontiers of Theology in Latin America*, 34-57.

40. See Gutierrez, *A Theology of Liberation*, 168-178; Segundo, *The Liberation of Theology*, 77-81. The intimate connection between theological method and Christology, from a Latin American perspective, can be seen from the way the two are consistently linked. For example, the August-September 1975 issue of *Estudios Centroamericanos* (San Salvador) is devoted to "theological method and Latin American Christology." Gutierrez explicitly makes the connection when he writes, "The great hermeneutical principle of faith, and hence the basis and foundation of all theological reasoning, is Jesus Christ" (*The Power of the Poor in History*, 61). The reason that Christology has played such a prominent role in the development of method is that it was an analysis of Christology which paved the way for recognition that action in solidarity with the poor is the "first step" on which theology builds as a "second step" Gutierrez can even define the incarnation as "God become poor." (*The Power of the Poor in History*, 13).

Noticeably absent from this brief Christological survey is the work of Jon Sobrino, *Christology at the Crossroads* (Maryknoll, N.Y.: Orbis Books, 1978). This work is a penetrating, systematic effort to confront the multitude of problems of a Christology understood from within a revolutionary context. The central thrust of Sobrino's work is to shift Christological questions away from abstractions about who Jesus is in himself, to questions pertaining to the preconditions for doing theology. Sobrino writes, "Jesus, strictly speaking, does not reveal the Father. . . . Jesus reveals the Son. And if we view Jesus in terms of his concrete history, we can say that what Jesus reveals to us is the way of the Son, the way one becomes Son of God" (105). The way one enters into relation with God, Sobrino argues, is by living and acting in solidarity with the oppressed: "the privileged meditation of God every day continues to be the real cross of the oppressed" (222-223). While Sobrino's work is helpful for understanding Christology from a Latin American perspective, it has also been critiqued as unduly influenced by European theology. See J. L. Sugundo, *The Historical Jesus of the Synoptics* (Maryknoll, N.Y.: Orbis, 1985), 190, n. 2.

41. For a brief biographical outline, see Gibellini (ed.), *Frontiers of Theology in Latin America*, 311-313.

42. The primary "newness" concerned the beginning of theology in praxis. Rather than beginning with the "products of reflection," as Dewey would say, the theologian begins with the problems of ordinary experience. In this case the problems of ordinary experience are those problems confronted in working for the liberation of the oppressed.

43. Gutierrez, *A Theology of Liberation*, 202.

44. Juan Luis Segundo, *A Theology for Artisans of a New Humanity,* published in five volumes: Vol. I: *The Community Called Church;* Vol. II: *Grace and the Human Condition;* Vol. III: *Our Idea of God;* Vol. IV: *The Sacraments Today;* and Vol. V: *Evolution and Guilt* (Maryknoll, N.Y.: Orbis Books, 1973-1974).

45. Juan Luis Segundo, *The Liberation of Theology* (Maryknoll, N.Y.: Orbis Books, 1976).

46. Juan Luis Segundo, *Jesus of Nazareth Yesterday and Today,* to be published in five volumes. To date only two volumes have appeared in English: Vol. I: *Faith and Ideologies* (Maryknoll, N.Y.: Orbis Books, 1984); Vol. II: *The Historical Jesus of the Synoptics* (Maryknoll, N.Y.: Orbis Books, 1985).

47. Segundo, *Our Idea of God,* Chapter Four.

48. *Ibid.,* 155.

49. See Segundo, *The Liberation of Theology,* 77-81, 162ff.

50. *Ibid.,* 77-81.

51. *Ibid.,* 8. Gutierrez also refers to a hermeneutic circle. He writes: "This is the basic circle of all hermeneutics: from the human being to God and from God to the human being, from history to faith and from faith to history, from love of our brothers and sisters to the love of the Father, and from the love of the Father to the love of our brothers and sisters, from human justice to God's holiness and from God's holiness to human justice, from the poor person to God and from God to the poor person" *(The Power of the Poor in History,* 15).

52. Segundo, *The Liberation of Theology,* 8-9. In a creative suggestion, Segundo keeps his circle open to new information by ensuring that

all phases are subject to critique; this he does by encouraging dialogue with humanistic atheists. For Segundo, the final appeal for the correctness of a particular action or program must be in terms of the welfare of those who will be affected by the action or program. One cannot jump out of history and appeal to divine guidance, whether in the form of direct illumination or "authentic" interpretation of a particular normative source. To do so is to divinize an ideology, it is to engage in idolatry. To guard against a tendency to become dogmatic in one's religious perspective, Segundo holds to the value of dialogue with those outside the Church. (See *The Community Called Church*, 124-128).

53. Segundo, *The Liberation of Theology*, 9.

54. *Ibid.*, Chapter Three.

55. *Ibid.*, 94.

56. As one illustration, in the discussion of theological method in John Macquarrie's *Principles of Christian Theology* (New York: Charles Scribner's Sons, 1977) there is no explicit reference to the social position of the theologian. On the contextual rootedness of all theology, see Robert McAfee Brown, "Context Affects Content: The Rootedness of All Theology," *Christianity and Crisis*, Vol. 37, No. 2 (July 18, 1977), 170-174.

57. This point has been made by numerous Third World and feminist theologians. One of the earliest statements was by Valerie Saiving, "The Human Situation: A Feminine View," *The Journal of Religion* (April, 1960).

58. Gutierrez writes: "Exegetes...are members of a very exclusive, expensive club. To become a member of this club you have to have assimilated Western culture—German and Anglo-Saxon culture, acutally—because exegesis in the Christian churches of today is so closely tied in with it." *The Power of the Poor in History*, 4. For the same point from a feminist perspective, see Jo Freeman, *Women: A Feminist Perspective*, 2nd edition, (Palo Alto, Cal.: Mayfield Publishing Co., 1979), Chapters Three and Four.

59. See Segundo, *The Community Called Church*, 1973.

60. Segundo, *The Liberation of Theology*, 208-237.

61. Segundo, *The Community Called Church*, Chapter One.

62. *Ibid.*, 78-86.

63. Cf. Segundo, *Faith and Ideologies*, especially Chapter One.

64. *Ibid.*, 3-10.

65. *Ibid.*, 16.

66. Segundo, *The Liberation of Theology*, 107. Also, Segundo, *Faith and Ideologies*, 10-15.

67. Segundo, *Faith and Ideologies,* 70-78.

68. Segundo, *The Liberation of Theology,* Chapters Three and Four.

69. Segundo, *The Liberation of Theology,* 82.

70. Segundo is here making use of Assmann's prologue to *Habla Fidel Castro Sobre Lose Cristianos Revolucionarios* (Montevideo: Tierra Nueva, 1972). Assmann, however, suggests a number of positive contributions that Christians can make to the revolutionary process, though he views their contributions as limited primarily to the "super-structure." (See Assmann, *Theology for a Nomad Church,* 139-145).

71. Segundo, *The Liberation of Theology,* 101.

72. *Ibid.,* 108-109.

73. *Ibid.,* 87.

74. John Dewey, *A Common Faith* (New Haven: Yale University Press, 1934), 9.

75. *Ibid.,* 33.

76. Donald A. Piatt, "Dewey's Logical Theory," in Paul A. Schilpp (ed.), *The Philosophy of John Dewey* (Evanston, Ill: Northwestern University, 1939), 106.

77. Dewey's claim that values are subject to experimental validation cannot be substantiated (see Chapter Two, note 143). This problem is particularly acute when we ask a question such as, "To what ideals is it worth committing one's life?" Segundo illustrates the dilemma by analyzing Albert Camus' play, *Caligula.* (See *The Liberation of Theology,* 103-104 and *Faith and Ideologies,* 3-10). The Roman emperor, Caligula, is absorbed with the problem of happiness. He eventually concludes that most people do not achieve happiness because they permit various distractions and affections to divert them from their goals. Caligula choses to eliminate all possible distractions, leading him to order the death of his closest friends and loved ones. In the end, however, Caligula becomes indifferent and dies.

For Segundo, "the thesis underlying that play is that most human beings are never satisfied in life because they do not manage to attain the ideal they had set for themselves." (*The Liberation of Theology,* 103). Segundo goes on to elaborate: "The 'parable' is clear:...no human being can experience in advance whether life is worth the trouble of being lived and in what ways it might be worthwhile" (103). The values to which one commits one's life cannot be experimentally derived. "Real life for a human being presupposes a nonempirical choice of some ideal that one presumes will be satisfying. It is this ideal, chosen ahead of time by nonempirical standards, that organizes and gives direction to the means and ends used to attain it" (104).

Commitment precedes specific analyses of ends and means. Segundo makes clear that this commitment, whether formulated theologically or philosophically, is a faith-commitment. While there are no "neutral" positions from which to dispassionately evaluate the relative merits of faith commitments, the Christian faith situates one within a community with historical depth and cross-cultural breadth. This does not provide "empirical verification" of the faith stance, but it does provide a comprehensive witness. This essentially is the same kind of empirical grounding on which Dewey bases his endorsement of scientific procedure.

78. John Dewey, *How We Think* (Boston: D. C. Heath and Company, 1933), 106.

79. John Dewey, *Logic: The Theory of Inquiry* (New York: Henry Holt and Company, 1938), 42.

80. Dewey's comment on this topic is that prior to inquiry the individual experiences "need." (Dewey, *Logic: The Theory of Inquiry*, 27). His understanding of "need" is that the organism is in disequilibrium with the environment.

81. Rosemary Radford Ruther, *Sexism and God-Talk: Toward a Feminist Theology* (Boston: Beacon Press, 1983), 159.

82. Segundo has a profound trust in the "ordinary experience" of church people. For example, he writes, "we must not underestimate Christian common sense as it has been applied to certain ambiguous things in the church *The Liberation of Theology,* 40. Segundo's circle is based upon a common sense interpretation of experience that raises profound questions. These questions are taken up and more formally analyzed in working through the circle.

83. John Dewey, *Art as Experience* (New York: Minton, Balch & Company, 1934), 37.

CHAPTER FIVE_____

1. Gordon W. Allport, *The Nature of Prejudice* (Reading, Mass.: Addison-Wesley Publishing Co., 1954, 1958, 1979?, xviii.

2. *Ibid.,* 406-407.

3. A comprehensive discussion of the relationship between prejudice and self-esteem can be found in C. Bagley, G. Verma, K. Mallick, and L. Young, *Personality, Self-Esteem and Prejudice* (Westmead, England: Saxon House, 1979).

4. Jack Levin and William Levin, *The Function of Discrimination and Prejudice* (New York: Harper & Row, 1982), 130-131.

5. Allport, *op cit.,* 153-157.

6. See Richard Apostle, Charles Glock, Thomas Piazza, and Marijean Suelzle, *The Anatomy of Racial Attitudes* (Berkeley, CA.: University of California Press, 1983). These authors have identified five "pure" explanatory modes that people use to explain the source of perceived racial differences. The *geneticists* assume differences are due to inferior racial inheritance; the *supernaturalists* attribute the differences to God. The *individualists* attribute differences to operations of human will. The *radicals* believe inferior status to have been deliberately imposed on blacks by the white majority; the *environmentalists* maintain that the social environment is the source of differences. Apostle, et al., also found that the type of explanatory mode that an individual used tended to be associated with what kinds of prescriptions (if any) that individual accepted for combatting racism.

7. The relationship between religion and prejudice is not entirely clear. In classic studies by Milton Rokeach, for example, greater religious commitment is associated with greater prejudice. There is also a significant body of literature to support the contention that while most Church members may be more prejudiced that the average nonmember, highly committed members — particularly those members who see religion as an open-ended process of pursuing ultimate questions — are significantly less prejudiced than the average person. See Milton Rokeach, *Beliefs, Attitudes, and Values* (San Francisco: Jossey-Bass, 1968), and "Religious values and social compassion," *Review of Religious Research,* Vol. 11, 1969, 3-23. For a review of studies on this question, see Richard Gorsuch and Daniel Aleshire, "Christian Faith and Ethnic Prejudice: A Review and Interpretation of Research," *Journal for the Scientific Study of Religion,* Vol. 13 (1974), 281-307. The findings of Gorsuch and Aleshire have been critiqued by several people. See especially the following articles: Thomas Cygnar, Donald Noel, and Cardell Jacobson, "Religiosity and Prejudice: An Interdimensional Analysis," *Journal for the Scientific Study of Religion,* Vol. 16 (1977), 183-191; Daniel Batson, Stephen Naifeh, and Suzanne Pate, "Social Desirability, Religious Orientation, and Racial Prejudice," *Journal for the Scientific Study of Religion,* Vol. 17 (1978), 31-41; and H. Paul Chalfant and Charles Peek, "Religious Affiliation, Religiosity and Racial Prejudice: A New Look at Old Relationships," *Review of Religious Research,* Vol. 25 (1983), 155-161.

8. Study quoted in Matthew Fox, *Original Blessing* (Santa Fe, N.M.: Bear and Co., 1983).

9. John Dewey, *Democracy and Education: An Introduction to the Philosophy of Education* (New York: Macmillan Publishing Co., The Free Press, 1916, 1944), 81.

CHAPTER SIX_____

1. The model I am proposing is indebted to the similar work of Thomas Groome, *Christian Religious Education: Sharing Our Story and*

Vision (San Francisco: Harper & Row, 1980). The differences in our approaches, however, are as significant as the similarities. There are essentially two issues which provide a clear contrast. In the first place, the model I suggest accepts the liberation theologian's view of reality as conflictive. The necessity of "taking sides" is explicitly acknowledged and built in as part of the model. Groome, on the other hand, pays little attention to this feature of Latin American thought.

The second issue over which our approaches diverge pertains to our understandings of praxis. Groome takes such a broad view of action that it loses its connotation of environmental transformation. For example, he writes, "Present action here means much more than the overt productive activity of the present moment. It means our whole human engagement in the world, our every doing that has any intentionality or deliberateness to it. Present action is whatever way we give expression to ourselves. It includes what we are doing physically, emotionally, intellectually, and spiritually as we live on personal, interpersonal, and social levels," (184). With this broad understanding of action "an articulation of a new awareness" becomes a praxis response (221).

Groome draws heavily upon Jurgen Habermas for his understanding of praxis. In Habermas' view, all knowing has a "knowledge constitutive interest" which orients it (See *Knowledge and Human Interest*, Boston: Beacon Press, 1973). For Habermas, an "interest" is an impelling way of organizing experience. Interests are "quasi-transcendental" and are species-wide. Such interests are "knowledge-constitutive" because they shape and determine what counts as the objects and types of knowledge: they determine the categories relevant to what we take to be knowledge, as well as the procedures for discovering and warranting knowledge claims. It is the "interest" we bring to the knowing process which unites theory and practice. This view of praxis has an idealistic thrust to it which allows the dialectic of theory and practice to be little more than the operation of a "quasi-transcendental" dynamic.

The liberation theologian holds to a definition of praxis which views knowledge as tied to action that transforms the environment. At this point, the liberation theologian (and the present writer) are more Deweyian than is Groome. The "self" does not come to reality with ready-made "knowledge-constitutive" interests; rather, "the self is created in the creation of objects." *Art as Experience* (New York: Minton, Balch & Co., 1934), 282.

2. See Paulo Freire, *Education for Critical Consciousness* (New York: The Seabury Press, 1973) and *The Politics of Education* (South Hadley, Mass.: Bergin & Garvey, 1985).

3. This approach was originally recommended by Frances Culbertson in "Modification of an Emotionally Held Attitude Through Role-playing," *Journal of Abnormal and Social Psychology*, 1957, 230-233. It has recently been advocated by H. Philip Constans, Jr., in "To Tip the Scale Against Prejudice: The Use of the Theory of Cognitive Dissonance in the Reduction of Racial Prejudice," *Focus on Learning* (1983), 18-24.

4. Quoted in Alfred Hennelly, *Theologies in Conflict: The Challenge of Juan Luis Segundo* (Maryknoll, N.Y.: Orbis Books, 1979), 109.

5. Matthew Lamb, *Solidarity With Victims: Toward a Theology of Social Transformation* (New York: The Crossroad Publishing Company, 1982), 1.

6. For a discussion of "active listening," see Thomas Gordon, *P.E.T.: Parent Effectiveness Training* (New York: New American Library, 1975).

7. See Beverly Gimmestad and Edith Chiara, "Dramatic Plays: A Vehicle for Prejudice Reduction in the Elementary School," *Journal of Educational Research,* Vol. 76 (1982), 45-49.

8. There are a number of very good resources available that approach prejudice reduction with a cognitive strategy. The elementary school teacher may wish to obtain David Shiman's *The Prejudice Book: Activities for the Classroom* (New York: Anti-Defamation League, 1979). Among the best for adolescents is Nina Gabelko and John Michaelis, *Reducing Adolescent Prejudice: A Handbook* (New York: Teachers College Press, 1981). A fine list of resources for combating racism and sexism can be found in Richard Simms and Gloria Contreras, *Racism and Sexism: Responding to the Challenge* (Bulletin 61 of the National Council for the Social Studies, Washington, D.C., 1980). The reader may also wish to obtain a current catalog of publications from the Anti-Defamation League of B'nai B'rith, 823 United Nations Plaza, New York, New York 10017.

9. Gordon Allport, *The Nature of Prejudice* (Reading, Mass.: Addison-Wesley Publishing Company, 1954/1979), 485. Ideas for action might be gained from reading the material available through Co-op America, 2100 M St., N.W., Suite 310, Washington, D.C. 20063. Co-op America is a non-profit association linking socially responsible businesses and consumers in a national network.

10. By "Christian Story" I am referring to "the whole faith tradition of our people, however that is expressed or embodied" (Groome, *Christian Religious Education,* 192). The Story is both a remembering which brings the tradition into the present and an announcement of hope which projects the Story into the future.

11. Groome, *Christian Religious Education,* 194.

12. Many helpful suggestions for developing a constructive, creative classroom in which students become responsible partners in the teaching-learning process can be found in Gene Stanford, *Developing Effective Classroom Groups: A Practical Guide for Teachers* (New York: Hart Publishing Co., 1977). The book is primarily for upper elementary and junior high school teachers, but could be adapted for older levels.

13. In addition to Groome's approach, other models that would be consistent with the perspective of the present work can be found in Joyce and

Weil, *Models of Teaching.* The section on "social" models, 220-323, contains a description of six approaches that are distinctly non-authoritarian. Three of these models are given greater elaboration in Marsha Weil and Bruce Joyce, *Social Models of Teaching: Expanding Your Teaching Repertoire* (Englewood Cliffs, New Jersey: Prentice-Hall, 1978).

14. These ideas are drawn from Richard Davies, "Creative Ambiguity," *Religious Education,* Vol. 77 (1982), 642-656.

15. Florence Davidson, "Respect for Persons and Ethnic Prejudice in Childhood: A Cognitive-Developmental Description," in Melvin Tumin and Walter Plotch (Eds.), *Pluralism in a Democratic Society* (New York: Praeger Publishers, 1977), 133-168.

16. Cf. David Shields, "Education for Moral Action," *Religious Education,* Vol. 75 (1980), 129-141.

17. T. Groome, *Christian Religious Education,* 189. Groome is indebted to the work of Martin Buber, *I and Thou* (New York: Charles Scribner's Sons, 1970) and Paulo Freire, *Education for Critical Consciousness* (New York: Seabury Press, 1973) and *Pedagogy in Process,* New York: Seabury Press, 1978) for his understanding of dialogue.

18. Many useful ideas, activities, and exercises for enhancing children's self-esteem can be found in Jack Canfield and Harold Wells, *One Hundred Ways to Enhance Self-Concept in the Classroom: A Handbook for Teacher and Parents* (Englewood Cliffs, N.J.: Prentice-Hall, 1976).

19. Irving Sigel and James Johnson, "Child Development and Respect for Cultural Diversity," in Melvin Tumin and Walter Plotch (Eds.), *Pluralism in a Democratic Society* (New York: Praeger Publishers, 1977), 169-206.

SELECTED BIBLIOGRAPHY

Apostle, Richard, Charles Glock, Thomas Piazza, and Marijean Suelzle. *The Anatomy of Racial Attitudes*. Berkeley, Calif.: University of California Press, 1983.

Bernstein, Richard. *Praxis and Action: Contemporary Philosophies of Human Activity*. Philadelphia: University of Pennsylvania Press, 1971.

Boff, Leonardo. *Church: Charism and Power*. New York: Crossroad, 1985.

Bredemeier, Brenda, and David Shields. "Values and Violence in Sports." *Psychology Today* 19:10 (October 1985), 22-32.

Brown, Robert McAfee. *Unexpected News: Reading the Bible with Third World Eyes*. Philadelphia: Westminster, 1984.

Canfield, Jack and Harold Wells. *100 Ways to Enhance Self-Concept in the Classroom: A Handbook for Teacher and Parents*. Englewood Cliffs, N.J.: Prentice-Hall, 1976.

Casse, Pierre. *Training for the Cross-Cultural Mind*, 2nd ed. Washington, D.C.: The Society for Intercultural Education, 1981.

Chalfant, H. Paul and Charles Peek. "Religious Affiliation, Religiosity and Racial Prejudice: A New Look at Old Relationships." *Review of Religious Research* 25 (1983), 155-161.

Christ, Carol P., and Judith Plaskow, eds. *Womanspirit Rising: A Feminist Reader in Religion*. San Francisco: Harper & Row, 1979.

Colca, Carole, Deborah Lowen, Louis Colca, and Shirley Lord. "Combatting Racism in the Schools: A Group Work Pilot Project." *Social Work in Education* 5:1 (October 1982), 5-16.

Constans, H. Philip Jr. "To Tip the Scale Against Prejudice: The Use of the Theory of Cognitive Dissonance in the Reduction of Racial Prejudice." *Focus on Learning* 9:1 (1983), 18-24.

Culbertson, Frances. "Modification of an Emotionally Held Attitude Through Role-Playing." *Journal of Abnormal and Social Psychology* (1957), 230-233.

Cygnar, Thomas, Donald Noel, and Cardell Jacobson. "Religiosity and Prejudice: An Interdimensional Analysis." *Journal for the Scientific Study of Religion* 16 (1977), 183-191.

Davidson, Florence. "Respect for Persons and Ethnic Prejudice in Childhood: A Cognitive-Developmental Description." In *Pluralism in a Democratic Society*. Ed. Melvin Tumin and Walter Plotch. New York: Praeger Publishers, 1977.

Davies, Richard. "Creative Ambiguity." *Religious Education* 77 (1982), 642-656.

Dewey, John. *Art as Experience*. New York: Minton, Balch & Company, 1934.

_____. *A Common Faith*. New Haven: Yale University Press, 1934.

_____. *Experience and Nature*. New York: Dover Publications, 1958.

_____. *Human Nature and Conduct: An Introduction to Social Psychology*. New York: Henry Holt and Company, 1922. Reprinted with a new introduction, New York: Modern Library, 1930.

_____. *Logic: The Theory of Inquiry*. New York: Henry Holt and Company, 1938.

Dunn, Dorothy. *The Problem of Dualism in John Dewey*. Unpublished doctoral thesis, St. Louis University, 1966.

Dykstra, Craig. *Vision and Character: A Christian Educator's Alternative to Kohlberg*. New York: Paulist Press, 1981.

Fiorenza, Elisabeth Schussler. *Bread Not Stone: The Challenge of Feminist Biblical Interpretation*. Boston: Beacon Press, 1984.

_____. *In Memory of Her: A Feminist Theological Reconstruction of Christian Origins*. New York: Crossroad, 1983.

Fox. Matthew. *Original Blessing*. Santa Fe, N.M.: Bear and Co., 1983.

Freire, Paulo. *Education for Critical Consciousness*. New York: Seabury Press, 1973.

_____. *Pedagogy in Process*. New York: Seabury Press, 1978.

_____. *Pedagogy of the Oppressed*. New York: Seabury Press, 1970.

_____. *The Politics of Education*. South Hadley, Mass.: Bergin & Garvey, 1985.

Gibellini, Rosino, ed. *Frontiers of Theology in Latin America*. Maryknoll, N.Y.: Orbis Books, 1979.

Gilligan, Carol. *In a Different Voice: Psychological Theory and Women's Development*. Cambridge, Mass.: Harvard University Press, 1982.

Gimmestad, Beverly and Edith Chiara. "Dramatic Plays: A Vehicle for Prejudice Reduction in the Elementary School." *Journal of Educational Research* 76 (1982), 45-49.

Gorsuch, Richard and Daniel Aleshire. "Christian Faith and Ethnic Prejudice: A Review and Interpretation of Research." *Journal for the Scientific Study of Religion* 13 (1974), 281-307.

Groome, Thomas. *Christian Religious Education: Sharing Our Story and Vision.* San Francisco: Harper & Row, 1980.

Gruber, H. and J. Voneche, eds. *The Essential Piaget.* New York: Basic Books, 1977.

Gutierrez, Gustavo. *The Power of the Poor in History.* Maryknoll, N.Y.: Orbis Books, 1983.

_____. *We Drink From Our Own Wells: The Spiritual Journey of a People.* Maryknoll, N.Y.: Orbis Books, 1984.

Haan, Norma. "Can Research on Morality Be 'Scientific'?" *American Psychologist* 37 (1982), 1096-1104.

_____. *Coping and Defending: Processes of Self-Environment Organization.* San Francisco: Academic Press, 1977.

_____. "A Tripartite Model of Ego Functioning, Values and Clinical and Research Applications." *Journal of Nervous and Mental Disease* 148:1 (1969), 14-30.

_____. "Two Moralities in Action Contexts: Relationship to Thought, Ego Regulation and Development." *Journal of Personality and Social Psychology* 36 (1978), 286-305.

Harrison, Beverly. *Making the Connections: Essays in Feminist Social Ethics.* Ed. Carol Robb. Boston: Beacon Press, 1985.

Hennelly, Alfred. *Theologies in Conflict: The Challenge of Juan Luis Segundo.* Maryknoll, N.Y.: Orbis Books, 1979.

Heyward, Carter. *Our Passion for Justice: Images of Power, Sexuality, and Liberation.* New York: The Pilgrim Press, 1984.

_____. "Ruether and Daly: Theologians Speaking, Sparking, Building and Burning." *Christianity and Crisis* 39:5 (April 2, 1979), 66-72.

Hodge, John, Donald Struckmann, and Lynn Trost. *Cultural Bases of Racism and Group Oppression.* Berkeley, Calif.: Two Riders Press, 1975.

Kohlberg, Lawrence, and Elliot Turiel. "Moral Development and Moral Education." In *Psychology and Educational Practice.* Ed. G. S. Lesser. Glenview, Ill.: Scott Foresman, 1971.

Lamb, Matthew. *Solidarity With Victims: Toward a Theology of Social Transformation*. New York: Crossroad, 1982.

Levin, Jack and William Levin. *Ageism: Prejudice and Discrimination Against the Elderly*. Belmont, Calif.: Wadsworth, 1980.

Metz, Johann Baptist. *Faith in History and Society: Toward a Practical Fundamental Theology*. New York: Seabury Press, 1980.

Miguez Bonino, Jose. *Christians and Marxists: The Mutual Challenge to Revolution*. Grand Rapids, Mich.: William B. Erdmans Publishing Co., 1976.

_____. *Doing Theology in a Revolutionary Situation*. Philadelphia: Fortress Press, 1975.

Moltmann, Jurgen. *The Power of the Powerless*. San Francisco: Harper & Row, 1983.

Phenix, Philip H. "John Dewey's War on Dualism." In *Dewey on Education: Appraisals*. Ed. Redinald D. Archambault. New York: Random House, 1966.

Piaget, Jean. *The Moral Judgment of the Child*. Glencoe, Ill.: Free Press, 1965.

_____. *Structuralism*. New York: Basic Books, 1970.

Rokeach, Milton. "Religious Values and Social Compassion." *Review of Religious Research* 11 (1969), 3-23.

Rose, Peter. *They and We: Racial and Ethnic Relations in the United States*, 3rd ed. New York: Random House, 1981.

Ruether, Rosemary Radford. "An American Socialism: A Just Economic Order." *Religious Socialism* 7:3,4 (Summer & Fall 1983) and 8:2,3 (Spring & Summer 1984).

_____. "Anti-Judaism Is the Left Hand of Christology." *New Catholic World* 217 (January-February 1974), 12-15.

_____. "The Becoming of Women in Church and Society." *Cross Currents* 17 (Fall 1967), 418-426.

_____. "Better Red Than Dead." *The Ecumenist* 12:1 (November-December 1973), 11.

_____. "Crisis in Sex and Race: Black Theology vs. Feminist Theology." *Christianity and Crisis* 34 (April 15, 1974), 67-73.

_____. "The Cult of True Womanhood." *Commonweal* 99:6 (November 9, 1973), 127-132.

_____. *Disputed Questions: On Being a Christian*. Nashville: Abingdon, 1982.

Ruether, Rosemary Radford. "Feminism and Patriarchal Religion: Principles of Ideological Critique of the Bible." *Journal For the Study of the Old Testament* 22 (February 1982), 54-66.

_____. "Feminist Interpretation: A Method of Correlation." In *Feminist Interpretation of the Bible*. Ed. Letty M. Russell. Philadelphia: The Westminster Press, 1985.

_____. "Feminist Theology in the Academy." *Christianity and Crisis* 45:3 (March 4, 1985), 57-62.

_____. "Home and Work: Women's Roles and the Transformation of Values." *Theological Studies* 36 (December 1975), 647-659.

_____. *Liberation Theology: Human Hope Confronts Christian History and American Power*. New York: Paulist Press, 1972.

_____. "Outlines for a Theology of Liberation." *Dialogue* 11 (Autumn 1972), 252-257.

_____. *The Radical Kingdom: The Western Experience of Messianic Hope*. New York: Harper & Row.

_____. "Rich Nations/Poor Nations and the Exploitation of the Earth." *Dialogue* 13 (Summer 1974), 201-207.

_____. "Sexism and the Theology of Liberation: Nature, Fall and Salvation as Seen from the Experience of Women." *The Christian Century* 90 (December 12, 1973), 1224-1229.

_____. "Social Sin." *Commonweal* 58 (January 30, 1981), 46-48.

_____. *To Change the World: Christology and Cultural Criticism*. New York: Crossroad, 1981.

_____. "Why Socialism Needs Feminism, & Vice Versa." *Christianity and Crisis* 40:7 (April 28, 1980), 103-108.

_____. "Women, Ecology and the Domination of Nature." *The Ecumenist* 14:1 (November-December 1975), 1-5.

_____. "Women in Ministry: Where are They Heading." *Christianity and Crisis* 43:5 (April 4, 1983), 111-116.

Russell, Letty M., ed. *Feminist Interpretation of the Bible*. Philadelphia: The Westminster Press, 1985.

_____. *Growth in Partnership*. Philadelphia: Westminster Press, 1981.

Segundo, Juan Luis. "Education, Communication and Liberation: A Christian Vision." *IDOC International—North American Edition*. (November 13, 1971), 63-96.

_____. *The Hidden Motives of Pastoral Action*. Maryknoll, N.Y.: Orbis Books, 1978.

Segundo, Juan Luis. *Jesus of Nazareth Yesterday and Today. Vol. 11: The Historical Jesus of the Synoptics.* Maryknoll, N.Y.: Orbis, 1985.

_____. *Theology and the Church.* Minneapolis: Seabury Books, 1985.

_____. *Theology for Artisans of a New Humanity. Vol. 1. The Community Called Church.* Maryknoll, N.Y.: Orbis Books, 1973.

_____. *Theology for Artisans of a New Humanity. Vol. 2. Grace and the Human Condition.* Maryknoll, N.Y.: Orbis Books, 1973.

_____. *Theology for Artisans of a New Humanity, Vol. 3. Our Idea of God.* Maryknoll, N.Y.: Orbis Books, 1974.

_____. *Theology for Artisans of a New Humanity. Vol. 4. The Sacraments Today.* Maryknoll, N.Y.: Orbis Books, 1974.

_____. *Theology for Artisans of a New Humanity. Vol. 5. Evolution and Guilt.* Maryknoll, N.Y.: Orbis Books, 1974.

Shields, David. "Christ: A Male Feminist View." *Encounter* 45:3 (Summer 1984), 221-232.

_____. "Sexism Is Not the Only Issue." *Lutheran Partners,* on press.

Sigel, Irving and James Johnson. "Child Development and Respect for Cultural Diversity." In *Pluralism in a Democratic Society.* Ed. Melvin Tumin and Walter Plotch. New York: Praeger Publishers, 1977.

Simms, Richard and Gloria Contreras. *Racism and Sexism: Responding to the Challenge.* Bulletin 61 of the National Council for Social Studies, Washington, D.C., 1980.

Sobrino, Joh. *Christology at the Crossroads.* Maryknoll, N.Y.: Orbis Books, 1978.

_____. *The True Church and the Poor.* Maryknoll, N.Y.: Orbis Books, 1984.

Stanford, Gene. *Developing Effective Classroom Groups: A Practical Guide for Teachers.* New York: Hart Publishing Co., 1977.

Washbourn, Penny. *Becoming Woman.* New York: Harper and Row, 1977.

Welch, Sharon D. *Communities of Resistance and Solidarity: A Feminist Theology of Liberation.* Maryknoll, N.Y.: Orbis Books, 1985.

INDEX

Allport, Gordon, 149, 152, 188-189

Anti-semitism, 14-15, 81

Apocalypticism, 14, 16, 21

Aquinas, Thomas, 30

Aristotle, 8

Assmann, Hugo, 115, 121, 124, 139

Bacon, Francis, 22

Bredemeier, Brenda, 92

Brown, Robert McAfee, i, 111

Buhlmann, Walbert, 110

Christ, Carol, 29

Christianity: anti-semitism and, 14-15; dualism and, 12-22; ecological crisis and, 20-22; liberation and, 29-33

Christology, 32, 125-129

Church: and dualism, 12-22, as liberating community, 29-33; Segundo's view of, 133-136

Classism, 7, 18, 35, 42, 61, 117, 119-122, 169

Collins, Sheila, 94

Constantine, 128

Counter-attitudinal advocacy, 183-184

Daly, Mary, 29, 30, 94

Democracy, 59-61, 169-170

Developmentalism, applied to Latin America, 120-121

Dewey, John, 39-64, 79, 83, 101, 110, 142-145, 161, 167, 168, 169, 170-171, 172, 173-174, 175, 178, 194, 195; on democracy, 59-61, 169; on education, 57-64; on esthetic experience, 55-56; on experience, 45-59, 168; on habit, 53-54, 171-172; on inquiry, 61-64, 170-175; on intelligence, 51-57, 173; on knowledge, 48-49; on nature, 47-48; on "quest for certainty," 40-43, 51; on sources of dualism, 40-45; on value, 54-56

Dialectic, 13-14

Difference principle, 181, 182

Dualism, 3-4, 9-11, 15-17, 21-22, 30-31, 43-44, 47-49, 50, 54-48, 58, 93, 127, 145, 168; body-soul, 8, 16, 31; clergy-laity, 31; culture-nature, 4, 44, 58; experience-nature, 47-48; experience-thought, 50; fact-value, 10, 54-56, 168; God-human, 31, 127, 169; good-bad, 4, 152, 160; home-work, 9-10; individual-community, 16; law-gospel, 15; male-female, 8, 16-17, 152; means-ends, 56; mind-body, 4, 7, 11, 24, 57-58, 169; nature-grace, 15;

243

Dualism (continued)
    public-private, 10; sacred-secular, 30, 127, 131; saved-damned, 17, 164, 169; science-art, 56; science-religion, 43; self-other, 5; spirit-matter, 4, 7; spirit-nature, 21, 22; strong-weak, 93; subject-object, 10, 17, 46, 48-49, 58; thought-action, 54, 169; thought-feeling, 55, 169. *See also* Hierarchical dualism

Ecological crisis, 20-22

Education, 57-64, 107, 177-207; cross-cultural, 205-207. *See also* Moral education, Religious education.

Ego processes, 24-25, 74-81; repression, 24; projection, 25

Experience: 45-49, 112, 132, 142-143, 145-147, 168-169; consummatory distinguished from instrumental, 52; direct and indirect, 62; primary distinguished from reflective, 46, 53

Faith: Dewey's view of, 143; Segundo's view of, 136-142, 144, 172

Feminist theology, 3-36, 110

Freire, Paulo, 107, 115, 179

Freud, Sigmund, 23, 74

Gender roles, 4-5, 7, 10, 94-95, 165, 197

Gilligan, Carol, 83

Gnosticism, 15

Greek philosophy, 8, 16, 21, 41-42

Groome, Thomas, 191, 203-204

Gutierrez, Gustavo, 114, 118, 121, 123, 125-127

Haan, Norma, 67-104, 161, 167, 168, 169-170, 171, 172, 173, 174, 175,

Haan, Norma (continued)
    194, 203; and habit, 53-54, 171-173, 180-182; compared to Collins, 103-104; compared to Kohlberg, 72-73, 81-83; coping and defending model, 74-79; theory of interactional morality, 81-93; view of moral development, 95-100; view of moral education, 103-104

Habermas, Jurgen, 83

Hermeneutics, 111-112, 129-133, 175; defined, 129

Hierarchical dualism, 3-10, 26, 79-81, 151-152, 156, 159-160; alternate forms of, 6-10; as rigid moral imbalance, 93-95; church and, 12-22; effects of industrialization on, 8-9; imperialism and, 17-18; morality and, 93-95, 99, 100-103, 168; origin of, 4-6, 80; repression and, 24; projection and, 25. *See also* Classism, Dualism, Prejudice, Racism, Sexism.

Hunt, Mary, 165

Ideology, Segundo's view of, 137-138, 140, 142, 172

Ideological suspicion, 131-133, 146, 174, 175, 191

Industrialization, 8-10, 18

Inquiry, 61-64, 142-147, 170-175

Johnson, James, 205

Kant, Immanuel, 116

Kohlberg, Lawrence, 69, 72, 73, 81-83, 84, 103

Lamb, Matthew, 185

Liberation, defined, 117; groups in conflict, 19; of women, 33-34; theology of, 110-125

Luther, Martin, 30, 109

Marx, Karl, 116, 119, 120

Miguez Bonino, Jose, 110, 118

Moral balance, 84, 86-89, 172, 173; legitimate and illegitimate imbalances, 91-92; legitimate and illegitimate regressions, 92-93

Moral development, 95-103; and prejudice, 100-103

Moral dialogue, 84-86, 160-161

Moral education, 103-104, 203-204

Moral truth, 84, 89-91, 169

Nature: Christian view of, 20-22

Political option, as prerequisite for theology, 130

Piaget, Jean, 69, 72, 74-75, 206

Piatt, Donald, 143

Plato, 8

Poverty, defined, 114

Praxis, 122-123

Prejudice, definition of, 2-3; discrimination and, 25-26, 154-155; and experience, 151-152; irrationality of, 161-162; morality and, 93-95, 154, 160-161, 168; oppression and, 25-26; prevention of, 201-207; pyramid principle and, 166; reduction of, 178-201; relation to psycholological structures and processes, 79-81; and religion, 163-164; self-esteem and, 153-154; and stereotyping, 159-160; sources of, 149; twelve summary statements about, 151-167; victim-blaming and, 13. *See also* Anti-semitism, *also* Dualism, Hierarchical dualism, Racism, Sexism.

Quest for certainty, 40-43, 152-153

Racism, 18-20, 26, 44-45, 81, 94, 100, 102, 181, 182

Religious education, 107-108

Reverse discrimination, 163

Romanticism, effects on images of women, 8-10, 80

Ruether, Rosemary Radford, 3-36, 39, 61, 68, 79-80, 102, 144, 160, 161; on anti-semitism, 14-15; on the church, 12-22, 29-33; on consciousness raising, 33-34; on the ecological crisis, 20-22; on ego defense, 23-24; on imperialism, 17-18; on origins of hierarchical dualism, 4-6; on prophetic dialectic, 14; on racism, 18-20; on sexism, 6-13, 18-20, 25, 28, 30-34; on socialization, 25-28

Salvation, 134-135

Sarton, May, 186

Scapegoating, 154

Secularization, 9, 42

Self-esteem, 102, 153-154, 204-205

Segundo, Juan Luis, 109-110, 121, 125, 127-147, 161, 169, 170, 171, 172, 173, 174, 175, 184, 194; and Dewey, 142-145; hermeneutic circle of, 129-133; on the church, 133-136; on faith and ideology, 136-142, 172, 173; on theological method, 129-142

Sexism, 4, 6-12, 23, 26, 29-36, 86, 94-95, 100, 163, 165, 166-167; as model for other prejudices, 10-12, 35-37, 156-157; effects of industrialization on, 8-9; Genesis myth and, 12, 30; in the Bible, 12, 192; and the pyramid principle, 166-167; racism and, 18-20; romanticism and, 9-10

Shields, David, 92-93

Siegel, irving, 205

Sobrino, Jon, 115, 116, 122

Socialization, 26-28, 94

Social learning theory, 70, 71-72

Sport, 92

Steinbeck, John, 186

Stereotypes, 100,102, 158-160, 168-169

Structural developmental theory, 69-74
Subordinationism, 127-128

Tertullian, 30

Theological method, 108-109, 128, 129-142, 146; distortion of, 132, 145-146; and the social sciences, 118-120

Urbanization, 7

Vicious abstractionism, 44-45, 62, 146, 168

Violence, 121

White, Lynn, 20